100 THINGS PHISH
FANS SHOULD KNOW & DO BEFORE THEY DIE

ANDY P. SMITH AND JASON GERSHUNY

TRIUMPH
BOOKS

The Library of Congress has catalogued the previous edition as follows:

Names: Smith, Andy P. author. | Gershuny, Jason, author.
Title: 100 things Phish fans should know & do before they die / Andy P. Smith and Jason Gershuny.
Other titles: One hundred things Phish fans should know & do before they die
Description: Chicago, Illinois : Triumph Books, [2018]
Identifiers: LCCN 2018002454 | ISBN 9781629375397
Subjects: LCSH: Phish (Musical group)—Miscellanea.
Classification: LCC ML421.P565 S65 2018 | DDC 782.42166092/2—dc23
LC record available at https://lccn.loc.gov/2018002454

This book is available in quantity at special discounts for your group or organization. For further information, contact:

Triumph Books LLC
814 North Franklin Street
Chicago, Illinois 60610
(312) 337–0747
www.triumphbooks.com

Printed in U.S.A.
ISBN: 978-1-63727-668-6
Design by Patricia Frey
Photos courtesy of the authors unless otherwise indicated

Jenna, my love, this book is for you. Thank you for encouraging me and believing in me when I said I wanted to be a professional Phish fan. Baby, we did it! Without your support, it wouldn't have happened. I love you so much!

And, if I may, I'd like to share this dedication with my parents, especially my mother, who took me and three friends to my first Phish show as a teenager. I can't imagine you fully understood what you were getting me into, but that's the best part: you just knew I wanted to go, and were kind enough to take the trip with me. I love you. Thank you so much!
—Andy P. Smith

I dedicate this book to the three most important and inspirational women in my world—the light of my life, my daughter, Izabella; my incredibly kind and understanding wife, Mindy; and my mom, Sylvia, who supported, encouraged, and loved me since my first breath.

I love you all so much, and owe much of my life's abundant joy to you.
—Jason Gershuny

Contents

Phish at Sphere in Las Vegas, April 2024. (Scott Harris)

Foreword

At the end of the day, the most obvious choice turned out to be the most surprising choice—and the right one. On December 31, 2023, Phish marked their 40th anniversary by performing one of their most cherished offerings, the story-song-cycle "The Man Who Stepped Into Yesterday," live for the first time in almost 30 years at New York's Madison Square Garden.

The group dropped the multimedia presentation, often referred to as a "rock opera" and commonly known as Gamehendge by fans, during the second and third sets of their 83rd show at Madison Square Garden as the clock struck midnight—just a few blocks from Times Square, the international epicenter of New Year's Eve revelry. A far cry from the previous oracle-like, Zappa-adjacent presentations that made Gamehendge a fan favorite in the '80s and '90s, this version featured costumed actors, larger than life props, and narration by *Orange is the New Black* star Annie Golden. And it instantly turned into a Mount Rushmore moment for the band and fans alike.

While performing an oft-requested suite of songs during a marquee show on one of the country's most iconic stages wouldn't seem like headline news for most bands, Phish has always played with rock-and-roll tropes in their own prankster way—subverting music-industry clichés for so long now that it was actually *more* surprising that the band busted out Gamehendge on New Year's Eve than if they had pulled the same stunt during an otherwise sleepy Sunday night show or at a low-key, out-of-the-way location just before a major-market stop.

But that ability to keep fans guessing, while still nodding to the past, has been a hallmark of Phish's current, latter-day period. Since reuniting in 2009 (and especially since their 13-night, repeat-free

Baker's Dozen residency at Madison Square Garden eight years later) Phish has tapped into a golden age of almost anti-nostalgia, turning their own musical traditions on their head and using their extensive back catalog to keep their setlists fresh and ever-evolving—without falling into the rote traps that have weighed down so many classic-rock acts.

Instead of covering another band's classic album in full on Halloween as they've done now many times, in recent years they've used October 31 as an opportunity to debut three record-length, high-concept sets of original material. They've grown their New Year's Eve "gags" from fun stunts into fully baked Broadway productions and they've remained pioneers on the streaming front by not only broadcasting the majority of their shows live but by also using the pandemic to launch their archival live show series, *Dinner and a Movie*, which gave fans around the world the much-welcomed opportunity to share recipes and commune during the COVID-necessitated Great Pause.

Along the way, they've also continued to seed their own songbook, working with bona fide producer legends like Bob Ezrin as well as modern tastemakers such as Vance Powell for full-band releases, as well as expanding their horizons through solo-project collaborations with indie-rock architects Shawn Everett and Peter Katis. Those sessions have produced hashtagable lyrics, which have no doubt inspired numerous yearbook pages and social media handles and become live favorites in their own right. In fact, the group's first set on December 31, 2023, was packed with anthemic, newer tunes like "Everything's Right," "Ruby Waves," and "A Life Beyond a Dream," as if to balance the scales of time against the forthcoming slate of songs written while the band members were still in college. It made for a fitting anniversary party too, though Phish has famously been loose with when and how they honor their time together. In 1998, they celebrated their 15th anniversary on October 30, mistakenly believing that to be date of their first show; in 2003, they hosted an official 20th anniversary concert on December 2, the *correct* date of their first gig, but really marked the occasion a night earlier by reuniting with former member Jeff Holdsworth for the first and only time since 1986; in 2013, they used their December 31 gig to look back and ahead as their 30th anniversary got underway; and in 2022, they kicked off their 40th anniversary campaign almost a full year early on the same date.

"Phish's biggest blessing has been not having a hit song," says Brian Harding of the Instagram account and print magazine *PHILM*. "If you revisit their '90s major label dalliance, they definitely attempted but beautifully failed. Which is to say, Phish's crowd is and has always been there for the entity of Phish. The public hasn't had the chance to get tired of them or to devolve to levels of parody like so many other legacy bands."

Of course, Phish's jamming style has continued to mature and evolve in both subtle and not-so-subtle ways during their so-called "3.0" and "4.0" periods, and new opportunities like their current partnership with the Sphere in Las Vegas have opened up unexpected creative doors. Phish's inaugural four-night stand at the Sphere was a truly immersive experience, boasting new ambient music created by Anastasio to soundtrack the atrium, psychedelic visuals that were loaded with both eye-candy and Easter eggs from throughout the group's 40-plus years, and a loose but thematic arc that kept fans guessing and engaged all the way through the run.

"Phish continues to produce new material and not settle for a comfort zone of constant familiarity," says Scott Marks, who tracks the band's setlists for Phish.net. "I'm not sure there really have been any events that have defined the current era of 4.0. The new material from *Lonely Trip* and eventually *Evolve* has helped define the era, but debuts and song appearances aren't events per se. The New Year's gags have been behemoth events (especially Gamehendge) but aren't defining a la, let's say, the Baker's Dozen or Big Cypress at the ends/twilights of 3.0 and 1.0, respectively. The big things of the current era would be the New Year's Eve gags and the four giant jams—8/31/21 "Soul Planet," 4/17/23 "Tweezer," 2/22/24 "A Wave Of Hope," and 2/23/24 "Chalk Dust Torture."

All of this is to say that Phish's story is still unfolding more than four decades after the group's founding members first crossed paths at the University of Vermont—and the musicians have long been able to reach a goal they set out for themselves while still a bar band in Burlington, Vermont.

"I remember going to see Modern Jazz Quartet," Anastasio told *Relix* in 2016. "They were so good—telepathic. They started playing in like 1952 and this must have been around 1985. We were all standing there going, 'We're gonna be that.'"

As they enter their next decade together, the members of Phish have proven their musical telepathy time and time again. And, in a world where bands come and go, or worse, fall prey to nostalgia, indeed the most obvious choice turns out to be the most surprising choice overall—to keep creating and evolving, together.

—Mike Greenhaus
April 2024

Thoughts on Sphere and the Year 2024

On Sunday, April 21, 2024—just a few hours before the final show of Phish's four-night run at Sphere—I had a quick check-in with Jason and Mike. We got on a call to talk about the Sphere shows, the current trajectory of the band, and the year that started with Gamehendge. Here's a small excerpt of our conversation.

—Andy P. Smith

ANDY P. SMITH: Having seen these first three Sphere shows now, where's the band at? How are the vibes?

MIKE GREENHAUS: It really was the first time in a long time that I think everyone going into the shows—whether they were streaming or there in person or just checking out the happenings in real time on the internet—went to a Phish show not knowing what to expect. Even though Phish change their show every single day, and have had countless stunts and gags over the years, this was a whole different experience, a whole different way of interacting with the music.

ANDY: I got the feeling that people felt a little bit underwhelmed by the visuals on Thursday? But come Friday and Saturday, it was a different story.

MIKE: I personally wasn't underwhelmed by the visuals. The visuals were great. From the get-go, there were different types of visuals. Some were more atmospheric, some were more video-centric, some were more scenescapes, and then some were kind of just like little Easter egg nods to the band's own history and songbook.

ANDY: Was the crowd only Phish fans or was there a contingent of industry folks and people just going for the Sphere experience?

MIKE: I'm sure there were music industry people who were just going to check out the experience, but in general most people there were pretty passionate Phish fans. It was obviously a tough ticket to get. It was a destination event for a lot of people. But it was one of the more high-profile shows that they've done recently, and got a lot more national media attention than your average Phish show, both because they were the second band to play the Sphere and because what they're doing with it is so different than what U2 did, which was a feat and a spectacle itself. But given that Phish is such an improvisational band, changing their show each night, they're coming at it from such a different perspective that they drew a lot of attention. And even though they were maybe under a microscope by the media world, Phish did a really good job presenting a Phish show: there were really long jams, really interesting song selections, and really thought-out transitions throughout the show. And also they can't help but be their prankster selves. The dog-licking video was the most obvious example of that, which is something that maybe to the outside world would elicit some head scratching, but it's just kind of the perfect little gag, if you will, to give the feel of a classic Phish show.

ANDY: Media coverage of these shows reminds me of the Baker's Dozen when Phish hit the radar for a lot of different people who didn't know much or anything about the band. *CBS This Morning*, *Spin*, etc. The Sphere coverage has been wild.

JASON GERSHUNY: Looking at this from the view of the rest of the world, I don't think Phish has ever been more nationally or internationally relevant. I was trying to think back, in 30 years of being a fan, I don't know a moment where there was more of a sort of casual attention being put on the band for people outside our scene. I think in an interview Trey did with *CBS Saturday Morning*, he said, "We're 40 years in and just hitting our stride." And seeing Phish in *USA Today* and the *Associated Press* is really cool. I don't know how many new people are going to now go to shows, I don't know if it's going to have that kind of a dramatic impact, but just seeing what we've come to love and known for so long being brought to attention, being bubbled up in different ways, it's kind of awesome. I think it was Page talking about the pride that the band members had in being the second band to play the Sphere. He was saying, "Most people were thinking it was gonna be Springsteen or The Stones, and it was us." And just how much that meant to them.

It's been really cool watching this all happen, watching the mechanisms of Phish, where they're already thinking about the summer festival and thinking about the summer tour and the album release, the train keeps rolling. And even though they're hitting this high mark of their career—where the world's attention is put on them and they're using I think the largest screen in the world and the best sound system in the world and having this moment—Trey's taking calls about the festival and thinking about how to constantly blow our minds and move things forward. It's great to see the health of the band in the 40th year. And the fact that they're still producing, they're still creating and writing music and finding ways to innovate at every opportunity they get...I think it's something to celebrate.

ANDY: I totally agree—what band does this? Really, what band rises to the level of doing musical costumes on Halloween and

Broadway production level shows with three sets on New Year's Eve? Even at the Sphere they're playing over three hours each night. They don't have to do that. It's just so incredible to see them still pushing the envelope in ways other acts don't. It's really remarkable.

I mean, beginning 2024 at the stroke of midnight with a full Gamehendge set, now Sphere, and a new album, and the tour, and the first festival in eight years. Like, this year is pretty beefy. If we jump cut 10 years down the road, like, how is 2024 gonna be remembered, or stand out among the 40-plus years of this band? To me it feels kind of momentous, but maybe that's just being in the moment.

JASON: Gamehendge, with the size and scope and mythology, what that meant to the fanbase, for that to be the starting point of this year—and for it to be done in that way, with the theatrics, and just really giving it their all for the first time in 30 years...it really was an emotional, heartfelt moment. And they just followed up: Mexico was great as always, and then to have the Sphere on top of that and the festival coming up. And then who knows what's gonna be happening the rest of the year. This will be one of those years that people talk about. And it makes sense because we're coming off their 40th anniversary. This is the launch to 40 and beyond. And they're killing it.

MIKE: I'm looking forward to seeing Gamehendge at the Sphere for Phish 50. [All laughing] They haven't played any yet!

Introduction

Phish is a band, and yet so much more.

Despite our combined attendance of close to 500 shows, boiling down this cultural phenomenon and the storied history of this American rock band into 100 things was a daunting task for Jason and me. We could have easily written 1,000 things or even separate volumes of whole books on the music, the tours, the festivals, the fans.

No fan base is more knowledgeable, more obsessed, than the Phish fan base. Any number of fans you'd find at a Phish show could tell you about their favorite performance of "Tweezer" (chapter 93) or regale you with stories from Shakedown Street (chapter 24) or gratefully share how they scored their Miracle ticket (chapter 66). Each fan of this storied band has his or her own tales and narratives. Each of us has our unique history and experiences with Phish, whether we've seen this band just once or dozens, hundreds, or countless times. This collection is merely our own version of this shared experience.

100 Things Phish Fans Should Know and Do Before They Die, we hope, is the beginning of a longer conversation. Our aim with this book is to inspire a dialogue among fans: chats between jaded vets and student noobs, Big Cypress attendees and Baker's Dozen crusaders, Cow Funkers, and Fuegoists. That said, some readers may disagree with some of our thoughts and opinions here. Even as coauthors of this book we have differing opinions. Hell, we're not the definitive archivists of this band that continues to perform and tour. We're just along for the ride, part of the process—and now you are, too.

As we wrote this book, one question kept popping up in our minds. Why Phish? Why Phish over so many other bands out there? Why Phish, still, after 40 years?

Why Phish? Because Phish is so much more than a band. Phish is a culture, a phenomenon, a dance party, a celebration, an inside joke, and a practical joke all the same. Phish is a 30-minute psychedelic improvisational meltdown followed by a two-minute, 100-year-old, a cappella barbershop quartet song. Phish is composition and improvisation. Phish is both humble and confident; spontaneous and rehearsed; four musicians larger than the sum of their parts.

A Phish show can reach religious heights, eliciting shared euphoria, as 20,000 fans revel in the band's exceptional tension/

All manner of Phish tickets and ephemera collected across 250-plus shows by 100 Things Phish co-author Jason Gershuny. (Jason Gershuny)

release improvisations. A Phish show can and will touch upon a plethora of musical genres and still be inherently, uniquely "Phish." No two shows are ever the same.

As clichéd as it may be to say, it's foremost about the music. These four virtuoso musicians, performing together for 40 years, have claimed their spot among the annals of great American music, recording 16 studio albums and releasing countless live albums from their more than 2,000 shows.

Why Phish? Because from the stage, they can do anything they put their minds to. To put it plainly: Phish is the best band in the world. There isn't another band today that could play 13 shows at Madison Square Garden and not repeat a single song.

Why Phish? We could give you a thousand reasons why Phish, but have attempted to distill that into 100 things, 100 whys, some objective, some personal, some historical, some magical, and yet, some still to be written....

This book was a collaborative project. Jason Gershuny wrote chapters 2, 7, 12, 17, 22, 30, 35, 38, 40, 46, 47, 49, 50, 72, 74, 83, 84, 88, and 89. All others were written by me, Andy P. Smith.

Start at the beginning and read cover to cover or skip around from chapter to chapter. We hope you enjoy reminiscing, discovering, relistening, and immersing yourself in the world of Phish while reading this as much as we did while writing it.

Thank you for checking out our book, and thank you for making the Phish community such a wonderful, joyful place.

See you on tour!

1 Four (or Five or Six) Dudes in Vermont

What is Phish? On its surface, that seems like an easy question to answer. But Phish is certainly more than the sum of its parts.

Phish is a band, a progressive rock fusion jazz psych jam band with a fervent following, performing live shows across America never repeating a single set, constantly exploring the vast possibilities within musical performance. To laymen, "Phish is kinda like the Grateful Dead, right?" But that's just uneducated presupposition, kind of like saying, "All pizza tastes the same."

Phish is surprising. Phish is inspiring. Phish is a community, a culture, a vibe. Phish is an institution, a religion, a kingdom, a world unto its own. Phish is a misspelling, a Secret Language, a middle-aged man wearing a muumuu. Phish is a vagabond circus, a classically trained pandemonium. Phish is a live performance, a jam, a journey.

But more literally, Phish is an American band formed in Vermont in 1983. Led by guitarist Trey Anastasio (b. 1964), Phish includes Mike Gordon (b. 1965) on bass, Jon Fishman (b. 1965) on drums, and Page McConnell (b. 1963) on keyboards.

The initial group included Jeff Holdsworth on guitar and vocals and briefly Marc Daubert on percussion. While Holdsworth was very much a cofounder of the band with Anastasio and penned a number of songs still included in Phish's repertoire ("Possum," "Camel Walk"), he left the band in 1986 after visiting Alaska and experiencing a spiritual awakening.

While Page McConnell, Phish's keyboardist, is undoubtedly vital to the sound of the group, he was not an original member of the band. He joined Phish in 1985, making Phish a five-piece group until Holdsworth left the band, thus cementing the Phish lineup that has remained unchanged for more than 30 years.

Ernest "Trey" Joseph Anastasio III, aka Big Red, was born in Fort Worth, Texas, and soon moved to Princeton, New Jersey, where he and his sister, Kristy, came of age. Both of his parents worked in education, his father as an executive of the Educational Testing Service and his mother as a children's book author and editor at *Sesame Street* magazine. Anastasio attended public and private schools, graduating from The Taft School, a private prep academy in Connecticut, where he met collaborators Tom Marshall and The Dude of Life (see chapter 10). It was at that time he formed his first bands, Red Tide and Space Antelope. He then enrolled at the University of Vermont, initially as a philosophy major, where he posted a flyer seeking a bass player.

Michael Elliot Gordon, aka Cactus, was the bassist who answered the ad. Growing up in Massachusetts as the son of an abstract painter and a founder and CEO of a chain of convenience stores, Gordon also attended prominent high schools as a student. He enrolled at UVM as an electrical engineering major and graduated with a bachelor of fine arts degree—and a new band.

Jon Fishman, aka Henrietta, grew up in Syracuse, New York, where he started drumming at a very early age. He was quite accomplished by the time he graduated high school and moved to Vermont to attend UVM, where he joined Gordon, Anastasio, and Holdsworth to form the band, initially and briefly called Blackwood Convention. Then, of course, the band changed their name, making Fishman the eponymous member, with just a slightly different spelling.

Page Samuel McConnell, aka Leo, aka The Chairman of the Boards, was born in Philadelphia, Pennsylvania, and grew up in Basking Ridge, New Jersey, where he fastidiously studied the piano, playing in bands as early as middle school. His father,

Dr. McConnell, worked in research and development at McNeil Laboratories, where he helped develop Tylenol and magnetic resonance testing. Page McConnell, like Anastasio, attended private prep academies, including a boarding school in Massachusetts, before attending Southern Methodist University in Texas. After two years he transferred to Goddard College in Vermont, where he would meet Anastasio, Gordon, and Fishman.

The band played their first gig at UVM on Friday, December 2, 1983 (see chapter 6). Phish's first gig to include Page McConnell was May 3, 1985. And the rest is history.

Over the decades, Phish has released 16 studio albums, hosted more than 10 weekend festivals, and played more than 2,000 shows. They've grossed hundreds of millions of dollars through album sales, live gigs, merchandise, webcasts, downloads, and films. And yet, Phish has never had a hit single, significant radio play, or mainstream accolades.

In 2000, they took a hiatus for a couple of years and then broke up for five years (chapter 75), and since returning in 2009, Phish has performed and toured regularly, though not as extensively as their prolific glory days in the 1990s. But many would say they're now playing as well as they ever have.

The Phish fan base is perhaps the only true link to The Grateful Dead, as both audiences embraced the counterculture lifestyle of living on the road, following the bands on tour from show to show, effectively building a traveling city with its own economy, rules, and traditions.

To that point, Phish is more than four dudes who met in college in Vermont. Phish have built something larger than themselves. Phish's grassroots growth is unprecedented, mainly due to their unique live performances. No two shows are the same.

Yes, Phish is a band, four musicians playing in a traditional rock band lineup of guitar, bass, drums, and keys. They've got it simple. But to say Phish is just a band is to miss the point entirely.

Phish is a cultural phenomenon, one that simply started with four (or five, or six) dudes in Vermont in the mid-1980s.

2 Career Overview

Since the new millennium, we have seen many tech companies launch, update, and reboot their products by using decimal-based designations such as 1.0, 2.0, and 3.0. Whole-number jumps often signify huge changes to the product. Within the world of Phish, there are three distinct eras (1.0, 2.0, and 3.0) that signify different phases in the band's history. These segments are based on periods of touring and marked by the breaks between those phases.

The designation 1.0 refers to 1983 to 2000, 2.0 is 2003 to 2004, and 3.0 is 2009 to present.

The 1.0 era is considered by most die-hard fans as the pinnacle of Phish. Phish 1.0 refers to original Phish, from their first concert in the Harris-Millis Cafeteria at UVM on December 2, 1983, until the final note of the October 7, 2000, show at Shoreline Amphitheatre in Mountain View, California.

Prior to Page McConnell joining Phish in 1985, Phish actually had two other members in the band—Jeff Holdsworth, who was a guitarist at the band's inception until he left for good in 1986, and Marc Daubert, who was an official member of the band for a few months in the mid '80s. Finally, in May 1986, the familiar Phish lineup of Trey Anastasio, Mike Gordon, Jon Fishman, and Page McConnell took shape.

For the next 14 years, Phish toured relentlessly, crisscrossing the nation, and at times, the world, traveling to Europe and Japan multiple times. They went from playing empty cafeterias to smoky bars to classic theaters to sold-out arenas and giant festivals. The miles, musical moments, and monster jams created a totally unique global Phish phenomenon.

Phish hit their self-proclaimed "high point" (as Trey, Mike, and Jon proclaimed in an interview with *Entertainment Weekly*) during the legendary Big Cypress Millennial Show in Florida during the New Year's run in 1999. Phish played two nights of incredible music, including a seven-plus-hour all-night set after the unofficial start of the new millennium. They felt they had created the greatest spectacle of their career, and were unsure where to go from there.

As Trey said to the *Burlington Free Times*, "For the first time, we had something [Big Cypress] we knew we couldn't out-do. Our whole career, we had been pushing this big, cool ball steadily uphill; not nine months after Big Cypress, it started to feel like it was starting to roll downhill."

In the fall of 2000, not nine months of Big Cypress, Phish announced they were going to take an indefinite "hiatus" as Trey penned a public letter explaining the motivation. Even though no time frame was given on the return, it was clearly worded to be a pause and not an end.

During the break, band members found a variety of outlets to keep their creative juices flowing. Side projects like the Trey Anastasio Band, Page McConnell's Vida Blue and the Spam All-Stars, Jon Fishman's Pork Tornado, and Mike Gordon's work on the movie *Outside Out* took the forefront of the band members' attention during the hiatus (see chapter 81).

Ultimately, the break didn't last long, and Phish returned after 26 months on December 31, 2002, at New York City's Madison Square Garden. Phish was back, and Phish 2.0 had officially begun. The tranquil opening notes of "Piper," built into a frenzied intensity, officially ringing in the new phase of Phish.

Phish 2.0 was brief, not quite 20 months, and was a time period known for some incredibly long and unique jams. As with any era of Phish, there were standout moments and shows that left the fans amazed, such as the It Festival, the legendary bust-out of "Destiny Unbound" at Nassau Coliseum in New York on February 28, 2003, and the bust-out-filled Star Lake show in Pennsylvania later that summer, on July 29, 2003.

But with all the good produced during Phish 2.0, under the surface, problems within the band were brewing. A series of infamously sloppy and uninspired shows in Las Vegas in 2004 made it clear that the band was not firing on all cylinders. Something was amiss.

A little more than a month after the Las Vegas shows, Trey sent a letter to the fans stating that he felt, in part, "Phish has run its course and that we should end it now while it's still on a high note." The end of Phish, or at least Phish 2.0, was at hand. They scheduled one final summer tour to say goodbye.

The final shows of Phish 2.0 took place at a festival in Coventry, Vermont. The intent was to have a giant final celebration of the band and their fans, but the weather leading up to the weekend and the lapses in the music left people feeling less than celebratory by the weekend's end (see chapter 86).

Unlike the end of Phish 1.0, this was a clearly defined breakup, not another hiatus. There was no guarantee that the band would ever get together again. In fact, Anastasio made it clear to everyone that this was indeed the end of Phish.

During the five-year breakup, the band members took some time away from the stage together, yet still found themselves engaged in creative solo projects and collaborations. Trey, Page, and Mike each had separate stints touring under their own names. In 2006, Trey and Mike teamed up with Joe Russo and Marco Benevento to form G.R.A.B. Trey also collaborated with some orchestras. Jon took on drumming duties for the Yonder Mountain

String Band for a while. There were opportunities to see the band members play, just not necessarily together.

Yet the most important event of this time period was also one of the darkest moments of the band's history. In 2006, Trey Anastasio was arrested in Whitehall, New York, for misdemeanor drug possession, driving while under the influence of drugs, and aggravated unlicensed operation. Trey had hit rock bottom and acknowledged this when he spoke to the Washington County Felony Drug Court in June 2016.

"The night I got arrested, I couldn't go 10 minutes without taking something," Anastasio said. "Nine years later, I don't think about drinking or drugging anymore." He added that it was "a gift to get arrested and be put through the paces to get sober."

Trey Anastasio used his experience to become an advocate for drug recovery programs. When speaking on behalf of the importance of the drug courts on Capitol Hill in May 2009, Trey said, "My life had become a catastrophe. I had no idea how to turn it around. My band had broken up. I had almost lost my family. My whole life had devolved into a disaster. I believe that the police officer who stopped me at 3:00 that morning saved my life."

And so, by 2009, by his own accounts, Trey had regained his footing and was clean and sober, and the band members were ready to give Phish one more reboot.

After five years of nonexistence, Phish once again graced the stage. They chose the legendary Hampton Coliseum—"The Mothership"—in Hampton, Virginia, to start things off. The Phish 3.0 era was launched with one of the most epic moments in Phish history. When they walked onstage for the first time in nearly a half a decade, the audience erupted in joy. When they began the first few notes of the classic "Fluffhead" for the first time in more than eight years, the crowd went absolutely wild (see chapter 88).

Phish 3.0 is a revelation. Phish fans around the world "feel the feeling" that we once forgot, and the band continues to create incredible moments, runs of shows, and tours.

Phish 3.0 has had its own microevolutions and epic tours. Fans are once again discussing and debating which 3.0 run was the best (*cough* Summer 2015, Baker's Dozen, Fall 2021 *cough*), or which Phish 3.0 jam was the deepest . They are even daring to compare the all-time greatness of Big Cypress to the immense achievement of the 13-show Baker's Dozen residency (see chapter 13).

We are in a new, mature, and healthy age of Phish. Much of the fan base has grown up along with the band and is introducing the musical magic to an entire new generation of phans. Trey has written a Tony-nominated Broadway musical, *Hands on a Hardbody*, and Mike Gordon has become a front man of his own nationally touring Mike Gordon Band (M.G.B.). Jon Fishman was even elected to public office in Maine on the Lincolnville Board of Selectmen. They've released new albums and have continued their longstanding New Year's Eve and Halloween traditions, and have even started new traditions, such the annual Dick's Labor Day run of shows in Colorado.

Phish 3.0 is becoming an entity all its own and is now fully hitting its stride. With this newfound vibrancy and health, it seems the catchy lyrics of "Blaze On" can be seen as a mantra: "the worst days are gone, so now the band plays on, you got one life, blaze on." Apropos for a band that's been playing and creating together for more than 40 years, wouldn't you agree?

Of course, there are many fans who believe we're now in the era of Phish 4.0—positing that the COVID break and 2020's rescheduled Summer Tour and the rescheduled New Years run of 2021 constitutes a break in performing and the beginning of this new chapter. And whatever era you may subscribe to, it seems that Trey Anastasio welcomed the 4.0 era with a new guitar.

On January 15, 2021, Anastasio shared a post and photo of his new guitar—this 10th guitar made by the band's former soundman and accomplished luthier Paul Languedoc (see more in chapter 39)—writing in the post: "The fact that this new guitar appeared during this downtime gives me hope for a new era of live music. I'll play it with love and gratitude, from the first notes of the next live shows. 'The 4.0' guitar!"

Whether it's 3.0 or 4.0, one thing is clear: the band continues to celebrate long-held performance traditions like musical costumes on Halloween in Las Vegas and New Year's runs at Madison Square Garden. And they continue newer annual stands as well. We've now had two three-night runs on the beach in Atlantic City. And since 2016's premiere four-night run at the all-inclusive Riviera Maya resort in Mexico, Phish has returned to Mexico six times, playing shows with long-awaited bust-outs (see chapter 76), with an encore guest sit-in from Dave Matthews (02/24/2022, see chapter 80).

Each year, Phish continues to play roughly two dozen shows across their Summer Tours, as well as a dozen shows for Fall and Spring Tours in 2022 and 2023. They've played their storied Labor Day run in Colorado every year since 2011, excluding the rescheduled dates from 2020, increasing from three to four shows in 2022 and 2023 (see chapter 92).

Hell—2023's Magnificent Seven at Madison Square Garden was a feat in and of itself. And with the 12/31/23 performance of Gamehendge, the spring 2023 Sphere shows, and the 2024 festival in Delaware…the momentum, creativity, and in many ways the culmination of a 40-year career that Phish is bringing into this current era is unprecedented and full evidence of a band with no plans to slow down or fade away.

3 Influences and Inspiration

Needless to say, as characterized by Phish's multigenre musicality, its band members have drawn inspiration from a variety of predecessors. Phish is influenced by 1960s rock, '70s disco funk, '80s pop, and more.

In an interview with Charlie Rose in May 2004 to discuss the band's decision to break up, Anastasio also shared some thoughts about which great musicians inspired him to pursue the art himself. When asked about the comparison between Phish and the Grateful Dead, Anastasio said, "It's not true in the sense that [the Grateful Dead] is probably the greatest band in American history." He continued, "Well, I'm just going to talk about Jerry now.... I probably only saw two rock concerts that completely transported me; one was Bruce Springsteen in 1978, he was doing "Rosaletta," and every single person in the entire arena was locked to that guy. That made me want to be a musician. The other times were the first and second times when I saw The Dead. And what I saw was a guy—Oh no no, another one, Zappa. I saw Zappa a number of times and he was just as intense—but Jerry Garcia was an absolute wonder to behold. When he walked onstage, he had every single person in that room riding on his every eyebrow move. And I've never seen it again. And now I know that some time has gone by how lucky I was. He was such a great singer and such a great songwriter. And that's the thing I don't see people talking about as much. But when I saw the Dead what I saw was people singing along. And hanging on this guy's every inflection. And it was done with tremendous soul; he was the most soulful singer I've ever seen. There's never going to be the next Jerry Garcia. There's never going to be the next Grateful Dead."

Anastasio then goes on to herald Bill Monroe as the inventor of bluegrass music, as well as Frank Zappa and Little Feat's Lowell George.

But let's be honest here. Many of Phish's early shows—1983, 1984, 1985—featured Grateful Dead covers such as "Scarlett > Fire," "Eyes of the World," "Help Is on the Way," and "Slipknot!," among others, an undeniable influence on Phish's early years to say the least.

Page McConnell was also a Deadhead. In a 2008 interview with ABC, McConnell said, "When I would see [the Grateful Dead] in concert, it would be a different song every night that would be my favorite of the evening. It wasn't any one song in particular that kept me coming back."

McConnell continued to list influences, including The Allman Brothers' "Jessica" and a handful of songs by Elton John, specifically "Amoreena," which, McConnell said, "I think I heard for the first time when I saw *Dog Day Afternoon*."

It's clear to see the band finds inspiration in the bands they've covered over the years, particularly Talking Heads, whose 1979 album *Fear of Music* peaked at No. 21 on Billboard and went gold. In 1980, Talking Heads released *Remain in Light*, which peaked at No. 19 and went gold. Trey Anastasio was 19 years old in 1980, and 16 years later he and his band Phish would cover the Talking Heads album in its entirety (chapter 11).

Looking at the variety of Halloween "musical costumes," the band members are also clearly inspired by The Who, The Velvet Underground, Little Feat, The Rolling Stones, The Beatles, and David Bowie. These are seminal acts whose canonical albums Phish has rehearsed and performed in Halloween homages since 1994.

But let's go back to the beginning—the late 1980s, Phish's college days at UVM. Back then it was all about Zappa.

In a December 2015 *Rolling Stone* article about the 100 greatest guitarists, Anastasio said of Frank Zappa's 1981 album *Shut Up 'n' Play Yer Guitar*, "When I was learning how to play guitar, I was obsessed with that album. Every boundary that was possible on the guitar was examined by him in ways that other people didn't."

According to Phish.net, Phish has covered Zappa's "Peaches en Regalia" 86 times since premiering the cover in 1986.

It's reported that the results of Phish's Halloween cover album fan vote in 1995 elected Frank Zappa's *Joe's Garage* album to be performed, but the band opted to choose the second-place winner, *Quadrophenia* by The Who. Rumored reasons for the alternate ranged from Zappa's complex song compositions and R-rated lyrics to Zappa's request for certain songs never to be performed live.

"Frank Zappa was a huge influence on how I wrote music for Phish," Anastasio wrote in *Rolling Stone* in 2010. "Songs like "You Enjoy Myself" and "Split Open and Melt" were completely charted out because he had shown me it was possible. And when I played at Bonnaroo with my 10-piece band, we did two covers, "The Devil Went Down to Georgia" and "Sultans of Swing." In both songs, I had the horn section play the guitar solos, note for note. I never would have thought of doing that if I hadn't seen Zappa do "Stairway to Heaven" in Burlington with the horns playing Jimmy Page's entire guitar solo, in harmony."

Concluding that article, Anastasio wrote plainly, "Zappa gave me the faith that anything in music was possible."

4 "You Enjoy Myself"

"You Enjoy Myself," aka "YEM," is perhaps the most quintessential Phish song. It's the song they've played the most, more than 635 times, averaging once every three shows, according to Phish.net. It's got it all: a delicate, composed section; solos for each band member;

The Title Though?

The song title itself reportedly comes from that same summer in 1985 in Europe, where Anastasio had been hanging out with some Italians who spoke little English. When they parted ways, the Italians said, "You enjoy myself, yes?" And yet, another origin story states something similar yet different: it wasn't an Italian couple but rather a German guy who reportedly said to Trey and Jon, "When I'm with you, you enjoy myself!" We may never know the truth.

a glorious peak buildup; strange lyrics; trampolines; open jam; and then what can only be described as a vocal jam.

"YEM" is Phish, unabashed, shameless, and entirely of its own. The song, as recorded on Phish's 1992 album *Junta*, is just short of 10 minutes, while most live versions land around the 20-minute mark.

If you were to dive into the catalogue of "YEM," well, it's difficult to pick a place to start. The song itself has changed over the decades. The first recorded version, on Phish's *The White Tape*, is entirely a cappella, while more recent versions of the Phish classic include Trey Anastasio's 2009 performance with the New York Philharmonic and his 2014 performance with the Los Angeles Philharmonic. Highly regarded performances of the song include an early gig in Washington, D.C., (November 16, 1991) and a Vermont gig with Carlos Santana (July 25, 1992). See also any "YEM" from 1995 (for example, October 31, 1995, or Albany's December 9, 1995).

To call the song epic is not to give it justice. "YEM" is a journey. "YEM" is a vision quest. "YEM" is sex, replete with an opening flirtation, dancing, the foreplay, the BOY!, leading up to an explosive orgasm, followed by a bizarre, post-coitus scat denouement.

Ultimately, YEM is a voyage into the unknown, exploring the relationship between man and the greater universe, unraveling the cosmic knot that is existence and, well…. Yes, okay, so the lyrics are a bit weird, even unintelligible.

"Boy, Man, what a jam! The tramps are transcendent!" (Andy Sinboy)

The main lyrical component is a series of single words shouted after what Phish.net's Charlie Dirksen once described as the "Charge," namely, *Boy, Man, God, Shit.* What follows is a mumbled, marbled amalgamation of what is historically considered to be the phrase "Wash uffitze, drive me to Firenze."

Now, only the band truly knows what they're saying or what it may mean. The question has been posed countless times and the handful of conflicting answers only furthers the debate. But here's what we know. Trey Anastasio wrote the song during a busking adventure through Europe with Jon Fishman in the summer of 1985. A common consensus is that they had hailed a cab driver to take them to Florence, Italy, known as Firenze in Italian, and the cab driver, perhaps slighted by their on-the-road appearance or smell, told them to "wash your feet." According to Phish.net, some 1995 performances include the band singing "washa you feetsie" in what could be considered an Italian accent.

Other translations of the intelligible lyrics include, as proposed perhaps comically by Mike Gordon in Phish's 1990s newsletter, "Water you team, in a beehive I'm a sent you," and "Yes, I'll play, but no I won't raise," and "Washer/dryer/freezer/fencing," and "Wash you face and drive me to Valencia," and "Washington fences, please, says me."

And that's not the strangest part.

During one segment of the song, someone backstage (for many years it was Phish's road manager, Brad Sands) brings out a pair of mini trampolines and, yes, Anastasio and Gordon then jump on mini trampolines onstage while Page McConnell jams. While jumping in sync, they also perform choreographed movements, turning from facing front to facing left, turning from facing left to facing right, then turning around the long way to face front again, for example. Some fans jump along with the guys as well. It's a strange and unique aspect to live performances of this opus.

Once joined by Grateful Dead bassist Phil Lesh, the band employed three trampolines so he too could bounce along.

And after what was thought to be the final performance of "YEM" at what was planned to be Phish's final festival, Coventry, in 2004, the band gifted the trampolines to the audience, who destroyed or dismantled the tramps so as to share in the relics among each other.

Still today, "YEM" is one of the most highly regarded songs in Phish's repertoire. It really does encapsulate many of the attributes of this band, from composed instrumentalism to lengthy freeform jams, to weird lyrics and onstage theatrics. Boiled down to its essence, "YEM" is Phish and Phish is "YEM."

When you hear it, be sure to enjoy yourself!

5 Welcome to Gamehendge

If Phish is a religion, and to many it is, then Gamehendge, aka *The Man Who Stepped Into Yesterday* (TMWSIY), is Phish's Bible, Qur'an, I Ching, Dhammapada….

There is nothing more highly regarded, more sought-after than a performance of Gamehendge. It is the ultimate white whale for all us Captain Ahabs.

Some fans head into a show praying for a full-on Gamehendge performance, as rare a feat as that may be these days. Surely, you'll find someone in the parking lot before every Phish show starting rumors or perhaps just personally manifesting, saying, "Tonight's the night." And it almost never is, just compounding the obsession.

For the uninitiated, here's the thing: Gamehendge is a place, a mythical, fictional place, that is the setting for *The Man Who*

Stepped Into Yesterday, which, for lack of a better term, is a rock opera.

Trey Anastasio wrote this opera, a sort of concept album, while in college at Goddard in 1987. *The Man Who Stepped Into Yesterday*, abbreviated as TMWSIY, is a collection of songs, connected through a narrated story, that includes such classic Phish

Trey Anastasio narrates the "Gamehendge" saga while characters move about the stage on 12/31/23. (Scott Harris)

tunes as "The Lizards," "Tela," "Wilson," "AC/DC Bag," and more. Anastasio turned it in as his college thesis.

The story is a bit complex and features dozens of characters, metaphors, and underlying themes. The whole thing is one big allegory. Here's my best attempt to summarize this 30-year-old epic and operatic story:

The plot involves a lonely, retired colonel named Forbin and his dog, McGrupp, who leave this world and enter Gamehendge through a strange, magical doorway. Colonel Forbin then meets Rutherford the Brave, who tells him of his land, Gamehendge, which is inhabited by a race of people called the Lizards who are "practically extinct from doing things smart people don't do."

Gamehendge Performed Live

The Gamehendge saga has been played in its complete or near entirety just a few times in Phish's career: 3/12/88 in Burlington, Vermont; 10/13/91 in Olympia, Washington; 3/22/93 in Sacramento; 6/26/94 in Charleston, West Virginia (the "GameHoist," show as it's known, with a first set Gamehendge with narration and second set of the entire Hoist album except for "Riker's Mailbox"); and lastly, 7/8/94 in Mansfield, Massachusetts. Since then, Phish has often performed many of the Gamehendge saga songs, but had yet to dive into the full epic with narration. That is, until New Year's Eve 2023, at Madison Square Garden, more than 29 years and 1,194 shows later.

For those in attendance at Gamehendge 12/31/23, the experience was nothing short of catharsis. For nearly 30 years, parking-lot rumors would latch on to certain shows ("Tonight's the night they do it"), only to mislead and continue to build the lure and lore of the Gamehendge saga and its white whale legacy. But come New Year's Eve 2023, Phish delivered a two-set treatment of the long hunted, narrated chronicle first written by Trey Anastasio in 1987 as a student at Goddard College.

Impeccably performed at the highest production, the 12/31/23 Gamehendge started with "Harpua," which included Anastasio telling stories about previous Harpuas, while actors playing Jimmy and his

Sadly, the Lizards are subjugated by an overlord named Wilson who came to power by stealing the Lizards' Helping Friendly Book, all of which Forbin learns from Rutherford. Furthermore, he learns of Rutherford's plan to overthrow Wilson and save Gamehendge with the help of various allies, including the beautiful Tela, "the jewel of Wilson's foul domain," with whom Forbin ultimately falls in love. Together they plot against Wilson, though it's revealed that Tela is Wilson's spy and is killed by the allies. Meanwhile, Wilson's accountant, Mr. Palmer, is discovered to be funneling money to fund the revolution, and he too is killed ("Time to put your money where your mouth is"), executed in public by the robotic hangman AC/DC Bag.

grandma, with a puppet of the cat Poster Nutbag, joined the stage to punctuate the narrative with pantomime and dialogue, concluding with her saying to Jimmy: "It's time…it's New Year's Eve and I can't let you ring another new year without knowing the real story of Gamehendge!" Amidst the roar of the crowd, the band played "The Man Who Stepped Into Yesterday" and a glowing rhombus rose to frame the stage. The subsequent two-hour performance included dozens of costumed, dancing lizards, actors, and large-scale puppets portraying the characters from Gamehendge, as well as aerialists, additional vocalists, an off-stage choir, a giant Famous Mockingbird puppet who flew over the crowd—as printouts of lyrics and other Phish lore descended from the ceiling, perhaps representing shredded pieces of The Helping Friendly Book—and a concluding jam of "Split Open and Melt" that saw the Lizards falling one by one into the story's mountain that was revealed to be a volcano, after which the rhombus was lowered, completing the saga.

Concluding a nearly 30-year wait of the fans and in many ways culminating a 40-year career of the band, the 2023 Gamehendge performance will undoubtedly rank as one of the greatest Phish shows of all time and serve as a launching pad for the next "Harpua," continuing to bolster and enrich both the mythology of Gamehendge and the legacy of Phish.

Battle erupts. The allies fight upon armed llamas—"Taboot taboot!"—as Colonel Forbin climbs the mountain to ask for help from the Supreme God, Icculus, who then employs the Famous Mockingbird to recover the Helping Friendly Book hidden in Wilson's castle. The book is recovered, and Wilson is then assassinated by the Sloth: "I'm so bad / He's so nasty / Ain't got no friends / Real out-casty."

The Lizards are saved and Wilson's reign is over, returning peace to the land of Gamehendge. Or perhaps not, as it's revealed that one of the allies, Errand Wolfe, decides to keep the book for himself, thus deeming himself king of Gamehendge. The story concludes with Forbin in a prison cell, listening to the repeated calls of "Errand, Errand, Errand," just like the beginning chants of the terrible dictator Wilson.

The story of Gamehendge and *The Man Who Stepped Into Yesterday* is one of corruption, the abuse of power, revolution, war, treason, deception, death, and, ultimately, how absolute power corrupts absolutely.

But it's not all gloom and doom; there are a few good songs in there too! Considering it's the work of a 1980s college student, it holds up damn well. Personally, the opening riff of "Wilson," with its call-and-response chant from the crowd, continues to excite me. It never gets old! And "The Sloth" is one of my favorite Phish tunes.

If you haven't already, to truly understand the Phish ethos, take a listen to TMWSIY front to back. It's about an hour long and there are more than a few YouTube videos out there that contain the whole thing. You can also read a full-fledged transcription of the work on Andy Gadiel's Phish page (gadiel.com/phish), if you're into that sort of thing.

Sure, it may seem a little dated at this point. And it has elements of musical theatre, for lack of a better term. But, for anyone looking to make sense of some of these seemingly nonsensical songs, well, this is the path…the path to Gamehendge.

Read it! Read the book! Read the Helping Friendly Book!

Pray to Icculus, the book's author. Let us all pray and congregate in the church of a Phish show.

And hopefully, one day, someday, we'll see you in Gamehendge.

6 "Do You Know Any Flock of Seagulls?"

As discussed in the 2000 Todd Phillips documentary *Bittersweet Motel*, Phish's first traditional gig was an ROTC dance at Harris-Millis Cafeteria at UVM. They were billed not as Phish, but rather as Blackwood Convention, the name of a popular bidding convention in the card game bridge. I suppose they were bridge fans?

At the time, Trey Anastasio was 19 years old.

"We played this ROTC dance…." drummer Jon Fishman recalls in the documentary. "We were using hockey sticks for mic stands, and we ran outta songs in an hour and started repeating the songs and at one point some girl came up and asked us if we knew any Flock of Seagulls. And that was the beginning of the end. We took a break and they brought down a stereo from somebody's room and started cranking Michael Jackson and stuff, and weren't really encouraging us to go back on."

In the documentary, Fishman and Trey Anastasio continue to reminisce, remarking that they repeatedly played "Long Cool Woman" and "Proud Mary" during their second set at that ROTC gig on Friday, December 2, 1983.

However, Phish.net lists the second set as just two songs: "Scarlet Begonias" and "Fire on the Mountain," the Grateful

Dead covers. Phish.net also notes that this show is often billed as a Halloween Dance, dated in October, though Phish archivist Kevin Shapiro has since unearthed a note confirming the December 2 date, corroborated by band members recalling rehearsals for this gig over Thanksgiving weekend. Furthermore, it was not an ROTC-sponsored dance, but rather a dormitory-hosted event in Mike Gordon's dorm, which happened to be occupied by predominantly ROTC students.

The band was then composed of Trey Anastasio, Mike Gordon, Jon Fishman, and Jeff Holdsworth, and on the recording of this show you can hear a woman at the dance talking presumably to Holdsworth, asking what they're going to play next. "Scarlet Begonia," Holdsworth says. "What?" she asks. Holdsworth is forced to repeat "Scarlet Begonias" a few times but she clearly doesn't know the title. She then continues: "Don't you know any slow songs, something we can dance to?" In response, Anastasio teases "Back in Black" by AC/DC before blurting into the microphone, "This is by request," which elicits a laugh from the band. They then kick off "Scarlet."

At the time, the band played a fair amount of Grateful Dead songs, an extension of one of Anastasio's earlier bands, The Space Antelopes, with Steve Pollak aka The Dude of Life, also a UVM student who attended The Taft School in Watertown, Connecticut, with Anastasio.

In the fall of 1984, percussionist Marc Daubert joined the band but left in early 1985. Not long after, Page McConnell, a Goddard student, joined the band as keyboardist and performed his first gig with the group on May 3, 1985, on campus at UVM. When Holdsworth left the band upon graduating in 1986, the lineup we know today was formed: Trey, Page, Mike, and Fish.

Then, as college students are often apt to do, Anastasio and Pollak planned and executed a prank that would ultimately end Anastasio's time at UVM. The details of this prank are varied and rumors continue to be shared among UVM graduates, but the general consensus is that Trey, a premed student, had access to a lab where he and Steve procured a human hand and heart they then mailed to a "friend" as part of an ongoing inside joke with a note that read, "I've got to hand it to you, you've got heart."

Whether Anastasio was expelled or merely suspended for one semester is debated, but McConnell, who received a $50 incentive for each transferee, took the opportunity to convince him and Fishman to transfer from UVM to Goddard College, about an hour's drive east in Plainfield, Vermont.

At Goddard, starting in mid 1986, the quartet Phish recorded and distributed as many as six different self-titled cassettes across campus, including *The White Tape*, aka *Phish*, aka *The White Album*, a now seminal collection of (roughly) 90 minutes and 16 wild, wonderful, experimental tracks the band initially used as a demo to share with venues and promoters.

The band now had a demo tape.

Phish had arrived.

7 Type I vs. Type II

Phish phans often talk in a language that is seemingly all their own. Whether it is rattling off details on 20-song setlists, dates of shows from many years ago, specifics on amazing versions of songs, or intricate plans for the upcoming summer tour, there is a lot of unique jargon thrown around. For anyone new to the Phish game, it is a lot to process. To fully understand the nuances of Phish, it is important to understand the differences between the jam styles— Type I and Type II.

These overly simplistic yet highly accepted terms within the Phish fan base were coined by a fan named John Flynn in 1997 on the original home for online Phish discussions (rec.music.phish). Through countless online discussions among fans, or via in-person spirited debates, these two designations have become commonplace in the Phish fan lexicon. The growth and acceptance of these terms serve as a linguistic case study in the evolution of a subculture's use of unique language.

Type I jamming can most easily be summed up as a classic rock-and-roll jam. The overall musical structure of a song remains in some distinguishable form as the improvisational jam takes shape. "Type I" Phish jams contain focused solos that often reach screaming tension-and-release peaks. Tension-and-release jams are a Phish specialty, and take place when the band and the audience are moving through a song together toward an inevitable musical climax. They make keeping your breath when dancing an accomplishment in itself. They tend to be found at every single show, and usually quite often. Throw on a classic "Antelope," "Slave to the Traffic Light," or "Maze" to feel the power of a "Type I" jam.

Type II jamming is quite different, and much more rare. For some fans, an extended Type II jam is the white whale they seek out at every show. Type II jamming is when Phish launches into a familiar jam (often starting as Type I), yet during the course of the jam, any resemblance to the original song melts away. What is left in its musical wake is improvisation that often, but not always, pushes the boundaries of the widely-used 20-minute barometer. "Tweezers," "Lights," and "Ghosts" often have the deconstructive power to reach "Type II" status.

These jams are never isolated on an island. Jams will often touch upon each of the styles as they develop, and often fans will be in disagreement as to when Type II status is even achieved. Still these terms are widely used within the fan base and are useful terms for any Phish jam discussions.

"Superstar Trey shining bright like a diamond." (AP Images)

8 Jam Vehicles: Tweezer, Ruby Waves, Mike's Song, and More

Phish has more than 300 original songs in their catalogue. And certainly Phish could jam on any one of their songs (see "Lawn Boy" from July 25, 2017). But there are a handful of songs that lend themselves to jams more than others, as proved through the vast history of Phish's live performances.

Considering the benchmark of 20-minute jams, which is agreed to be the timely characteristic of a solid jam, you'll find a variety of songs that have earned their medals and accolades in that regard. You'll find plenty!

If you just want the jams, and jams alone, there's more than a few "jams only" YouTube supercuts you can check out. Or head straight to PhishJustJams.com, which is exactly that: live Phish songs with the composed sections and vocals cut out.

And if only to further assist your search for renowned "heady" jams, here's a list of Phish jam vehicles.

"Runaway Jim"
"Runaway Jim" may fool you into thinking it's a bluegrass folk number, but that minimalist moment early on will always break into a full-on roar...where it goes from there is anyone's guess! Not bad for a song about a dog stealing the singer's car, clothes, and rent money. (Check out the nearly hour-long version from November 29, 1997.)

"Chalk Dust Torture"
The refrain "Can I live while I'm young?" is the backbone of this arena rock staple, but don't get caught sleeping during "Chalk Dust Torture." Just when you think you know what's happening, the

band will take this one deep into Type II territory with peaks the size of Everest. (Listen to the performance from July 10, 1999, or, more recently, July 28, 2017.)

"Harry Hood"
Good ol' "Harry Hood".... Like an underwater explorer or an astronaut in orbit, this song may go this way or that way, may find treasure or life forms or nothing at all. Hood is all of us, searching and seeking and eventually, ultimately, returning home. (See July 31, 2003, and August 5, 2013.)

"Bathtub Gin"
Some say "The Riverport Gin" (July 29, 1998) is Phish's best "Bathtub Gin," if not their best jam. Ever. Perhaps. The band has played the song more than 300 times. And even though there may be some "bests" and "favorites" of those 300-plus performances, even though some may have heard it one too many times at shows and would rather skip it, one thing is for sure: like pizza and sex, "Bathtub Gin" is good even when it's bad, and you can have it just about a thousand different ways. (After Riverport, check out performances from August 13, 1993, or December 29, 1995.)

"Mike's Groove"
Let's just take a look at "Mike's Groove," the pairing sandwich of a jam that features "Mike's Song" > another song > "Weekapaug Groove." Traditionally, that middle song, the meat of the sandwich, has been "I'm Hydrogen," but these days they'll play anything, sometimes many things, in that middle slot. And that's part of the jam, man. As one of Phish's oldest songs—it's been played over 548 times—I'm surprised that I still get excited when they start to play it. But that right there is a testament to its versatility and jamability. Then, there's the 'Paug Groove that follows, which always

gets people moving—or *Sharin' in the Groove*, as they say. (Check out August 16, 1996, or July 17, 1998.)

"Ghost"

"Ghost" is one of those special songs. Phish can play it fast or they can play it slow. They can play it funky or they can play it bluesy. I've heard "Ghost" played bouncy and bubbly early in a show, and dark and brooding late in the second set. Any which way you get a "Ghost," you're guaranteed to get spooked—spooked by an awesome jam, man. (See July 23, 1997, November 17, 1997, or July 6, 1998.)

"You Enjoy Myself"

"You Enjoy Myself," aka "YEM," is the most quintessential Phish song. They've played it more than any other song. It's one of the oldest songs in their repertoire. But really, folks, Phish's "YEM" is an epic, multifaceted opus, strictly composed with an improvised element than can happen quickly or extend for 30 minutes, though in later years it seems to be more of the former, and thus No. 4 on our list. On "YEM," just two more words: vocal jam. (Check out July 25, 1992, March 14, 1993, and October 31, 1995.)

Vegas Golden Age

I must mention what is widely considered to be one of the greatest jams in recent years—my personal favorite jam perhaps ever—the "Vegas Golden Age" (10/28/16). The jam on this incredible 25-minute version of TV on the Radio's 2008 single is intense and emotive, to say the least. This jam will make you feel the feels, man.

Sure, The Baker's Dozen brought some heavy hitters. And Big Cypress alone (December 31, 1999) had nine jams eclipsing the 19-minute mark. "Tahoe Tweezer" is pretty good too. But that "Vegas Golden Age!" That performance may very well be the "Riverport Gin" of Phish 3.0—just sayin'!

"David Bowie"

"David Bowie," not unlike "YEM," has a compelling composed section that often, but not always, leads into an expansive improvisation. Made famous in 1994—a year that brought us more than a few "Big Bowies"—the song's structure cues up a jam from near silence, which may very well be its majesty: Bowie forces the band to practically start from zero, building and building, often toward dissonance or general angst before hitting the frenetic, start-stop composed section, and then it's done! (Check out December 29, 1994, or July 30, 1997.)

"Ruby Waves"

While phish premiered "Ruby Waves" in Toronto, Ontario on 06/18/2019, the song was written by Trey Anastasio and initially performed by TAB, before joining the Ghosts of the Forest repertoire in Portland, ME (04/04/2019). But it would show it's full force at Alpine Valley in East Troy, Wisconsin (07/14/2019) to conclude the Summer Tour where fans would bear witness to an enormous monster of a multi-faceted jam across a 38-minute "Ruby Waves," of which Phish.net writes: "Listening to this masterpiece is non negotiable." It's one of the longest songs Phish has ever performed and only time will tell if its historically known as the Alpine Ruby Waves or simply *The* Ruby Waves. (See also 10/20/21, 7/14/23, and 10/11/23, all of which run 25-30 minutes.)

"Down With Disease"

Played as a second-set opener more than any other song, Phish seems to have elected "Down With Disease" as the premier song to get the jam going. And it almost never fails. Beginning with a garbled gurgle from Mike Gordon, "Down With Disease" often heads into Type II territory rather quickly…and from there? It can go literally anywhere. (See August 17, 1997, or December 29, 1997.)

"Tweezer"

If we were to claim one song above all others as the preeminent jam vehicle, yes, it's "Tweezer." So much so that I will dare to use it as a verb. Goddamn, Phish can "Tweezer!" They can shred it, space it, funk it, and dark it. "Tweezer" jams are distinctive. Since its premiere in 1990, Phish has played "Tweezer" over 440 times. So dive in, y'all. Step into the freezer. (Perhaps start with May 7, 1994, December 2, 1995, or June 14, 1995. And see more in chapter 93.)

Of course, there's plenty more. We could have easily made a top 20 list. As such, honorable mentions include "Carini," "Piper," "Simple," "Stash," "Twist," and "Crosseyed and Painless," to name a few.

CK5

Beyond the four musicians onstage, there is one man without whom Phish would not be the band and live act they are today.

While commonly referred to as the fifth member of the band, he is not a musician. You won't see him onstage. But without him, you wouldn't see anything.

His name is Chris Kuroda, aka CK5, and he is Phish's lighting director, responsible for the visual spectacle that makes Phish shows all the more special.

Kuroda has worked as Phish's lighting director since March 1981. He has also worked as lighting director for Ariana Grande and Justin Bieber, having designed, written, conceived, and programmed all aspects of stage lighting for Justin Bieber's Believe Tour from 2012 to 2014.

Wanted: Creative Light Person

Phish ran an ad for a light designer in the March 1989 issue of the *Phish Newsletter*, which at the time was printed and distributed by Trey Anastasio's sister Kristy. It read:

WANTED: CREATIVE LIGHT PERSON TO RUN NEW LIGHT SHOW FOR PHISH ON A SALARIED, PERMANENT BASIS. THIS VERY VALUABLE PARTNER WILL TRAVEL WITH THE BAND AS A 5TH MEMBER. WE ARE LOOKING FOR SOMEONE FROM THE NEW ENGLAND AREA—NO NEED TO LIVE IN BURLINGTON. CALL (802) 654-9068.

Even in the late 1980s, Phish had a vision that included a significant lighting show. But for the record, Kuroda never even responded to the ad.

In a *New York Times* article published August 3, 2023, "How Phish's Lighting Designer Jams With the Band," Marc Tracy writes that Kuroda also "designs the lights for the New York Knicks and Rangers, and the Golden State Warriors. He has lit the Black Crowes, Aerosmith, R. Kelly, Ariana Grande, and, a decade ago, Justin Bieber, a show which involved 2,900 lighting cues and no punting."

Phish's light show is no ordinary light show. It is a spectacle unto itself. And while seemingly all other bands' lighting merely supports or accents the musical performance, the work of Chris Kuroda will sometimes genuinely influence the band's improvisation. The relationship this lighting artist has developed with these four musicians over the decades touches on a group mind, a psychic synchronicity.

In fact, while listening to a live Phish show from the annals, one may hear a loud, unexpected roar from the crowd seemingly out of context from the music. Well, that's Kuroda working his magic, literally wowing the audience.

Surely, Kuroda is a master of his trade, but recently some of his wizardry is a result of his tireless endeavors to do more, to be bigger and better. He never stops learning, never stops pushing the envelope, and is constantly developing new techniques as well as new technologies.

For Phish's summer 2016 tour, Kuroda and production designer Abigail Rosen Holmes developed an addition to their traditional lighting rig: an LED panel array onstage behind the band that showcased an infinite color palette as well as geometric animations during the first sets. And then, for the second sets, however, the large panel would split into dozens of individual panels and rise high above the band, a positioning that reminded some fans of classic arcade games like Galaga: colorful, independent aliens descending upon the stage.

While some fans praised the new addition, others disliked the added technology, calling it a distraction or otherwise overkill. Of course, no one knew what Kuroda had in store for summer 2017.

But let's step back for just a minute. How did Kuroda come to work as Phish's lighting director for now over 30 years?

According to Phish.com, Kuroda, already a Phish fan, was taking guitar lessons from Anastasio at the band's house in Winooski, Vermont the day before a two-night stint at local club The Front when Trey asked him if he knew anyone who would be interested "in carrying some gear in and out of local gigs for $20."

"I'll do it," Kuroda said.

Originally from Princeton, New Jersey (where Anastasio and lyricist Tom Marshall went to high school), Kuroda, aka Topher, grew up in Westchester County, New York, spending many of his teenage days in Manhattan. After initially attending New England College in New Hampshire, Kuroda transferred to UVM in 1986 to major in computer science. While studying in Burlington, Kuroda worked as manager of a silk screen shop.

As an avid fan and follower of the Grateful Dead—Kuroda caught 232 Dead shows—it was there, watching the work of the Dead's longtime lighting director, Candace Brightman, that he discovered his interest in and love for live production light shows.

The dynamic lighting rig designed and operated by Phish's Lighting Designer Chris Kuroda, sometimes referred to as "the fifth member of the band" on 12/28/22 at MSG, NYC. (Trevor Anderson)

Then suddenly, at 24 Kuroda found himself part of the Phish team as a roadie. As the story goes, back then, a man named Chris "Steck" Stecher was the band's lighting director. But not a week later, during an April 7 show at Stone Church, Steck left the lighting board to use the bathroom during "Famous Mockingbird" and Kuroda took over. According to Phish.com, Trey was impressed by the lighting work during "Mockingbird" and complimented Steck after the show, only to later discover it was indeed Topher at the helm for that song.

And the rest is history. Chris Kuroda has worked as Phish's only lighting designer and director ever since.

One of Kuroda's greatest accomplishments was his 2017 expansion and upgrade to Phish's lighting rig, which premiered in Chicago to kick off Phish's 2017 summer tour. Featuring a completely unprecedented automated truss system that allows Kuroda to move clusters of lights in sync or independently, this lighting rig is a sight to behold. In some instances, the lights themselves seem to have life, ascending and descending at free will. Again, this is Kuroda's wizardry at work. The 2017 rig is revolutionary. For a unique glimpse at its wonder, check out the handful of time-lapse videos on YouTube capturing the scope and scale of the rig's movement.

For more on the 2017 rig, check out the podcast *The Light Side*, hosted by lighting designer and audio engineer Luke Stratton, where in episode five Stratton sits down with Kuroda and associate designer and programmer Andrew Giffin.

The latest addition to Kuroda's rig? 144 LED tetra bars a couple feet long mounted to the moving truss pieces that light up, spin, and arrange themselves into patterns: swirls, squiggles, beams, bleeds, bops, soars, chases, and more. And as part of the MSG lighting director, Kuroda has also added programmable ceiling lights and LED section entrance lights that only enhance the full-room experience of his lighting.

Needless to say, Chris Kuroda, while not a performing musician, is an integral member of Phish. Can you imagine a Phish show without its brilliant, dynamic lighting?

No. Because, well, that just wouldn't be a Phish show.

10 Words and Lyrics: Tom Marshall and The Dude of Life

Within the world of Phish, there are a few key players without whom Phish would not be the band we know and love. And for all intents and purposes, the realm of Phish lyrics and poetry is ruled by a man named Tom Marshall.

Currently hosting the podcast *Under the Scales*, on which he interviews Phish fans, collaborators, and for two episodes Phish guitarist Trey Anastasio himself, Tom Marshall is a longtime collaborator with Anastasio and the primary lyricist of Phish. Marshall has songwriting credits for more than 100 Phish songs, including three on the recent *Big Boat*, 10 out of 15 on 1993's concept album *Rift*, and all 14 songs on *The Story of the Ghost* (see chapter 62).

Marshall is the man behind the words to such iconic songs as "Guelah Papyrus," "My Friend My Friend," and "The Squirming Coil," the latter of which concludes as follows:

Stun the puppy!
Burn the whale!
Bark a scruff and go to jail!
Forge the coin and lick the stamp!
Little Jimmy's off to camp

And, of course, who doesn't love the lyrics to "Stash"?

Smegma, dogmatagram, fishmarket stew
Police in a corner, gunnin' for you
Appletoast, bedheated, furblanket rat
Laugh when they shoot you, say
"Please don't do that"
Control for smilers can't be bought
The solar garlic starts to rot
Was it for this my life I sought?
Maybe so and maybe not

But not all of Marshall's lyrics are absurdist. Personally, I love the lyrics in "Waste":

don't want to be an actor, pretending on the stage
don't want to be a writer with my thought out on the page
don't want to be a painter 'cause everyone comes to look
don't want to be anything where my life's an open book

don't want to be a farmer, working in the sun
don't want to be an outlaw, always on the run
don't want to be a climber, reaching for the top
don't want to be anything where I don't know when to stop

a dream it's true
but I'd see it through
if I could be
wasting my time with you

In the early 1980s, Marshall and Anastasio attended Princeton Day School, a private middle school and high school in Princeton,

New Jersey, where they met and became friends, collaborating on songwriting beginning in the eighth grade.

As the legend goes, youths Marshall and Anastasio would meet at The Rhombus, a public park sculpture in Princeton, where they would write and collaborate for hours on end. Subsequently, The Rhombus ("New Piece," 1966, by Tony Smith) is prominently featured in *The Man Who Stepped Into Yesterday* as the portal from our world to the world of Gamehendge (or merely a part of Gamehendge?), and thus the sculpture in Princeton has grown to become a destination for many Phish pilgrims.

Tom Marshall is also an accomplished musician, fronting the band Amfibian after releasing his 2000 solo album *Amfibian Tales*. The band Amfibian featured Marshall on vocals and keyboards with guitarists Scott Metzger and Andrew Southern, former Ween bassist Matt Kohut, and two drummers, Pete Cottone and J.P. Wasicko. The band played actively for about a year before retiring, only to be reformed in 2004 when the band released their first studio album, *From the Ether*. The band then dissolved again after touring to support the album, and Marshall revived the group in 2006 and in 2007 released *Skip the Goodbyes*, which features Trey Anastasio, among others.

Over the years, Tom Marshall has joined Phish onstage to sit in on vocals on a handful of occasions, singing mostly covers, notably "Champagne Supernova" (December 29, 1996), "500 Miles (I'm Gonna Be)" (December 30, 1997), and "Born to Run" (July 16, 1999).

Today, Tom Marshall continues to collaborate with Phish as their lyricist, delivers two episodes of *Under the Scales* every month, and can occasionally be found sitting in on vocals with a variety of Phish tribute bands all across the country.

But Marshall isn't the only person with Phish song credits to his name. Of course, Trey Anastasio, Mike Gordon, Page McConnell, and Jon Fishman, as well as early band member Marc Daubert, all have writing credits for a variety of songs. Other authors include Richard "Nancy Taube" Wright, who wrote "Halley's Comet" and "I Didn't Know," as well as Susannah Goodman, who wrote the lyrics to "Bathtub Gin," after which Anastasio composed the music to match.

Then there's Steve Pollak, aka The Dude of Life.

While it may be confusing, the prolific poster artist Jim Pollock (see chapter 71) and The Dude of Life, Steve Pollak, are two very different people.

The Dude of Life, Steve Pollak, is a musician and lyricist in his own right. He met and befriended Trey Anastasio in high school, where they subsequently formed a band with two other friends called Space Antelope, primarily a Grateful Dead cover band. Together, Pollack and Anastasio attended UVM, collaborating on a number of musical projects, including a few songs now considered Phish staples, such as "Dinner and a Movie," "Fluffhead," "Suzy Greenberg," and the Space Antelope number "Run Like an Antelope."

The real Suzy Greenberg

Since debuting "Suzy Greenberg" in Johnson, Vermont on 2/13/87, Phish have performed the song 449-plus times. Written by Anastasio and Steve "The Dude of Life" Pollak when they were both college students, the lyrics are anything but mature: "Suzy's 'bout as faithful as a slot machine / Pays off once in a while, but then she robs you clean." But the song's joyous, singalong chorus never fails to get the crowd going, often awash in CK5's bright white lights.

As it turns out, there is a real Suzy Greenberg. Legendary, yes, but also an actual human who reportedly attended her very first Phish show on 4/12/22. As the band took the stage, Anastasio spoke to the audience, saying "The hero to this first song is in the audience tonight. She's at her first phish show. So could you guys sing along and welcome her? This song's about her." Then they launched into a fun-loving rendition of "Suzy Greenberg."

In 1991, Pollak recorded his first solo project, backed by the band Phish, titled *Crimes of the Mind*. He toured in support, and followed up with 1999's *Under the Sound Umbrella*.

Over the decades, The Dude of Life has appeared as a guest onstage with Phish a few times, performing, singing, or otherwise. In the 3.0 era, Pollak joined Phish and lyricist Tom Marshall to sing the lyrics to "Run Like an Antelope" to conclude the second set of the first night of Phish's 2012 SPAC run (July 6, 2012).

More recently, Phish busted out "Crimes of the Mind," the eponymous single by Marshall's Phish-backed musical project, at their 2016 Halloween run in Vegas (October 28, 2016) for the first time in nearly 300 shows.

While the breadth of Phish's lyrics is only outshined by the intricacies of their music, many of Phish's songs feature inspiring visuals, vexing questions, poignant observations, bizarre narrations, heart-wrenching poetics, and, to put it lightly, pure gobbledygook.

Phish's postmodern approach, meshing and intermingling different musical genres, is all the more apparent in their often absurd or silly lyrics. It's part of the fun!

11 Building a Musical Costume: Halloween 1.0

How does a band dress for Halloween? What kind of costume can a band wear?

While Phish's 1994 Halloween show may perhaps be their most memorable, it wasn't their first. Phish played four straight Halloween shows in '88, '89, '90, and '91, which featured costume contests for fans, but in 1994 the band kicked off a new tradition.

And this tradition is perhaps the most distinctive element of Phish's live performance history.

Before their fall 1994 tour kicked off in Bethlehem, Pennsylvania, in early October, Phish announced via their fan newsletter, *Doniac Schvice* (chapter 57), that their Halloween show at Glen Falls Civic Center would of course continue the fan costume contest and also include not two but three sets of music, one of which would be a cover of a classic album in its entirety. What album? Well, Phish invited their fans to vote! Via snail mail, of course—this was 1994, after all. Reportedly, Phish received just 50 votes and had a clear winner.

That night, October 31, 1994, Phish opened with "Frankenstein" (with Trey Anastasio wearing some sort of cloud head mask) and delivered stellar versions of "Reba," "Divided Sky," "Julius," and "Harpua," to name a few of the first set highlights. Then, as they returned to the stage for the second set, the audience heard a familiar voice over the PA. It was Ed Sullivan's famous introduction that concludes with, "Ladies and Gentlemen, The Beatles!" And Phish immediately ripped into "Back in The U.S.S.R." That night, for the second set, Phish played all 29 songs on The Beatles' *White Album*. It was revolutionary and totally unique.

Phish certainly made the songs their own, changing lyrics, teasing their own songs within the Beatles' songs, singing the end of Helter Skelter a cappella. "Cry Baby Cry" concluded with Jon Fishman playing the vacuum and "Revolution 9" just got weird as a background tape played "He Ent to the Bog" from Phish's *The White Tape* and Fishman pulled his dress up and over his head, getting completely naked as the other band members blew bubbles. Eventually, strobe lights blasted the stage and the audience as the band departed. Now setbreak, with the venue's house light on, The Beatles' song "Good Night" played over the PA and someone announced the band would be returning (for the third set) in about 15 minutes.

Phish then returned and played another nearly hour-long set before encoring with "Amazing Grace," selecting the winner of the costume contest, and playing "The Squirming Coil" to end their four-hour musical performance (concluding at 3:30 AM) that would later be released as Live Phish Vol. 13 in 2002.

Phish's 1994 Halloween concert is a landmark show for many reasons. Here is a band, so versatile in their abilities, that can show up for the 20th gig of their 46-date fall tour and play a four-hour show that features a 29-song Beatles album. Here is a band who engages their audience, involving them in a costume contest as well as a democratic vote as to what album to cover. Here is a band, 10 years into their career, pushing themselves into new territory by performing what many critics have heralded as one of the greatest albums of all time.

In 1968, Jann S. Wenner wrote of the *White Album* in *Rolling Stone*:

> As to the Beatles, it is hard to see what they are going to do next. Like the success of their earlier albums and the success of all others in this field, whether original artists or good imitative ones, the success of it is based on their ability to bring these other traditions to rock and roll (and not vice versa, like the inevitable excesses of "folk-rock," "raga-rock," and "acid-rock") and especially in the case of Dylan, the Stones, the Beatles, and to a lesser extent all the other good groups in rock and roll, the ability to maintain their own identity both as rock and roll and as the Beatles, or as Bob Dylan, or as the Rolling Stones, and so on.

It's interesting to think of replacing "The Beatles" with "Phish" in Wenner's 1968 article when he writes, "Thus, [Phish] can safely afford to be eclectic, deliberately borrowing and accepting any outside influence or idea or emotion, because their own musical ability and personal/spiritual/artistic identity is so strong that they make it uniquely theirs, and uniquely [Phish]."

In many ways this show cements Phish in the canon of American music as a premier rock band among many, certainly. But it also showcases the wholly unique band called Phish.

Nearly 19 years later, Phish returned to the Civic Center in Glen Falls, New York (October 23, 2013). The band opened with "Back in the U.S.S.R." and closed the show with "While My Guitar Gently Weeps," both songs from The Beatles' *White Album*.

In 1995, Phish again asked their fans to vote for what album they would cover in "musical costume" for their Halloween show at Rosemont Horizon in Rosemont, Illinois, about 20 miles outside of Chicago. That night (October 31, 1995), rumors abounded that Phish would cover Michael Jackson's *Thriller*.

Phish opened the show with "Icculus" for the first and only time in their career, setting a wild, unpredictable tone for the evening right away. After a spirited set of music, Phish closed the first set with "Harpua," featuring narration by Mike Gordon and pointed *Thriller* teases from Anastasio. In fact, throughout their fall tour Phish had teased and hinted at the *Thriller* album many times over, perhaps deliberately misdirecting the audience regarding the forthcoming Halloween album of choice.

Like the year before, Phish had again asked their fans to vote for what album they would cover, and allegedly the band received the most votes for Frank Zappa's 1979 three-part rock opera album *Joe's Garage*. But when the band set out to learn and rehearse the songs, they thought better. Zappa's complex compositions, R-rated lyrics, and public request that some of the songs never be performed live perhaps lead Phish to abandon the album and choose to cover the album with the second most votes: The Who's *Quadrophenia*.

But continuing to build this *Thriller* red herring at the show, setbreak music included Michael Jackson songs and Phish even teased "Thriller" when taking the stage for the second set, only to open instead with *Quadrophenia*'s "I Am the Sea," replete with ocean wave sound effects. For the cover album performance the band was joined by Dave "The Truth" Grippo on alto saxophone, Don Glasgo on trombone, Joey Sommerville on trumpet, and Alan Parshley on French horn.

Released almost exactly 22 years prior to the day Phish covered the album, *Quadrophenia* was The Who's sixth studio album and second rock opera, a follow-up of sorts to *Tommy*. Written and compsed by Pete Townshend, the album is about a young mod named Jimmy set in 1965 London.

As a touring band in the mid 1960s, The Who was famous, or infamous, for destroying their instruments at the end of their shows. Pete Townshend is heralded as the first rock star to smash his guitar onstage. And perhaps most famously, when The Who appeared on the Smothers Brothers' show in 1967, their U.S. television debut, drummer Keith Moon loaded his kick drum with explosives and as the band started smashing their instruments during the finale performance of "My Generation," Moon detonated the drum, injuring himself and Townshend.

But back to Phish. After the *Quadrophenia* set, the band returned to the stage and made their next move in the band vs. audience chess game they'd been playing throughout the tour. Then, Anastasio led Phish through an incredible third set, featuring a 40-minute "You Enjoy Myself" of epic, space-crunch-disco proportions and a horn-infused, very apropos "Jesus Left Chicago."

Then, before the encore, stagehands set up a replica Keith Moon drum set. Phish returned to the stage and performed an acoustic "My Generation," after which Fishman and Anastasio destroyed the replica drum kit. In true unpredictable Phish style, a stagehand brought out an oversized plunger that Trey pressed down, setting off a large explosion backstage.

This nearly four-hour show was officially released as Live Phish Vol. 14 in 2002.

In 1996, Phish would once again return to perform on Halloween night in "musical costume," this year at Atlanta's Omni Coliseum. But this year's album would be no surprise. As fans entered the venue they were given a Phishbill, which was a spin on the classic Broadway theatre magazine *Playbill*, with cover artwork featuring the cover of the 1980 Talking Heads album *Remain in Light*.

Phish continued their tradition of creating musically stacked, Halloween-themed first sets during Halloween shows, opening with "Sanity" > "Highway to Hell." For the second year in a row the Halloween show had some first-set narration, referencing David Byrne of Talking Heads during "Colonel Forbin's Ascent."

Phish returned to the stage for the second set and performed all eight songs from *Remain in Light* featuring Santana percussionist Karl Perazzo and Dave Grippo and Gary Gazaway on saxophone and trumpet, respectively. There are some incredible moments in this set, including the debut of the now-modern Phish staple "Crosseyed and Painless" and an over-the-top version of "The Great Curve," a performance so raging as to elicit an audible cheer from someone on the stage when the song ends. Phish concluded the set with "The Overload," a performance that included strange, onstage, TV-laden theatrics.

Since premiering "Crosseyed and Painless" at the Omni on Halloween night 1996, Phish has performed the Talking Heads classic more than 60 times and have opened second sets with the song two dozen times.

The layered approach necessary to recreate an album of this magnitude may be one of the contributing forces behind the band's musical transformation in the late 1990s. Covering *Remain in Light* may at least be partly to thank for spurring on the evolution of the band toward the lauded 1997 Cow Funk era, which many fans consider the band's best time period, as Anastasio discusses in Richard Gehr's *The Phish Book*.

Phish then played a third set with Karl Perazzo on percussion. The "2001" > "Maze" is perfectly paired. They appropriately encored this Halloween with "Frankenstein," thus completing their third annual musical costume tradition, released as Live Phish Vol. 15 in 2002.

In 1998, Phish kicked off their fall tour with a one-off show in Los Angeles, followed by two nights on Halloween weekend at the Thomas & Mack Center in Las Vegas.

Once again, rumors swirled regarding what album the band would play in "musical costume," and in repeating the previous year's Phishbill concept, the band revealed immediately to attendees that they would cover *Loaded* by The Velvet Underground.

After a solid and funky first set, Phish took the stage for the second set and kicked off the storied 1970 album with "Who Loves The Sun?" And while some may argue that previous Halloween cover albums featured Phish jamming or otherwise improvising on the songs, this performance is perhaps the only cover album show where Phish does truly deviate from the compositions, exploring jams on a number of the songs (see the high-energy exploration of "Lonesome Cowboy Bill").

The *Loaded* set is a perfect example of the band giving their all to make another band's music their own. "Sweet Jane" and "Rock and Roll" were songs made for live Phish, and "Oh! Sweet Nuthin'" was powerful and poignant. They weren't trying to recreate or recite someone else's music; they were building upon a classic foundation to create new and original Phish magic. This set shreds.

Without a doubt, the Halloween costume set is one of Phish's most legendary traditions. And the payoff goes well beyond the cover set. Because they are so laser-focused on honoring and expanding on another artist's music, their practiced execution spills out into striking and memorable sets for the rest of the run.

One of the more controversial sets in Phish history was the third set that night, which featured just three songs. "Wolfman's Brother" opened the set and took a dark and spaced-out turn, winding and churning for 30 minutes. Some loved the dark theme for this Halloween show and others thought it was wandering directionless. And then one of the weirder moments in Phish history occured. Concluding "Ghost," just the third song of the set, Anastasio seemed to unceremoniously end the song and simply walked offstage. Some speculate that the moment may have been a little too intense, for one reason or another.

The set left many fans scratching their heads. Phish encored quickly with "Sleeping Money" and "Tweezer Reprise," thus ending the third show of the fall tour and the fourth "musical costume" show of Phish's career. The *Loaded* October 31, 1998, show was eventually released as Live Phish Vol. 16.

The Beatles, The Who, Talking Heads, and The Velvet Underground—Phish's 1990s musical costume Halloween sets have proved to be some of the most inspired, well-executed live musical performances of the decade. They offer not a glimpse but a full-on immersion into the musical greats that propelled this band to carve out their own spot in the canon of classic rock, albeit by covering the very rock gods that came before them.

What band can take another band's album and make it their own? What band can deliver, year after year, a spectacle of both nostalgia and originality? What band involves their audience through a democratic voting process, then still surprises, even misleads their audience? What band? Only the Phish from Vermont.

12 Big Cypress: NYE 1999

Pinnacle. Peak. Apex. Zenith. Acme.

In the realm of Phish, there is one show and one show alone that brings forth this kind of praise. The Big Cypress Millennial Festival in December 1999, nestled deep in the Florida Everglades, was the moment when Phish's legacy reached dizzying new heights.

There is so much that can be said about this festival, but the easiest way to describe the magnitude of the event is to let the band speak for themselves. A few months after the festival concluded, Phish was asked in an *Entertainment Weekly* article which show they considered to be a highlight of their career, and three out of four of them said Big Cypress. It was that special and worthy of all of the accolades it received.

To understand the power of Big Cypress, one needs to travel back to that moment in time. The world was sitting at the tail end of one millennium, on the precipice of another. The cold war had ended, and the war on terror had yet to begin. America was knee-deep in her 1990s golden age.

Computer technology and social media were just taking hold of our collective consciousness. Even cell phones were not yet a modern requirement. For those younger than 30, imagine going to a show and not seeing dozens of bright screens taking crappy pictures and video throughout. Imagine trying to meet up with friends by pinning handwritten paper messages to physical message boards, hoping your friend would actually find them among the hundreds of other dangling scraps of paper. It's true—Phish concerts really used to be like that. And with this as the backdrop, Phish was on top of their game.

Leading up to the year 2000, computer scientists recognized that a common programming shortcut may have dire consequences. It was the age of Y2K paranoia, where adding an apostrophe instead of typing out the full "19" at the beginning of the year could have somehow caused all the world's technology to freak out and fail simultaneously. The question became, what would happen when the calendar struck 2000, and computers thought we went back in time to 1900?

Wild theories began to surface that planes would fall out of the sky, nuclear missiles would launch, and technological chaos would reign supreme. Certainly, Isaac Asimov would have been proud of the technohysteria scenario. Meanwhile, Phish hatched their grandest plan of all.

Phish's idea was to throw an all-night dance party deep in the Florida Everglades at the Big Cypress Seminole Reservation. According to Liveforlivemusic.com, this party wound up being the largest concert happening in the world, drawing a larger crowd than musical heavyweights Sting, Barbra Streisand, Aerosmith, Billy Joel, and Eric Clapton. Even Phish's performance of "Heavy Things" was featured on national TV as part of ABC's New Year's Eve 1999 coverage with Peter Jennings.

Over two days Phish played an incredible 16 hours of music with no assistance from any opening acts. The crown jewel of the weekend was the nonstop New Year's set from just before midnight until sunrise the next morning. Phish meant business, even installing a port-a-potty on the side of the stage just so they could do their personal business without leaving the stage.

It was a picture-perfect weekend in the Florida Everglades, with weather in the mid 80s and great vibes all around. With a heavy majority of the band's fans being from the Northeast, the unseasonably warm temps in December felt heaven-sent. From a typical lot perspective, there was little vending compared with the number of folks there, simply because this was seen as a vacation for all involved. Most brought what they needed for the weekend, and if they didn't, they had to do a little more legwork than usual.

Everything about the venue's setup was perfect. It was flat and spacious—there were even dried mangrove forests on the perimeter that provided some midday shade. Alligators normally lived in those forests, but the revelry may have temporarily scared them off. There was a built-up faux New Orleans–themed main street boardwalk where fans congregated and occasionally jammed with one another. There was even the "Meatstick Time Capsule," which is scheduled to be opened in 4020 to educate the future on what occurred at Big Cypress.

What often gets lost in the shuffle in talking about Cypress are the four other sets that weekend that were not seven-hour-long

The Boardwalk at Big Cypress in Florida, 1999. (Nicoelle Danielle Cohen)

marathons. The December 30 show was a three-set extravaganza in its own right, and if not overshadowed by the midnight set it would be lauded as one of the most complete shows of their career. Two cover songs (Taj Mahal's "Corrina" and Traffic's "Light Up or Leave Me Alone") were busted out for the first time in more than 1,000 shows; two songs were sung with Seminole Indian Chief Jim Billie on guitar and vocals. This just scratches the surface of the three extended sets of amazing music that set the stage for the weekend.

Another oft-forgotten detail of this weekend is that the millennial show also had a nearly two-hour extended afternoon set. There were musical gems like the "Split Open and Melt" > "Catapult" and the debut of J.J. Cale's "After Midnight" that foreshadowed the late-night hijinks. Still, all of these amazing moments get overshadowed by the avalanche of music that took place right after midnight.

An entire book can be written about the millennial set. Just find yourself a long road trip, press play, and take it all in. At around 15 minutes to midnight, the marathon set begins. There is a Father Time figure on a bicycle powering a giant clock on the back of the stage toward the magical midnight moment. It seemed that Father Time was getting winded, as the eerie clicking of the millennial clock slowed down to a crawl.

Luckily for Father Time, Phish was on hand to save the day. Deep in the audience, spotlights revealed a giant swamp airboat emerging from cover. But just as quickly as it was revealed, the airboat "exploded" with some pyrotechnics, and from within Phish emerged in their famed flying hot dog float, with a pre-recorded version of "Meatstick" as their triumphant soundtrack. They flew across the adoring crowd, throwing leis and waves as they stepped in to help Father Time and propel the crowd to the new millennium.

The band brought along giant meatstick (sausage) links to give Father Time a protein boost. Father Time was recharged, his celestial bike was in motion, and he was able to push the clock to midnight. With that the countdown resumed, the band picked up their instruments and began to play "Meatstick," and the millennium was saved.

"Down with Disease," backed by an incredible fireworks display, launched the set into the stratosphere, and the rest is incredible Phish history. On a personal note, during this momentous moment in time I was surrounded by 15 or so of my closest friends from around the country. Someone snuck champagne into the show, and at the stroke of midnight we were hosed down with bubbly like we won the World Series. All in attendance were world champions that night.

There is little in Phish history, let alone music history, that compares to Big Cypress. One seven-plus-hour, 37-song set of music to rule them all. It had everything—epic long jams, flying hot dog hijinks, rock-and-roll shredding, tender ballads, deep funk,

"The Hot Dog Flight on the New Millennium's Eve." (Alanna Smith)

Phish classics and covers, rare bust-outs, literal fireworks, and even natural phenomena in a glorious sunrise.

This was a stamina check of Herculean proportions for every single person there. If jamming is your thing, there are nine songs from this single show that top the 19-minute mark. For comparative perspective, according to JamBase.com there were a total of 10 20-minute songs over the course of the heralded 13-show Baker's Dozen run. If sentimentality is more your style, "Wading in the Velvet Sea" during a radiant pink sky sunrise was a delicate moment for the ages. Even the choice of P.A. music at the end of the show, The Beatles classic "Here Comes the Sun," created a surreal and unforgettable moment in time.

Big Cypress was the peak of Phish. Despite the bizarre ratings battle among fans on Phish.net after the 2023 NYE Gamehendge show, Big Cypress will forever remain a peak moment in the 40-plus years of this band. Even with the collective creative imagination Phish is well known for, it is hard to imagine that Big Cypress will ever be topped.

13 The Baker's Dozen

The number 13 is baked with superstition and myth. Those who fear the supposedly unlucky number, triskaidekaphobics, may use a variety of evidence to support their beliefs: Jesus was one of 13 at the last supper, in tarot decks the 13th card is Death, and ancient monks who chronicled the lunar calendar foretold unfortunate circumstances in years with 13 full moons instead of 12.

Mathematically, the number 13 is a "happy number," a Fibonacci number, and one of only three known Wilson primes (wink, wink).

But the history of 13 being known as a "baker's dozen" dates back to the Middle Ages or medieval period. Ruled by kings, the public peasants and villagers relied on baked bread as a daily staple but were often taken advantage of by bakers overcharging for loaves. After much outcry, King Henry II established the Assize of Bread and Ale law that correlated the price of wheat to the price of bread, meant to keep the bakers honest and fair. Bakers found cheating their customers were severely punished with fines, flogging, or even amputation. And so, to avoid such penalties at all costs, bakers would overserve their customers, adding the "in-bread" or "vantage loaf" to orders, ensuring they were working above board. And so, a baker's customer purchasing a dozen loaves of bread would be given 13 instead, what would come to be known as a baker's dozen.

Similarly, when Phish announced a 13-show run at Madison Square Garden in the summer of 2017, fans who opted to purchase the 13-ticket package paid a discounted rate, effectively getting the 13th show for free. Was this meant to keep Phish honest? To ensure that they delivered? A preemptive apology of sorts for lack of touring?

Of course, heated discussions erupted in the fan base as soon as Phish announced the Dozen in January. Those far from New York City were disappointed not to have a full-fledged tour or shows closer to home. With just five shows across Chicago, Dayton, and Pittsburgh before the 13-show residency at Madison Square Garden, this summer "tour" announcement left many fans scratching their heads.

Having already played Madison Square Garden more than 80 times, Phish was no stranger to the room. They love The Garden, its size, its sound, its renown. Sure, many others have played The Garden many, many times over; the Grateful Dead performed there 52 times in their career. Sir Elton John? 64 times. Billy Joel? Now more than 100 times.

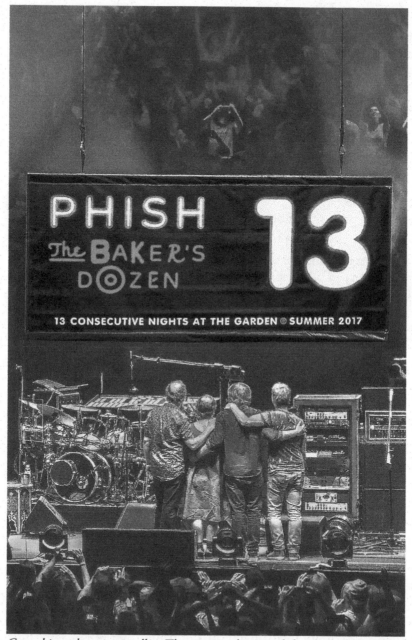

Carved into the cavern wall… The moment they raised the esteemed banner (08/06/17) that now hangs in Madison Square Garden to commemorate the Baker's Dozen and Phish's 13 consecutive nights at MSG in 2017. (Scott Harris)

But Phish, over the years, has made MSG their adoptive home, hosting storied New Year's Eve runs at the venue many times over. And so, with Phish very much moving into The Garden for three weeks, a baker's dozen run of shows, well, what could we expect?

Would Phish repeat songs? Would they play Gamehendge? Would they welcome special guests? Theatrics? Much was speculated and discussed in the months leading up to the July 21 residency kickoff.

But despite all this chatter in the lead-up to the Baker's Dozen, the shows didn't sell out. In Facebook groups and forums, only a small percentage of fans voiced their intention to "hit all 13." (I would guess 800–1,000 fans saw all 13 shows.) With the shows taking place across three weekends, including Tuesday and Wednesday shows, it seemed most fans were content to hit one or two weekends, especially those traveling from out of town. In the week leading up to the residency, tickets were still available.

But the hype was real. For those who purchased the full 13-ticket package, round, illustrated doughnut tickets were delivered in pink Baker's Dozen doughnut boxes. Eight different artists, including longtime Phish collaborators Jim Pollock and David Welker, were tapped to design unique, limited-edition posters. Pollock also designed a four-inch pewter statue to commemorate the residency. Local promoters and musicians planned a full calendar of preshow and postshow parties at nearby bars and music venues. Ben and Jerry's was there, having launched a new, limited edition ice cream flavor called Freezer Reprise, which they distributed freely outside The Garden the first night of the residency.

The morning of the first show, Phish revealed that Philadelphia doughnut company Federal Donuts would be at MSG giving away free doughnut to attendees each night, each with its own flavor. The first night's doughnut flavor? Coconut—a coconut-cream glazed doughnut with toasted coconut topping.

What had perhaps first germinated 10 or more years ago was now suddenly under way. Let me explain: the idea of a doughnut-concept run of shows was first discussed in a 2007 *Relix* magazine feature, "The Salvation of Page McConnell" (July 2007). in the article, McConnell talked about some of the more creative ideas they were unable to execute. One idea was for Phish to do a seven-show tour just to hit the seven U.S. states they had yet to play. Another idea was to play a "baker's dozen" of shows at Madison Square Garden or, say, the Dunkin Donuts Center in Providence, Rhode Island, where the band would offer free doughnuts to the audience and base the theme for each show around that night's doughnut flavor. McConnell continues, giving the example of a "Boston Crème" doughnut night that might include covers of songs by Boston and Cream.

And 10 years after that article, eight years after the band reunited, Phish was now finally kicking off The Baker's Dozen.

Inside Madison Square Garden, in the moments before lights out, the air was electric. People came dressed to impress. Some traveled from the far corners of the world to be there. The place was packed and the fans were ready.

Lights out! The crowd roared and the anticipation was palpable. The moment the house lights cut off is undoubtedly the most exciting moment because, quite frankly, Phish could come out and do just about anything to start the show. Ben and Jerry's hosted a contest where fans could enter their prediction for Phish's opening number of the run for a chance to win tickets to the final show. And that night they opened with a song that I don't think anyone could have predicted: "Shake Your Coconuts" by Danish pop duo Junior Senior. Of the 60,000 entries Ben and Jerry's received, not one contestant submitted "Shake Your Coconuts" to open the show. Phish surprised yet again.

And with that we were off and running! After the first song, looking down the barrel of 13 shows, as warm applause bathed the band, Anastasio joked with the audience, asking, "Are you tired yet?" The crowd roared!

Over the next 13 shows, Phish would perform nearly 35 hours of music. A book could be penned solely about The Baker's Dozen in and of itself with all its highlights, nuances, bust-outs, debuts, and extended jams. And much has already been written and published about the now-legendary residency. Jesse Jarnow's *Rolling Stone* recap is only outdone by his *New York Times* interview with Anastasio. And don't sleep on Scott Bernstein's "The Number Line: Phish Baker's Dozen Residency by the Numbers" at JamBase. com, where you can also find individual show recaps, including this author's outline of Night Two.

Only time can confirm that these 13 shows were the biggest thing Phish has ever done, arguably just ahead or just behind Big Cypress. But one thing is for certain: these 13 shows encapsulate the career of a band more than 30 years and some 1,600 shows after they started.

This is Phish right now, giving their best effort to every song, not repeating a single one, and keeping with a ridiculous theme for each night. An idea birthed 10, 20 years ago, perhaps only in jest, now executed so perfectly, so meticulously, that it may never be eclipsed by Phish or any other band.

What band would even attempt to play 237 different songs, including 61 covers, across 13 shows? What band? They even debuted 19 songs!

Not only did Phish deliver a stellar performance each and every night, but they pushed themselves to get creative with their themed setlists. In true prankster fashion, each morning's dough-nut announcement made gumshoes out of all of us, researching and predicting songs to match. And in true Phish fashion, we were never disappointed.

The musicianship, endurance, and originality of the Baker's Dozen are certainly unprecedented. Looking at the residency as a complete run, it's easy to gloss over the details and niceties of each single show. As such, we would be slipshod not to include brief night-by-night rundowns here.

And so, for those of us who were there, well, relish and cherish the memories here and forever. For those of you who weren't there, I hope what I've written showcases the unique magnitude of what is undoubtedly the single greatest musical experience of my life.

My favorite night was Jam-Filled, followed closely by Powdered. "Izabella" was incredible, pure fire. Of course, "Sunshine of Your Feeling" was a damn special moment and "Everything in Its Right Place" > "What's The Use" was the trippiest Phish I've ever seen.

So blessed to have shared it all with the rest of you lumps in the cosmic gravy!

Night One: Coconut

Opening and closing with coconut-themed songs, the latter of which was Harry Nilsson's "Coconut" performed a cappella, Phish proved they were down to play along with the doughnut flavors.

In the first set, Phish played "Moonage Daydream" for the first time since their Ziggy Stardust Halloween gig and Anastasio brought the house down with a rousingly powerful guitar solo. The second-set-opening pairing of "Tweezer" > "Seven Below" showcased true Phish brilliance, though it would be completely overshadowed in the shows to come.

Night Two: Strawberry

Perhaps to get it out of the way, or otherwise to reward those playing along at home, Phish opened with an a cappella rendition of "Strawberry Fields Forever," followed by "Halley's Comet" ("How would you like to have your thick strawberry goo?"). That night's first set featured an epic Type II jam on "Moma Dance" > "Breath and Burning." Clearly these guys were here to play. Ending the first set with impassioned versions of "Foam" and "Roggae,"

Phish concluded with "The Squirming Coil," featuring a beloved McConnell solo in the spotlight.

For the second set, Phish opened with "Down with Disease," stretching the jam over 20 minutes. Just when you thought it was over, it went deeper, and then, pow: "Strawberry Letter 23," the Brothers Johnson funk ballad made famous by Shuggie Otis. If there was any doubt left as to how much Phish would incorporate these doughnut themes into their shows, well, here's "A present from you / Strawberry letter 22."

Phish went deep with "I Always Wanted It This Way," as Anastasio played the Marimba Lumina, and this version of "Split Open and Melt" is a gooey one to say the least. What's this? A "Down with Disease" reprise?! Yes! For seven minutes, Phish revisited "DWD," with a little extra oomph and zest.

As if that's not enough, Phish delivered a three-song encore: Zappa's "Peaches en Regalia" > "Cities" by Talking Heads, concluding with the quick bluegrass romp "My Sweet One," after which everyone picked their faces up off the floor and headed out into the night.

Night Three: Red Velvet

Lights out. The band took the stage...but Trey headed to the drums? Kuroda painted the stage and the arena floor with a deep, crimson light, and the first sweet notes of "Sunday Morning" rang out as Fishman, clad in a bishop's outfit, took center stage singing the cool lyrics made famous by Nico of The Velvet Underground. As Fishman sang, he swung incense and splashed "holy" water on the crowd. Gordon took an epic bass solo on his knees, front of stage, practically bulging out of his pants...ladies and gentlemen, welcome to Red Velvet night!

My favorite from the first set is "It's Ice"—lengthy, dark, and atmospheric. The second-set opener of "AC/DC Bag" is perhaps one of the few subpar moments of the entire residency, but Phish quickly moved on, performing an incredible block of music, heavy with Type II jams: "Wolfman's Brother" > "Twist" > "Waves." The "Twist" was especially funky, as McConnell pushed for MVP status on the synth.

Encoring with "Sweet Jane," once again awash in red light, Phish logged Red Velvet Night in the record books.

Night Four: Jam-Filled

For a jam band like Phish to take the stage under the pretense that they'll incorporate a "jam-filled" doughnut theme into their performance was to establish an expectation that most of us were concerned they could not meet. Well, we were wrong. So unequivocally wrong.

Not three minutes into the opening number of "Sample in a Jar," the band went off book, to the surprise and delight of the crowd. Next was the short lounge-music act that is "Lawn Boy" with Page sauntering around the stage. During Gordon's customary bass solo, McConnell headed back to his station, but wait—instead, he returned to stage front armed with his keytar. The band then jammed on "Lawn Boy" for 30 incredible minutes (Page for President!), a first for the band and proof positive this night was indeed "Jam-Filled." This was Phish at their best: loose and limber, having fun, and trying something new.

This jam would be heralded as the moment of the Baker's Dozen residency, inspiring many to jokingly ask, "Is this still Lawn Boy?" (More on that later.) McConnell continued his campaign leading a dank, dark jam on "My Friend, My Friend," and Phish closed out the five-song first set with "Bathtub Gin."

"Fuego" opened the second set, with McConnell once again performing splendidly. "Thread" had its moments too, but the "Crosseyed and Painless" was massive, epic, and one of the top jams of the run, so awesome that Phish had to call the cops to stop it > "Makisupa Policeman." Anastasio got a rise out of the crowd, singing, "We be jammin'."

Encoring with rock stalwart "Julius," Phish still wasn't finished, > "Lawn Boy" reprise... God bless Leo! My only question is: was this the best show of the Baker's Dozen or the best show of Phish 3.0?

Night Five: Powdered

Yes, a "powder" theme...yikes! Never have so many people been seen openly booting before the lights went down. The first song, "White Winter Hymnal" by Fleet Foxes, performed a cappella, was delightful. "Roses Are Free" was rocking, into "Very Long Fuse." And "Pebbles and Marbles" held the highest regard until that killer "Tube" at the end.

"Carini" > "Mr. Completely" opened the second set with pure fire and brimstone, and when Phish launched into "1999," the crowd simply opened up and exploded. Notably, Phish had only played the classic Prince tune once prior, on New Year's Eve 1998. And I think it's safe to say no one thought they would play it again. Then Phish played it again! Bravo!

To conclude the "Powdered" night, Phish encored with Neil Young's "Powderfinger," giving the impression that Anastasio had yearned to perform this classic for years and years, perhaps always. Nicely done.

At this point Phish had proved two things: they would likely not be repeating songs, and they were performing and improvising at heights perhaps not seen since the late 1990s. As such, by Friday night, compelled by nights four and five, fans opted in and tickets for the remaining shows sold out. In short: shit just got real.

Night Six: Double Chocolate

Phish opened with "Chocolate Rain" by Tay Zonday—are you kidding me?! Incredible and hilarious! The band members even mimicked the YouTube celebrity's oft-mimed head movement after the lyrics "I move away from the mic to breathe in."

As all but Fishman moved to their instruments, we were treated to the 10th performance of "Ass Handed." And then we were off and running. "Free" delivered a solid jam as usual; "Weigh" was a welcomed oldie; and even "Undermind" was fun. "Destiny Unbound" got the crowd moving, followed by perhaps the most patient, perfectly performed "Divided Sky" I've ever heard. "Things People Do" was up next and they could've called it a set but then, "Sand" with a solid jam to boot.

The second set's "Have Mercy" > "Chalk Dust Torture" was everything, even teasing "Hood." Now for the double chocolate: "You Sexy Thing" > "Mercury" > "You Sexy Thing"—pure, unadulterated Phish, with Gordo working hard to sing those high notes. "Backward Down the Number Line" came next with a heady jam, and "Rock and Roll" closed the set.

The "Fee" encore gave Anastasio the opportunity to sing "Have a chocolate doughnut and catch your breath," followed by a stunning rendition of "Space Oddity," all the more powerful in the arena than in the previous summer's open-air venues.

Night Seven: Cinnamon

Before the show started, an announcement came over the PA system: "Ladies and gentlemen…we have an important announcement to make…." Mimicking the infamous Woodstock LSD warning announcement, the speaker continued: "Do not eat the brown doughnuts. If you eat the brown doughnuts, please report to the Water Wheel table."

The band opened with "Llama," perhaps a bit of a misstep, then "Wilson" got everyone focused, dialed in. "Stealing Time" > "Ya Mar" was lots of fun. Then "Tela" for the Gamehendge folks. "Vultures" got people moving again, perhaps pushing for a call and response "Woo!" > "Train Song" > "Horn" (a nice deep breath)

A jimmies doughnut from Federal Donuts handed out to concertgoers at Night Eight of the Baker's Dozen. The Universe is a doughnut, take a bite.
(Stephen Olker)

then an epic, cacophonous "I Am the Walrus," complete with crowd "Woos!"

For the second set, "Blaze On" > "Twenty Years" was fun, but the heart of the set was the "Alumni Blues" > "Letter to Jimmy Page" > "Alumni Blues," particularly for the older heads in the audience. "Meatstick" happened. "Dirt," perhaps a nod to the Cinnamon theme; then, as teased and promised the night before during "Chalk Dust Torture," we got our "Hood."

Encoring again with a Neil Young cover, Phish closed the evening with "Cinnamon Girl."

Night Eight: Jimmies

After opening with "The Curtain/With," the band then dove right into the theme with "Runaway Jim." Phish played "Esther" flawlessly, followed by the narrated double-shot of "Forbin's" > "Mockingbird." Phish closed out the set with "David Bowie."

Opening the second set with a jam-heavy powerhouse duo "Drowned" > "A Song I Heard the Ocean Sing," well, that was awesome. After 40 minutes of music, we got our "Omm pah pah, oom pah pah, oom pah pah, oom pah pahhhhhhhh-ahhhhhhhh...."

Trey and Mike took seats at the front edge of the stage and pretended to read the newspaper like old chums, casually discussing the lumps in the cosmic gravy, a prewritten narration for this special "Harpua." The universe is a doughnut! > "2001" and an encore of "The Wind Cries Mary," are you kidding me? Incredible.

What's more is that before the encore, some front-row fan tossed a T-shirt onto the stage. Sure enough, Anastasio would return for the encore wearing said shirt, blue with white text that read simply, IS THIS STILL LAWN BOY?

Bravo, y'all.

Night Nine: Maple

Opening with a Hendrixesque "O Canada" (on Canada day—they're Vermonters, eh) with the Canadian flag spotlit above the crowd, the band then moved into "Crowd Control" and "Sugar Shack," which gave each band member some time to warm up and ease us all into what was palpably the slowest-moving, most ass-dragging show of the run thus far. "When the Circus Comes to Town" got everyone misty-eyed with the lyric "never thought I'd make it this far," perhaps with more poignancy on the ninth night of thirteen.

"Daniel Saw the Stone" came next and finally got the show going. "Army of One" saw Page crush it yet again (BD MVP, baby) and "The Wedge" was fun as usual, but no significant jams yet. "Guelah Papyrus" came and went, then Page soloed "Maple Leaf Rag," then Guelah came back! "McGrupp" was easily the highlight, with Leo straight running the game, into "Limb By Limb," which had its moments > "Walk Away," which let Trey work the room into a frenzy, building and building each time until Kuroda had the whole arena lit bright white.

The second set opened with "Golden Age." It was initially promising, and I love that song, but perhaps they should shelve that one, because I don't think they'll best that 2016 Vegas "Golden Age." They gave it a good treatment this time, but abandoned it for "Leaves," which is just a poor man's "Free." "Swept Away" came next, which no one wanted, but sounded nice and sweet and felt good in the room. "Steep" > "46 Days" was incredible, nicely done, gentlemen > "Piper," yes, another solid showing, with a "46 Days" tease and spooky reprise > "Possum," again, with Kuroda trying to keep up.

Phish encored with "Rock 'n' Roll Suicide." Neil Young it is not, but I'll take Bowie any Tuesday night, and the Phish done well with it for the second time around, wrapping a relatively short show.

Ending 15 minutes early isn't a Phish anyone wants to see, but at this point I think everyone was in need of a little respite heading into a midweek Night 10. And even still, the band had played two 80-minute sets.

Night Ten: Holes

Phish came out and opened up with what I know as the theme song for the HBO show *The Wire*. It's a Tom Waits song called "Way Down in the Hole," and they crushed it. After that, it was a perfectly played and perfectly placed "Buried Alive," and things were really rocking. "Kill Devil Falls" smoothed things out before a welcome "Guyute," featuring some strange and impressive vocalizing from all members. "I Didn't Know" came next, keeping with some vocal play, then "NICU," which felt like home. Up next was "Meat" > "Maze," an incredible section of music, with "Meat" just diggin' deep and "Maze" going hard. Highly recommended! After this, "Ginseng Sullivan and "Waiting All Night" gave us a breather, then "Heavy Things" and "Antelope" brought the energy back full on for a romp through space to close the first set.

Looking back on the second set, it's one of the best of the run, no doubt. It featured an extended "Mike's Groove," to say the least! "Mike's" opened up strong, to the roar of the crowd, and got weird and spooky as fog filled the stage for a baritone rendition of "O Holy Night" that gave way to "Taste," which jammed as hard as it ever will, wow. "Wingsuit" came next, and that was a top-tier performance as well. "Sneakin' Sally" snapped us all back real quick before > "Weekapaug" (though the intro was not played). Wow, what a "Mike's Groove!"

Phish encored with "A Day in the Life" with the third verse referencing "4,000 holes in Blackburn, Lancashire / And though the holes were rather small / they had to count them all / Now they know how many holes it takes to fill the Albert Hall / I'd love to turn you on...."

Night Eleven: Lemon Poppy

Opening with what sounded like a Bob Dylan song, "See That My Grave Is Kept Clean" (Blind Lemon Jefferson), quickly moved to "Punch You in the Eye" > "Party Time," which seemed to energize all the weekend warriors in the arena. Phish can certainly read a room, that's for sure! "Big Black Furry Creature from Mars" really punked it up, and then they brought it back down with a welcomed bust-out of "Dinner and a Movie." "Ocelot" came next, perhaps Phish's most Dead-sounding song. "Bold as Love" in the middle of the set > "First Tube" sent MSG shaking up and down as 20,000 fans peaked at the same time.

The second set opened with an a cappella "Dem Bones," perhaps just to help everyone get settled, stretch it out a little bit, then "No Men in No Man's Land" came out with a vengeance, but holy shit > "Everything in Its Right Place"—wow wow wow!

"Sucking on a lemon…" Incredible; so wild and unexpected and perfectly executed as a Phish song, the trippiest I've ever seen, but wait, there's more > "What's the Use?" Wow. Kuroda outdid himself with this one! MSG was in outer space, rotating and orbiting high above New York City. "Scents" helped people return to earth, and offered a solid jam to boot > "Caspian" was fun but then > "Fluffhead," and the crowd went wild! Complete with "Everything in Its Right Place" teases and quotes galore.

For the encore, McConnell once again strapped on his keytar, joined Anastasio and Gordon at the front edge of the stage, and sent us all home with a silky, funky "Frankenstein."

Night Twelve: Boston Cream

This was the night we were all waiting for—the doughnut flavor theme that started it all, now famously foreshadowed in that 2007 *Relix* article. Well, here we are!

Marley's "Soul Shakedown Party" was a nice, easy way to start the show, a gentle groove to loosen up. "Uncle Pen" is always welcome. And "The Sloth," hell yeah! They did a nice number there. "Gotta Jibboo" felt a little funkier than in the past, and had a nice little jam. "Fuck Your Face" brought the punk, following in the success of the previous show's first punk/funk set balance. And then, they hit us with it: "Sunshine of Your Feeling," a medley of Cream and Boston songs, with teases and quotes of "Sunshine of Your Love," "More Than a Feeling," "Tales of Brave Ulysses," and the "Long Time" portion of Boston's "Foreplay/Long Time," and man, did they kill it. The crowd applauded earnestly, the band was all smiles, everyone was dialed in, it was just pure joy.

Afterward, as the applause died, Trey said, "Tomorrow's doughnut is Kansas Metallica flavored." And everyone laughed. Fishman: "We've been waiting 20 years to make that joke." And the band nodded, Page grinning ear to ear. "Seriously," Fishman said.

"Frost" came next, a TAB song > "Scent of A Mule," that featured some incredible work from Page McConnell, teasing all those Boston and Cream songs while Kuroda hit us with a nice yellow hue as if to apologize that Zeppelin's "Lemon" song was omitted on the night. Next came Hendrix's "Fire" again, perhaps making up for the absence on the Jimmies night? Then "Alaska" > "Plasma" to wrap an incredible first set of jams, smiles, covers, and the punch line to a joke that started 20 years prior.

Set two kicked off with "Ghost," a classic jam vehicle, which most were waiting for since Night One. They jammed, but not too deep > "Petrichor", well-executed, perhaps the best-executed? > "Light" > "The Lizards" to get everyone back on track. "The Horse" > "Silent in the Morning" to cool things down then > "Quinn the Eskimo" > "Rocky Top."

With a "Joy" encore, you could tell they hit their peak with "Sunshine of Your Feeling" and had nothing left to give…full of joy, the band concluded the penultimate night of the Baker's Dozen.

Night Thirteen: Glazed

To say we were "glazed" after 13 shows is an understatement. We were fully glossed, glazed, dazed, and raged. A welcome "Dogs Stole Things" kicked off the set, with a nicely performed "Rift" as a one-two punch. "Ha Ha Ha" fittingly came next, followed by the disco funk of "Camel Walk," which allowed everyone to settle into a groove. "Crazy Sometimes" got the crowd going hard > "Saw It Again" > "Sanity" > "Bouncing around the Room" was a nice block of music: well-performed, well-placed, more than a wink and a nod to this extended run at the Garden, but it didn't stop there. Next was "Most Events Aren't Planned", from Page's Vida Blue project, perhaps as a hat tip for the MVP of this run? "Bug" got the crowd energized, followed by a brief pause to cool down, as Trey asked Page how he was feeling. "A bit glazed," Page answered > "I Been Around." But wait, there's more!

"Izabella"—wow. A true bust-out of this Hendrix song, perhaps neglected on Jimmies night, but on Night 12 fans on the floor close to the stage held up a large, bright-pink sign that read IZABELLA. And now, delivered on the final night of the run, well, the crowd went absolutely wild. They went crazy! The whole place was bursting with emotion and joy and shock—bewilderment, really. This was a shining moment of the run, and certainly a highlight for many, including my coauthor, Jason, who caught Phish's performance of his daughter's namesake song in 1997.

The second set opened with the long-awaited "Simple," which reached new heights, though not perhaps higher than the Northerly Island version three weeks prior. "Rise/Come Together" came next > "Starman," hell yeah, more Bowie! Well done, guys. Now "YEM," rocking the trampolines, extended vocal jam. Then "Loving Cup," gimme one drink!

The encore had everyone waiting with bated breath. Returning to the stage, Phish gently rolled into "On the Road Again," which had both Trey and Page tearing up, choking up on "playing music with my friends," perhaps finally letting it all sink in: the massive accomplishment of this run, the survival of this band, the continued jams and new music, only continuing to grow this wholly unique and special experience. Concluding the song, as the crowd applauded, Page moved from behind his rig towards the front of the stage and Trey played a little reggae riff that sounded a lot like...Page said, "A lot of people have been asking me, is this still 'Lawn Boy?' Yes, it is." And the crowd roared; an Olfactory Hues reprise! Then Mike hit the introductory bass solo for "Weekapaug Groove," unplayed from Friday, and then the band launched into "Tweezer Reprise," an encore for the ages.

After exiting the stage, the band returned to witness a Phish banner hoisted up at the edge of the stage, exalting their unprecedented run of 13 consecutive shows. After a quick band photo with the banner, it ascended to its home at the ceiling at Madison Square

Garden, a testament to an incredible musical experience—one that may never be topped.

For 13 nights, this band delivered beyond anyone's expectations. And now complete, with the band gone from the stage, the house lights back on, the PA played Billy Joel's "New York State of Mind" as attendees slowly made their way out of the arena.

14 Madison Square Garden

For a venue to proudly claim the nickname "the world's most famous arena" takes some boldness; such claims must be backed up by hard evidence. Since its inception in 1979, Madison Square Garden (MSG) has earned that moniker by hosting legendary concerts, sporting events, political rallies, and more from deep in the heart of New York City. Technically, the current incarnation of MSG is the fourth building to bear the title Madison Square Garden. Without a doubt it is a must-see landmark in one of the greatest cities in the world.

Phish graced the stage at "The Garden" for the first time on December 30, 1994. In an *Entertainment Weekly* interview, Page McConnell said this was his "Phish high point," and on the *Inside Out with Turner and Seth* podcast in 2017, lighting director Chris Kuroda agreed that the '94 MSG show was his favorite show.

From that incredible moment through the heralded "17 in 17" (17 MSG shows in 2017), Phish played the Garden a whopping 56 times. Seeing Phish play MSG is a destination event that all fans should experience.

The Baker's Dozen run was record-breaking, as it topped Billy Joel's MSG consecutive-show record of 12. At the conclusion of Phish's residency, MSG honored the band by hanging a banner high in the rafters and NYC mayor Bill de Blasio formally proclaimed August 6, 2017, "Phish Day."

At this point, however, we'd be remiss not to mention Harry Styles' now historic 15-show run at MSG, whose own banner now hangs beside the banners for Phish and Billy Joel. And for those of us counting along at home, Billy Joel holds the record for the greatest number of appearances at the Garden with 134 shows as of February 2023. As of January 2024, Phish has performed 83 times at MSG.

At 83 shows, we certainly can't dive into each one here, but let's take a look at a handful of the magical nights that have taken place in the Garden.

1. **December 30, 1994:** "Wilson" was the first song played in this hallowed hall, and it is doubtful that any other "Wilson" chant was louder.

2. **December 31, 1995:** This performance is considered by most as one of the greatest Phish shows in history. With the Gamehendge Time Machine and a rare "Mike's/Weekapaug Groove" split between two sets, amazing jams, Forbin's narration, Fishman's setbreak shave and a haircut, and an audience chess match, this show had it all.

3. **December 30, 1997:** This show reportedly cost the band $10,000 in fees because they played past the venue's curfew. Robert Palmer's "Sneakin' Sally" was busted out for the first time in nearly 1,000 shows and then reprised well in the encore. An absolutely huge second set included an "AC/DC Bag" for the ages, a "Harpua" that set the stage for the New Years' gag, and a giant four-song encore.

4. **December 31, 1998:** Prince's "1999" may have been the greatest show opener in the band's history. With crazily

costumed dancers onstage, Mike and Trey had a coordinated dance routine planned, and they even jammed on their backs while they laid down a funk nasty groove. Rarely does the top moment of a show happen in the opening slot, but you better party like it's 1999 when it's about to turn 1999.

5. **December 31, 2002:** The grand return from hiatus opened with "Piper" to build up the anticipatory energy to climax, and the second-set, seven-below indoor "disco snowstorm" was a great way to ring in NYE.

6. **December 31, 2010:** This show featured a second set with a short but ever-so-tight "Ghost," followed by a "YEM" > "Manteca" > "YEM" in all of its glory. The third set was a United Nations of "Meatstick," with dancers, costumes, and

A pseudo-aerial shot of Madison Square Garden (as seen from Gershuny's buddy's hotel room balcony). (Jason Gershuny)

72

singers singing the song's chorus in many languages. The band reprised the flying hot dog from NYE 1994 and 1999.

7. **December 31, 2011:** A "Steam"-themed NYE had floating fans flapping and flipping furiously to the flow. After midnight, Mike and Trey were raised in the air during the "Down with Disease" jam. This was a highly underrated show that used 3.0 staples as jam vehicles. Just don't bring up the mid-third-set "Alaska," "Velvet Sea" combo.

8. **December 31, 2012:** A golf-themed New Year's Eve set completed the three-year acronym trifecta of "Meatstick," "Steam," "Golf" (MSG). There was an insane "Kung"-based golf-cart marathon with a track of high-speed golf carts racing over and under the stage while the band was playing. The entire third set was composed of songs with golf references.

9. **December 31, 2013:** This performance is also known as the JEMP Truck 30th-anniversary set. The entire second set was played in the middle of The Garden on top of a run-down JEMP Truck (an acronym of the band members' names, Jon, Ernesto, Mike, and Page, and also the name of their own record label). This was an old-school set; none of the songs played debuted after 1991. Hockey sticks were used as microphone stands and milk crates as stools to replicate the same jerry-rigged setup as the first show in 1983. Phish served their 30th-birthday cake, which was decorated to memorialize their iconic 1988 Colorado band photo, to fans near the stage. Commemorative videos were shown to celebrate the anniversary and introduce the second set and encore.

10. **December 31, 2015:** Demonstrating the power of the new songs, "No Man's Land" and "Blaze On" served as centerpieces

to the New Year's Eve virtual hourglass disappearing magic trick psychedelic meltdown.

11. **December 31, 2016:** Petrichor was a beautiful production with synchronized dancers, floating LED umbrellas, and an indoor fake rain. Phishing with a touch of class until it literally rained (balloon) cats and dogs during the gag and the "Suzy Greenberg" dance party erupted.

12. **July 21–August 6, 2017:** The Baker's Dozen—a career-defining, catalog-spanning 13 shows with no repeated songs. They played 237 unique songs, which was a virtual anthology of Phish. This—13 straight MSG shows over two and a half weeks, where each night had a theme tied to a type of doughnut—was the greatest accomplishment of Phish's career since Big Cypress.

13. **December 31, 2017:** "In a minute I'll be free, and we'll be splashing in the sea." Not only were we splashing in the sea, we were the sea. All audience members were given "cosmic wristbands," which were remotely controlled LED bracelets that created a venue-wide oceanic setting. Phish used the annual tradition of New Year's theatrics to create a set-spanning nautical/pirate theme, as they turned the stage into a giant pirate ship, complete with enormous rotating sails and masts, cannons that shot off imaginary disco cannonballs into the crowd, all the while under a Phish themed jolly roger flag. (The December 30, 2017, show should not be overlooked, either.)

14. **December 31, 2019:** Send in the clones! Someone call the Rescue Squad! This show has it all: the band members wearing monochromatic outfits, each playing on their independent raised and moving platforms, armies of monochromatic clones

Right angle rooms drive me crazier each day... Lighting Designer Chris Kuroda (CK5) lights up the crowd before the imminent balloon drop on New Year's Eve 2018 at MSG. (Scott Harris)

singing along, and *gasp!* technical difficulties with Trey Anastasio's platform stuck high above the stage through the encore until he was indeed rescued by the band's crew. Of course, rumors would quickly spread that the "broken" platform was itself a gag, but those who were there say they could see genuine fear and concern on Trey's face. (Also, don't sleep on 12/30/19 and that face-melting "Tweezer.")

15. **April 22, 2022:** After canceling the 2021 New Years run, Phish rescheduled the four shows for April, kicking off on Earth Day, with 4/22 functioning as the replacement date for the band's traditional three-set New Years Eve show. For the third set, the

stage was raised to feature projected imagery on screens below the band and during "Waves," a large-scale whale flew around the venue, eventually flanked by flying dolphins, to the shock and delight of the fans awash in blue light.

Don't you see anything you'd like to try? Trey Anastasio appreciates the lifesize whale and dolphins "swimming by" at MSG on 04/22/22. (Scott Harris)

16. **August 5, 2023:** The final show of what some fans call "The Magnificent Seven"' at MSG, perhaps confirmed only by the arena's walk-out music played after the show: Elmer Bernstein's "Main Theme" score for John Sturges's 1960 film *The Magnificent Seven*. And what a conclusion this show was! Featuring a notable first set "Prince Caspian" and a full-on, full-band Type II jam "Tweezer" wrapped around "Guy Forget," played for the first time in 425 shows (9/4/11).

17. **December 31, 2023:** This show started out relatively normal and as expected: "Everything's Right" opener, followed by "Tube," some other tunes…"Character Zero" to close out the first set. Hell, even the second set *started* out with a rather uneventful eight-minute "Down with Disease," but then…oh, but then…. "Om-pa-pa oom-pa-pa oom-pa-pa oom-pa-paaaaa…" The energy in the room at that moment is indescribable. And even as they band played "Harpua" and gave narration and everyone felt like it was really happening, they were finally doing it, no one dared fully believe until Jimmy's grandmother said it out loud: "Gamehendge." (See chapter 5)

15 *Junta* (1989)

For me, *Junta* always felt like a bootleg. It's strange—a double album, black-and-white artwork—and the songs are weird, man. This is Phish? In many ways, yes.

Junta is Phish's first official studio release. Independently recorded at Euphoria Sound Studio in Revere, Massachusetts, this album was initially released on cassette tape in 1988, arriving in stores officially in May 1989. Elektra Records would re-release the album in October 1992.

The album is named for Phish's first official manager and agent, Ben "Junta" Hunter, whose nickname is pronounced with a hard J and a short U, according to Wikipedia.

The album, clocking in at more than two hours, was released as a double cassette and double CD. At the time, bands like Nine Inch Nails, Pixies, The Beastie Boys, and The Cure had chart-topping albums. And it was unheard of for a band to premiere with a double album. To say this album, featuring black-and-white cover art by Jim Pollock, was esoteric or largely inaccessible is an understatement. But if nothing else, that's what *Junta* was: a statement.

Elektra's re-release in 1992 had the album on record store shelves next to albums by Bon Jovi, 10,000 Maniacs, Journey, R.E.M., and Amy Grant. It took five years for the album to be certified gold (October 1997) and another seven years for it to go platinum (July 2004).

Part prog, part prank, part epic chronicles of myth and fable—not to mention its three 11-minute tracks, each nearly completely instrumental performances—*Junta* stands alone as an unabashed, brazen collection of compositions and songs.

Steven McDonald writes in his review on AllMusic.com, "With great sound and better playing, Phish's debut *Junta* is highly recommended whether you're starting to discover Phish or are backing up to the beginning. It may be a bit long-winded and unfocused, yet it establishes their dedication to musical exploration effectively—not to mention the typical wild and woolly Phish humor spilling out all over the lengthy tracks."

The Elektra re-release, with additional time available on the CD, added three "bonus" live tracks that did not previously appear on the album: "Union Federal," "Sanity," and "Icculus," the latter two from July 25, 1988, at Nectar's, though the "Union Federal" track comes directly from a private rehearsal session, aka an Oh Kee Pa Ceremony (see chapter 29).

A look back at Phish's albums in a 2000 issue of *Entertainment Weekly* gave *Junta* a "C" grade. Will Hermes wrote, "The formula crystallizes: frat-hippie fantasias high-fiving folk-rock guitar heroics and iffy lite-jazz fusion grooves. Highlight: the gnarly 25-minute improv 'Union Federal.'"

Disregarding *The White Tape*, this is Phish's first release for the public. Many fans across the country would be introduced to the band via Anastasio's megaphone-laced story of "Fee" the weasel or the dark carnival world of "Esther" or the six-part "Fluff's Travels."

And while fans may scoff at the idea of listening to the studio album versions of improvisation vehicles like "You Enjoy Myself" or "David Bowie," the first stone-carved versions of these songs, forever preserved here in *Junta*, provide just a bit of context to the windy, winding origin story of this American band who called themselves Phish.

That "Icculus," though? Yes, please.

16 Dance Like No One Is Watching, aka Surrender to the Flow

Seriously. Dance. Go to a Phish show and dance. Dance your ass off. Dance like nobody's watching.

And if booze or otherwise can help you lose your inhibitions and get you dancing, well, then, please do imbibe. But I would argue that none of us need help dancing. Just listen to the music and let go. Go with the flow. *Surrender* to the flow!

> **#STFU**
> Here's the thing, very simply: please don't talk at a show. Just don't talk! It's disturbing to your neighbors, and quite frankly, it's keeping you from the Flow.
>
> Sure, make some quick exchanges with your buddies, inside voices, even whisper in ears; that's fine, expected. But don't just gab, y'all. Please! Tickets are expensive, people want to dial in, so don't chat like you're catching up with an old friend. And if you are? Then go to a bar.

Whether you're in the pit, near the rail, behind the stage, in the last row, or roaming the aisles, spinning in the hallways, dance! Wherever you are! Please, dance!

Because here's the thing: dancing is contagious. People see other people dancing and it makes them dance. Suddenly, you have a few people dancing, then a few more people dancing, then everyone around you is dancing, and the whole section is dancing, the whole arena is dancing!

And I promise you, the band sees that. They *feel* that. It's a transfer of energy between the band and the audience, with the music connecting us all.

Maybe you've heard of "The Hose"?

Trey Anastasio and Mike Gordon explained The Hose, referencing remarks by Carlos Santana, with whom Phish toured in 1992 and briefly in 1994, in an NPR radio interview in the spring of 1994, just after *Hoist* was released.

Trey says, "We actually have exercises that we do, where we work on improving our improvising as a group. It gets rid of the ego. It's an exercise to get rid of the ego. And the more that we do it the more we find that our improvisations are less concerned with showing off flashy solos or whatever, and more concerned with making a group sound. There's a feeling that we always talk about. When we went out with Santana, he had brought up this thing about The Hose...where the music is like water rushing through you and as a musician your function is really like that of a hose. And, and well his thing is that the audience is like a sea of flowers, you know, and you're watering the audience. But the concept of music going through you, that you're not actually creating it, that what you're doing is—the best thing that you can do is get out of the way. So, when you are in a room full of people, there's this kind of group vibe that seems to get rolling sometimes."

Mike adds, "It really starts to seem like It's not the audience or the band. This *Thing* that gets rolling is its own Thing. When things are going really well, and a jam has taken off, there's this feeling of motion that is created by the rhythm. And at that point my bass that I'm playing feels like this sort of vehicle, or like a hitch for me to hold on to, like I was thinking if you were on a ski lift, maybe. A chair lift. Or just something that would hook you on to the motion that's going, and pull you along with it."

As audience members we also have a responsibility to the band: to be present and listening and at our best, giving back in whatever way we can. Because it truly is a "group mind" out there during a Phish show. This "thing" Mike describes is real, and it only happens when everyone surrenders to the flow—and that means you, too.

17 Audience Participation (How Many Times Should I Clap in "Stash"?)

In the immortal words of the timeless poet Ladies Love Cool James—or as he is better known, LL Cool J—"Clap your hands everybody, and everybody just clap your hands." Rap is not the only corner of the music realm where audience participation is strongly encouraged. In the Phish world, these responses are often more complicated, goofy, and sometimes require a Secret Language to understand.

At any Phish show, there can be many opportunities to interact with the band, the music, and those around you. Here is a brief description of a few of those collaborative moments.

"Stash": Audience members clap along with the musical break in the composed section before the lyrics. What is interesting about this is over time the number of claps has evolved. Back in the early '90s, four claps used to match up with Fishman's four hits to the woodblocks. Somewhere in the mid '90s that all changed, and the audience now predominatly claps three times.

"Wilson": One of the keystone songs of the story of Gamehendge begins slowly with Trey strumming two repeated power chords. Audience members paying keen attention then shout "Wiiillllllsoooon!" before the same bar and response are repeated. The intensity of the audience's chant seems to get louder each time. This usually happens three times before the song kicks into gear on the fourth go 'round. This audience call and response is repeated in the middle of the song, as well.

"Harry Hood": The "Hood" chant is less popular than the two examples mentioned above, but has been in the Phish/audience repertoire for more than 20 years. During the introduction of "Harry Hood," when the band shouts, "Harry!," audience members reply shouting, "Hood!"

"Twist": "Wooing" at Phish shows is a touchy subject among the fan base. It's not trying to pick someone up with sweets or affection, but rather shouting a short "Woo!" at specific moments during the show. Some love it, some abhor it, but "Twist" is one place where it is generally accepted by all. After the lyric about "substituting every sound," fans shout "Woo!," and after "wouldn't twist around that way," they "Woo!" again. Also, after the chorus there are two distinct "Woos!"

"Meatstick": Phish wanted to create a dance craze to sweep the nation. They even tried to break the *Guinness Book of World Records* record for a group dance performance at Camp Oswego Festival. The "Meatstick" dance is a pretty complicated series of moves, but it's not too hard to pick up on with some practice. Ultimately, it's a move with outstretched arms, a mimicked water pump motion, a fake clap followed by a real clap, twirling your pointer finger in the air like Hulk Hogan and then pointing it at your head, and some Japanese lyrics to add some international flavor to the mix.

"Contact": Following the midpoint funk jam of "Contact," and during the final verses of the song, Mike, Page, and Trey will begin to throw their hands in the air and wave them back and forth like they just don't care. Fishman is the only one still playing his instrument while the others are still singing. The audience mimics the band's arm motions in beautiful synchronicity.

"Moma Dance": One of the lesser-known audience participation aspects of a Phish show takes place during "Moma Dance." During the June 20, 1998, debut of "Moma Dance" in Denmark, Trey taught the audience the Moma Dance. This is possibly the easiest way to participate, although few are aware it is even happening. There are two beats near the chorus of the song where you are supposed to stomp your right foot along with Fishman's two snare drum hits. It happens twice in the middle and twice at the end.

"The Howling": The musical highlight of the 2021 Sci-fi Soldier set may have been "The Howling." It is almost an instinctual impetus to howl in ecstasy when the band throws down this newfound, crowd-pleasing funk favorite.

18 Phish and the Internet

In the early days, the early 1990s, Phish was only just beginning to play 1,000-person-capacity rooms. In October 1991, Phish played The Cubby Bear, a small sports bar across the street from the storied Wrigley Field. Fifteen years later, Phish sold out two nights at the Cubs' 40,000-capacity stadium.

Similarly, in 1990, the World Wide Web was only just born, and today the Internet has nearly four billion users.

As Phish's fame and popularity grew across the United States, so did access to the Internet. Phish and the Internet basically grew up together. Like neighboring children in the suburbs, Phish and the Internet dared and encouraged each other to explore and experiment, ultimately developing into handsome, successful individuals who now perhaps reminisce about their childhood and the innocence and privilege of youth.

In the 1990s, Phish's fan base, and the early adopters of the Internet within it, worked as missionaries spreading the good word to the farthest corners of the country via message boards and newsgroups. The very nature of Phish's live performances, unique setlists and musical teases—all that data!—begged to be archived and made freely available to all.

The proliferation of Phish setlists, live shows, and gossip on the Internet surely gave rise to this band, beyond mere grassroots growth through touring. Hell, Phish certainly wasn't played on the radio!

"I came across Phish in 1993 and wanted to learn everything I could about it," says Scott Bernstein, editorial director of JamBase. com and founder of YEMblog.com. "And I realized that to do that I would have to connect to this thing called the Internet. Fans who were either at college or otherwise had access to the Internet started a newsgroup, rec.music.phish, and that was the first real foray. Anyone who had access to the Internet could get to this newsgroup."

A newsgroup, for younger readers, is effectively an online message board where anyone can post or respond to posts. At the time, that's mostly what the Internet was: email and message boards.

This small group of Phish fans obsessively collected and confirmed setlists and jam teases from every Phish show. Their goal from the very beginning was to become the ultimate fan-produced guide to Phish and initially operated as a group of independent contributors. At the show? Write down the setlist and share on rec.music.phish.

At the time, the Internet was still a strange frontier. In 1995, America Online would add the Internet as a feature to its service, and that's when things really took off. Suddenly, other Phish-related sites appeared on the frontier landscape, including Andy Gadiel's Phish Page.

"Andy Gadiel launched Andy Gadiel's Phish Page in 1996," Bernstein says. "And that became a central repository for Phish fans on the Internet. He had links to anybody else who had a Phish page, he would have setlists that night. And people would literally call him from a pay phone after the show and tell him the setlist and he'd put it on the site. Then you get to '97, '98, when the majority of Americans started to get the Internet... that's when Phish.net launched their site."

Phish.net focused on tirelessly cataloging and archiving Phish's setlists, ultimately publishing a book, *The Phish Companion*, now a massive tome in its third edition. And they incorporated The Mockingbird Foundation, a nonprofit organization that donated all proceeds from their book sales to fund musical education (see chapter 100).

Phish on IG: memes, fashion, film, and more

There's plenty of Phish content to be found on Instagram, check out: @thingsyouseeatphish, @phishchicks, @phishmeme, @phishmemeisreal, and my personal favorite, @phishdanceparty who takes video of people dancing and overlays synced Phish tunes. Ever curious about what Trey, Mike, and Page are wearing on stage? (We know what Fishman is wearing.) Then check out @Phish.phasion where you'll find details on Phish fashion like brands and pricing. Also, for our Phish photographers and film enthusiasts, there's Philm @phishonphilm, a film photography account and publisher of books and magazines.

But where does the band fit into all of this? What about Phish.com?

"They launched Phish.com in 1996," Bernstein says. "It was very basic; just had the tour dates. And then in 1997 they made the site a lot nicer, added a minisite for The Great Went, and by '98 it was a full-blown thing with all sorts of information about the band and Dry Goods and people were more using the website than *Doniac Schvice* [the now-defunct Phish paper newsletter]."

People were also using peer-to-peer FTP sites to exchange audio files, both soundboard recordings and audience recordings of live Phish shows. And in 1999, PhantasyTour.com launched, which would become the main message board for fans. "It all just spawned from there," Bernstein says. "And it all started with rec, a newsgroup that maybe 100 people had access to when it premiered."

Then, Bernstein himself came to be a valued pioneer on the frontier. Through his postings about Phish in a private message board, he came to run a blog on *Glide Magazine* called Hidden Track, which he grew from 2006 to 2010 to include an annual readership of more than one million people. He then moved to JamBase.com (founded by Andy Gadiel), where he remains as editorial director. In fact, in 2017, Trey Anastasio only gave a handful of interviews, and one of those few went to Bernstein at JamBase.

But in the middle of it all, circa 2008, Bernstein also founded and launched his own website dedicated to Phish called YEMBlog. com. "The idea was to have this website where I would share all this new Phish content I was finding," says Bernstein. "But what really hit was the Twitter feed." In 2009, Bernstein, or a trusted friend, would live-tweet the setlist from the show. Followers could follow along in real time. "It was the beginning of Twitter," Bernstein says. "And it just blew up. All of a sudden I had 10,000 followers, and all these years later [I] now have 35,000 followers."

Of course, now the technology is more readily available, and social media is more accessible than ever. "There was a long period of time where you had to be technologically inclined to talk about Phish online and connect with people online," Bernstein says. "And now social media has brought that down to make it so that anybody can easily talk about Phish and meet people through the Internet.

And so in 2011 Scott Bernstein stopped live-tweeting Phish show setlists. The demands of the practice began to take away from his Phish show experience. It wasn't fun anymore. "I said, 'enough,'" he explains. "There are enough people on Twitter and elsewhere; we don't need to be the source for the setlists anymore. And quickly after that Phish started tweeting the setlists themselves with Phish: From The Road (@Phish_FTR)."

Another premier figure at the time (circa 2009) was a writer and blogger known as Mr. Miner who published extensive reviews of every single Phish show on his website, PhishThoughts.com. In 2011, he too published a book—Miner's Phish Thoughts—a large compilation of his reviews clocking in at nearly 700 pages.

And it doesn't stop there. Today, Phish.com, Phish.net, PhantasyTour.com, Reddit.com/r/phish/, and YEMblog.com are all fantastic, active resources for everything Phish. And there are a few Facebook groups, as well—Addicted to Phish and Phish Tour 2014 (named for the year it was founded) both have around 25,000 members. Just beware of the Facebook group Phish Tour 2017; that's where the trolls live, watch out!

19 NYE 1995: Gamehendge Time Machine

There are moments in Phish history that set precedents, close one chapter and open a new one, and define a "before" and "after" period for the band. Phish's New Year's Eve 1995 show is one such moment, from which Phish would emerge newly accomplished and rightfully heralded, and by all means established a new level of live performance and pageantry.

The fall 1995 tour saw the band playing in their biggest venues yet, moving from Seattle's Paramount Theatre to the Seattle Center Arena or from Austin's Liberty Lunch to the Austin Music Hall. That summer, Phish released their first live album, *A Live One* (see chapter 53), and performed the now-famous 50-minute rendition of "Mud Island Tweezer" at an amphitheater in Memphis, Tennessee. It's also notable that, using a giant chess board, Phish played chess with the audience, who were instructed to meet at setbreaks at the Greenpeace table to make up their collective move.

The first set of the December 31, 1995, show is remarkable for many reasons and memorable for others. This was the first NYE Phish played at The Garden, and if you listen to the recording (released for the 10th anniversary in December 2005), you can hear absolute joy and excitement from the crowd at lights out as the band comes out swinging with "Punch You in the Eye." The

"Reba" jam is noteworthy and "Fly Famous Mockingbird" features a narration by Trey Anastasio about the recipe for time being stolen and everyone being stuck in 1994 and hearing the same songs… which leads into "Shine" by Collective Soul, the No. 1 rock song of 1994, performed that night with vocals by Phish lyricist Tom Marshall. So, yes, remarkable for the jams and the Mockingbird story, while perhaps memorable for their take on Collective Soul's ubiquitous grunge ballad.

During the setbreak at the 1995 New Year's Eve show, a representative of the band announced that they would not be making a chess move and would resign after losing their queen, thus concluding the year's friendly competition with each side having won one game.

Phish's second set that night begins with a cover of The Who's "Drowned." It's well worth the listen, and includes a subtle (or perhaps not?) tease of the Grateful Dead's "Fire on the Mountain" before the transition into "The Lizards." The band ultimately turns to "Runaway Jim" for the set's next big jam, clocking in at 15 minutes. After a couple more songs and a palate cleanser of "Hello My Baby," we get an absolutely incredible 20-minute "Mike's Song" into a tripped-out cacophony—what's now called the "Digital Delay Loop Jam"—to end the set.

As if that wasn't enough, during the following setbreak the crew wheeled out a barber's chair to center stage, where Fishman sat before the audience for a shave.

The band then returned to the stage wearing lab coats and playing synths surrounded by all manner of laboratory props, including Van de Graaff generators. Borrowing from some kind of Frankenstein laboratory, the "Phish Time Factory" set out to right the passage of time and return us to the precipice of 1996. And so, Fishman, portraying Father Time, was loaded into an "electrified" box that was closed and lifted above the stage as the band counted down to midnight. Then—"Happy New Year!" The box opened, the sides fell out, and there was Fishman, high above the stage, dressed as a baby—diaper, bonnet, and all!

The band moved through "Auld Lang Syne" as balloons dropped from the ceiling, and then Mike Gordon ripped into the opening bass solo of "Weekapaug Groove," concluding the "Mike's Groove" pairing from the end of the second set. Never had the band bridged the "Mike's Groove" gap across a setbreak, and, to say the least, this version is one for the books. "Sea & Sand" allows everyone to take a breath, and then Phish delivers a masterful "You Enjoy Myself"—the first of 1996, of course. "Sanity" is next, and then "Frankenstein" closes out the set. The band encores with "Johnny B. Goode."

The weird spectacle, narration, incredible jams, Gamehendge songs…all of it culled together to level up the band Phish. None of us would be the same after this momentous journey from 1995 to 1996. This three-and-a-half-hour show has everything Phish and then some. If you're looking to roll back the clock and listen to the precise moment when Phish, in their 12th year as a band, grew into their own with both style and humor, precision and "Digital Delay," well, ladies and gentlemen, carve out some time and head back to December 31, 1995. This is Phish with a capital "P."

20 The Clifford Ball: A Beacon of Light in the World of Flight

Before Bonnaroo, before Outside Lands, before Gov Ball and Sasquatch Festival…before all of these massive, weekend-long music festivals that now regularly happen every summer, there was The Clifford Ball.

As the story goes, Phish named The Clifford Ball after an airplane enthusiast, aviator, prolific businessman, and WWI and

WWII veteran, Mr. Clifford Ball. Rumor goes that The Clifford Ball was the initial name of what would be the 1990s' traveling H.O.R.D.E. Festival. Furthermore, the liner notes of Phish's first live album, *A Live One* (see chapter 53), list all of the songs as being recorded at The Clifford Ball, a full year before the festival itself.

But in 1996, for two days in mid August, The Clifford Ball happened at the site of a former Air Force base in Plattsburgh, New York. And 70,000 Phish fans would attend, camping on-site. For the weekend, The Clifford Ball was the ninth-largest city in New York and four times the population of its host city.

The whole spectacle included a weekend of festivities, such as overhead flights by various aircraft, carnival rides, stilt-walkers, jugglers, and various circus-themed decor. Other musicians besides Phish also performed throughout the weekend, including a choir, a blues quartet, classical violinists, and the "Clifford Ball Orchestra," which performed an afternoon set of classical compositions.

Over the weekend Phish played seven sets of music, not including Friday night's sound check, but most certainly including a late-night fourth set on the first night (3:30 AM, actually) that featured the band performing on a flatbed truck slowly driving through the festival grounds.

Other musical highlights include Friday's hour-long 11:00 PM sound check jam featuring Trey Anastasio on a tiny drum kit. For jams from the first show (August 16, 1996), check out Anastasio's solo in "Esther." And for the second set, after the band's mini acoustic set, cue up "Mike's Song" > "Simple" > "Contact" > "Weekapaug Groove." For third-set highlights, listen to "Down with Disease," a nice rendition of "Life on Mars?", and the explosive "Harry Hood" > Jam, performed synchronously with a fireworks show.

For the second night of two, Phish returned to the stage for another three-set performance, featuring solid jams on "Reba," "It's Ice," "Fluffhead," "Scent of a Mule," and "Slave to the Traffic Light." Phish also invited Ben and Jerry of ice cream fame to join

Plattsburgh Says No

Reports indicated that every store along the Northway leading to the Clifford Ball site in Plattsburgh was bought out of all beer, soda, snacks, everything. The festival apparently injected more than $20 million into the local economy.

After The Clifford Ball, Phish immediately petitioned to host a festival again the following summer, but despite raking in $20 million, Plattsburgh officials denied them.

As reported at JamBase.com in August 2016, Mark Barie, the CEO of Plattsburgh Airbase Redevelopment Corporation, the company responsible for marketing the Air Force base, which had been decommissioned the September prior to Clifford Ball, wanted to focus on selling the property as an airport instead of hosting music festivals. And so, Phish was not invited back to Plattsburgh.

Plattsburgh International Airport is now a county public use airport where passenger service began in 2007. In 2011, the airport serviced nearly 140,000 passengers.

them onstage to sing "Brother." During "Antelope," a female acrobat performed circuslike aerial feats suspended above the stage, and during "Tweezer" a pair of large trampolines graced both side stages featuring more acrobatics. For the encore, Phish performed the narrative tune "Harpua" as a stunt plane flew overhead. Though "Harpua" was unfinished, perhaps in part due to miscues from the stunt plane, Phish would only leave their fans hanging for the conclusion for...oh, about a year (see chapter 59).

The Clifford Ball gave Phish one of their rare moments in the mainstream spotlight as MTV aired a three-part, 30-minute documentary of the festival that featured interviews with the band, fans, Phish road manager Brad Sands, and then-mayor of Plattsburgh, Claude Rabideau.

In March 2009, Phish released their own film, a seven-DVD box set documenting the festival. And in November 2021, Phish announced a 12-LP Box Set of the six complete sets of music from

The Clifford Ball for the 25th anniversary of the festival. Phish Dry Goods also launched an exclusive bonus LP of Phish's late-night 37-minute "Flatbed Jam."

21 Phish Destroys America and Island Tour

In the fall of 1997, Phish set off for a 21-show run from Las Vegas to Albany, New York, a now-legendary tour known as "Phish Destroys America." It was deemed such by an official poster for the Las Vegas show by Ames Design that featured a martial artist with text that read, THEIR HANDS ARE FASTER THAN GUNS AND PHISH DESTROYS AMERICA.

Phish played nearly 80 shows in 1997 and have yet to play even half that amount in a single year since. Many fans and critics alike consider the 1997 shows, particularly the Phish Destroys America tour, as some of the best Phish shows of all time.

And while listening to even just the fall '97 tour would take between 50 and 60 hours, you can start at the beginning and make your way with the band from Vegas to points east, hand-pick the best of the best shows, or just focus on recommended jams. A nearly eight-hour supercut of the best jams of the tour is available on YouTube. And it's incredible.

Phish's prolific 1997 touring left the band eager to keep playing in early 1998. The band was hot and certainly didn't want to lose momentum.

Enter the Island Tour.

In late February, less than two months after their 1997 New Year's Eve show, Phish announced the Island Tour. The run would kick off about a month later, on April 2, 1998. At just four shows, two at Nassau Coliseum and two at Providence Civic Center, this minitour has come to be a high-water mark for the band in a moment of musical growth and increasing popularity.

The band then hit Trey Anastasio's recording studio, "The Barn," on his Vermont property for a few days of prolonged jam sessions, which they recorded and would develop into *The Story of the Ghost* (see chapter 62).

What's special about the Island Tour, beyond its blitzkrieg approach, is its extended jams and incredible improvisation. These shows include remarkable performances across Phish's core catalogue and include premieres of *Ghost* songs including "Birds of a Feather" (played two nights), "Franky Says," and "Shafty."

But really, it's about the funk—the "Cow Funk." On the final night (April 5, 1998), out of a blistering "Possum," Trey led the band into a sweet, funky jam, during which he spoke to the audience, saying: "So it's getting near the end of this little four-day run here, so we gotta, uh…It's been really fun and it's kinda weird having to stop after four days, but, for those of you who came to a lot of the shows or for those of you who just came tonight, thank you very much, we really appreciate everything. And, um…I started this little funk groove because we can't end this whole thing without a little more funk, since that's kinda been the theme. So for those of you who wanna take off, take off, but for those of you who just wanna dance to the funk, ya know, we're gonna stay around and keep grooving…."

And that's exactly what they did with "Cavern," quite possibly the funkiest version yet.

These four shows in April 1998 showcase the band in a loose, confident period that yielded a collection of jams. In 2005, Live Phish would release the Island Tour on CD and for download.

Please; find the time over a long weekend or perhaps a few days in April to listen to these extraordinary shows called the Island Tour.

22 The Grateful Dead/Phish Conundrum

There is no more sensitive topic in the Phish world than the connection and comparison between Phish and the Grateful Dead. It should be unequivocally stated that these two distinctly different acts have carved out their own unique places in American counterculture, and have made an impact on thousands, if not millions, of people in their independent 30-plus year touring careers. Their overall sound is different, their lyrical style is different, their compositional writing is different, their overall tempo is different, and their paths to success have been vastly different.

Even if the comparisons are uncomfortable, it is hard to deny that there aren't overall similarities in their storied histories. Both bands have wildly devoted fan bases who have traveled to the ends of the earth to see them play. At any given show, set, or even song, both bands can tap into a variety of musical genres and improvise within those structures. And both bands are true American success stories that are honest reflections of their generations.

Even at Phish's first show in 1983, they played the classic Grateful Dead pairing of "Scarlet" > "Fire." It is hard to find a Phish show in the mid 1980s without a Grateful Dead song peppered in. Without a doubt, the Grateful Dead were an early influence on the members of Phish. At the Connecticut Forum panel with Bob Weir, Trey described the impact of seeing his first Grateful Dead show in 1983 as "like getting hit in the head with a baseball bat."

But over time things changed. As Phish began to carve their own path in music in the late 1980s, any Grateful Dead covers just evaporated from their sets.

From an outsider's perspective, it seemed Phish wanted to create a legacy of their own, and they had a difficult time shaking the shadow of the Grateful Dead. Comparisons between the two bands were commonplace, and it was hard to find articles on Phish from this time period that didn't reference the Grateful Dead.

When Jerry Garcia passed away in August 1995, there was an observable shift within the size of the Phish scene. The ugly expression of "passing the torch" was thrown around by many journalists. The Phish phenomenon was no longer under the radar, and their days of playing intimate theaters were a thing of the past.

In the years following Jerry's death, Phish honored the legacy of the Grateful Dead a few times. At the Shoreline Amphitheater in the Bay Area on July 31, 1997 (the day before Jerry's birthday), during a "Weekapaug Groove," Trey teased "Happy Birthday to You" and later talked about keeping Jerry's spirit alive with music.

In a much grander gesture, Phish took the opportunity on the third anniversary of Jerry's death on August 9, 1998, in Virginia Beach to encore with the Grateful Dead masterpiece "Terrapin Station." Fans were beside themselves for this once-in-a-lifetime moment. This is a must-hear for any fan of Phish and the Grateful Dead.

In 1999, Phil Lesh, the Grateful Dead's bass player, having just recovered from lifesaving liver transplant surgery, announced his return to the stage with a three-night run of Phil and "Phriends" shows at The Warfield in San Francisco. Without an official lineup, tickets went on sale. Rumors swirled hinting at members of Phish joining Phil's band, and subsequently the shows sold out instantly.

Soon it was revealed that Phil had tapped Trey Anastasio, Page McConnell, Steve Kimock, and John Molo as his Phriends for this show. More than 20 years later, these shows still hold up as some of the best live music created during this generation. With only around 2,000 incredibly lucky fans in attendance, members of Phish and the Grateful Dead graced the stage together for the first

Trey Anastasio, Phil Lesh, and Bob Weir perform at Fare Thee Well 2015. Everybody's playin' in the band. (AP Images)

time in history. Seeing old-school members of both the Grateful Dead community and the Phish community intermingling was an incredibly beautiful sight and long overdue.

When they opened the show with a nearly 34-minute "Viola Lee Blues," the musical wall that had separated these bands for so long crumbled before our eyes and ears, and a new age of collaboration was born. Run, don't walk, to check out these shows if you haven't heard them yet. And if you have, wouldn't you agree it's time for a relisten?

From there, the collaborative floodgates were open. Later that year, Phil Lesh returned the favor by sitting in on, or rather jumping into, a Phish show at Shoreline Amphitheatre. When Phish played their classic "YEM," instead of bringing out two trampolines, they brought out three. Phil continued playing for the rest of the show, which included "Wolfman's Brother" and "Cold Rain and Snow." To add to the historic nature, prolific guitarist Warren Haynes joined in for the "Viola Lee Blues" encore.

In the following year, 2000, Grateful Dead's rhythm guitarist Bob Weir played with Phish at a Shoreline gig for the very first time, which also happened to be the penultimate show before the 1.0 hiatus. Weir joined the band for a three-song encore that included "El Paso," "Chalkdust Torture," and "West L.A. Fadeaway."

Sporadic collaborations took place between members of both bands through the years that followed, but in 2015 a new opportunity presented itself.

"Fare Thee Well," the Grateful Dead's 50th-anniversary celebration, brought the collaborative relationship between these bands to a whole other level. The members of the Grateful Dead wanted to celebrate the golden anniversary in epic form, but there was an obvious need to attempt to fill the unfillable lead guitar role of Jerry Garcia.

Promoter and impresario Peter Shapiro was the driving force behind this celebration and thought Trey would be a perfect fit. Shapiro is a jam music scene chessmaster whose resume includes owning the NYC music mecca Wetlands in the 1990s, creating the Brooklyn Bowl music venue dynasty, refurbishing and revitalizing the Capitol Theater, and launching the LOCKN' Festival.

When asked, "How did you get Trey Anastasio to do the shows?" by *Fast Company*, Shapiro replied, "I think the band and myself knew he was the right fit for this moment. I think we all felt that power this moment would have, and a melding of these two generations felt like the appropriate thing for this moment."

There were five Fare Thee Well shows in total—two in Santa Clara, California, and three in Chicago, Illinois. These shows were an incredible celebration of the history of the Grateful Dead as well as the full embrace of Trey and Phish as modern musical partners. The shows created beautiful moment after beautiful moment.

Trey wasn't the only one who toyed with the idea of joining a Grateful Dead incarnation. Shortly after Fare Thee Well, Mike Gordon was recruited to play bass on the current Grateful Dead touring band, Dead and Company. In the *Star Tribune*, Mike spoke about his week of rehearsals, saying, "It's such a dream gig. I love the Grateful Dead." But his solo band and Phish's own recording plans made it hard for him to make the commitment, and ultimately he declined the opportunity.

Since Fare Thee Well, Bob Weir has joined Phish one more time, for an emotional show in Nashville, Tennessee, on October 18, 2016. This was a very special collaboration, because Bob not only sang his songs, but added complex rhythmic layers to the jams for most of the second set. Weir even sang lead on the heart-wrenching Phish ballad "Miss You" that Anastasio wrote for his departed sister Kristy. It was an incredibly poignant and beautiful moment that left many wondering whom exactly he was singing to.

Then, in March 2018, The Grateful Dead's Bob Weir and Phil Lesh set out on a six-date Spring Tour that included two nights at NYC's Radio City Music Hall, where they welcomed Trey Anastasio to sit in for the second set of the second night. An emotional and joyful crowd was treated to "The Wheel," "Dark Star," "Eyes of the World," and "St. Stephen" before the band encored with "Ripple."

These moments, shared between all these musicians, are incredibly special and something to cherish. The real beauty is that nowadays there is no reason to think these magical collaborations won't happen again.

23 Meet the Phans

Phish shows attract all types of people. Phish fans include the entire spectrum, from old to young, party animal to straightedge, music professor to raver, parent to bachelor. You never know whom you'll meet at a Phish show.

As a means to offer you a glimpse into the types of characters you'll see at a Phish show, here are a dozen different groups of fans and their terminology.

Wooks

Chewbacca, Han Solo's copilot in *Star Wars*, is a Wookiee: long-haired and speaking in roars and grunts. The term *Wook* in Phish culture is debatable in regards to its disparaging nature, but in my experience no one is proudly calling oneself a Wook.

Generally, Wooks are grungy and unkempt from living on the road. They often have dreadlocks, and their fashions include patchwork pants and flat-brimmed hats. Wooks often sell crystals or rocks and many, not all, have perfected cons and scams as part of their survival on the road. This is where the line between good and bad gets fuzzy.

You see, not all Wooks are gentle giants like Chewbacca. Many consider the lot to be their home and will often take advantage of those with less experience or know-how. Is this inherently evil? Or is this just the natural dynamic of the lot ecosystem, not unlike the cheetah taking down the gazelle on the Serengeti? The cheetah is not bad. The cheetah is just doing what it needs to do to survive.

Chads and Custies

Custies are the prey of Wooks on lot. Custies are customers. They're the locals coming to shows with little to no experience of the scene. They're often taken advantage of when looking to buy lot items. That said, some Custies are not Phish fans at all and go to lot solely to buy drugs. And then some Custies grow up to be Wooks.

Are there rules when selling to Custies versus Wooks versus other fans? Rules? Man, there ain't no rules!

Chads are often Custies, but not always. Chads are bros—like, fraternity bros—often identified by preppy fashions, such as polo shirts and fancy wristwatches. While Chads may not be looking to spend money or buy drugs like Custies, if they do, you can expect prices to be marked up just the same. But I think generally Chads are observers and mocked for their lack of participation. At least Custies contribute to the lot economy.

Tarpers

Tarpers are the folks who arrive early to line up before the doors open so they can be among the first inside the venue and lay out a large blue vinyl tarp on the floor of the general admission area to claim space for themselves and their friends yet to come. And unless you're a Tarper yourself, you probably don't like them very much.

The common thought among fans regarding Tarpers is that you can't rightfully stake claim to a swath of floor space in a general admission area. To put it bluntly, you can't save space or otherwise ask someone not to use available "general admission" space.

But people do it anyway, and often it's a cause for confrontation or even conflicts at shows. In recent years, Phish have disallowed tarps in venues, to varying levels of impact.

Noobs

Noob is a derogatory term for someone relatively new to Phish. The term, short for "newbie," originates from video gamer communities to describe someone who doesn't really know what they're doing.

A Phish Noob may not know what song the band is playing or be able to speak to the differences in jamming techniques. And while a Phish Noob may or may not know the names of the band members, he or she most certainly would not know the name of the band's lighting director (see chapter 9).

Just a reminder, folks: at one point, we were all Noobs.

Jaded Vets

These are the Phish fans who cannot be impressed by current Phish concerts. They're older; they were there in the 1990s "heyday" of 1.0, and you'll know this because they'll tell you. They'll tell you how great it once was and how mediocre it is now.

Chompers

You've seen these guys at Phish shows. They're the ones rolling on so much Molly they're clenching their teeth and literally chomping on the air. Molly, aka MDMA, will do that to you sometimes. Generally speaking, Chompers are so high they lose their sense of personal space and some level of motor skills. Read: they'll dance on you, bump into you, and/or grab you in excitement!

There's a second definition of *Chomper*—someone who talks during the set. They're constantly chomping and gabbing and blabbing, either as a result of too many drugs or otherwise. Perhaps the Chomper behind you is also a Chad and just won't shut up, though he's likely only imbibing light beer. Nevertheless, this person may also be referred to as a Chomper.

Spinners

If you've been to a Phish show you've seen them: fans who are literally spinning in circles at the outskirts of the crowd, in hallways—really in any open and available space to spin, you'll find Spinners. They're likely on drugs, LSD for example.

Really, though, I have no idea why they spin. It seems fun for a little while, maybe for a song, but perhaps that's where the drugs come into play? Sure, religious sects have been spinning for ages; folks like turning Sufis and whirling dervishes. But I think something different is happening for the Spinners at Phish shows. Maybe so, maybe not!

Statisticians

You may find yourself in line for the bathroom at a Phish show and overhear a conversation that goes something like this:

"Dude, that 'Bathtub Gin' was the longest since MSG 2015."

"'Magna Gin' was 21 minutes."

"Nothing will beat 'Riverport,' though."

These guys are statisticians. They pride themselves on their esoteric knowledge of Phish song stats, including length, gap since the last time it was played, particulars of the jam, and more. Phish statisticians are not unlike baseball statisticians: accurate as fuck.

They know exactly how many shows they've been to. They know exactly when the last time Phish played "Manteca" was.

The Baker's Dozen run featured nine songs more than 20 minutes in length. It had been 574 shows since Phish last performed "Izabella" (July 31, 1998) when they busted it out at Madison Square Garden on the final night of the Baker's Dozen.

There are clear leaders and fact-checkers in the world of Phish stats—namely, Phish.net, the official scorekeepers and setlist scribes, not to mention the collective authors of *The Phish Companion*. Another valuable resource is Phishtistics by Phish.net staffer and author David "ZZYZX" Steinberg. Both websites offer users the opportunity to create an account and select the shows you've attended to then get a personalized statistical overview, if you're into that sort of thing.

Rail-Riders

As with anything, Phish too have their superfans. These guys are serious—just a heads-up. To put it lightly, this community of fans sticks together. These fans will often camp out for hours, sometimes sleeping overnight in line outside the venue, to ensure they're among the first inside when the doors open so they can grab their position at the rail at the base of the stage.

And boy can they dance! The Rail-Riders are often the most engaged, dialed-in fans at a show. There's no room for half-assed participation at the foot of the stage. Respect the culture of the rail and you'll be welcomed. Otherwise, take two steps back.

Families

With Phish coming of age in the 1990s, many fans are now parents looking to share the experience with their young children or otherwise bringing along their young'uns. Most outdoor amphitheaters will have makeshift family zones in the lawn demarcated with strollers or a dotted line of glow sticks on the grass.

It's important to give these guys space to enjoy themselves. That means no partying near the family zone. Keep it clean, guys, or head into the throng and party there.

Tapers

Tapers are the missionaries, the archivists, the purists, the historians. From the very beginning, this select group recorded and disseminated live Phish shows, spearheading the band's grassroots growth. Phish, like the Grateful Dead, has always supported audience recordings, offering tapers the opportunity to purchase tickets for an exclusive taper section.

While these days Phish releases every single live show for purchase and download at Live Phish, back in the day, you needed blanks and postage to collect your favorite shows. And still, some fans prefer audience recordings (AUD) that capture the tone of the venue over the crisp, official soundboard recording (SBD). For more on that, see chapter 45.

Vendors

Phish shows have always been a traveling circus, with hundreds or even thousands of fans moving down the road with the band from show to show. This gives rise to a bona fide economy where fans can find and purchase or barter for just about anything. Of course, the heart of this economy is the vendors.

Ranging from a full-on brick pizza oven cooking on the back of a pickup truck to a George Foreman grill on the trunk of a sedan, vendors operate at varying degrees of professionalism. To that point, some are just looking for a few extra bucks to buy beer in the venue, while some are working hard to finance their entire monthlong tour.

While most are there for the music first and foremost, some are less interested in the band and are focused on making profit. Shakedown Street, where vendors set up in organized rows, has always been a safe haven for entrepreneurs who, for one reason or another, have chosen a cash-only lifestyle. That said, competition can sometimes lead to conflicts, and Shakedown is not always a peaceful place. But for the most part, everyone gets along selling their food and wares.

Personally, I love to support the vendors at shows. I imagine the same $5 bill circulating on lot, exchanging hands over and over again for weeks, but never leaving Shakedown. Keep it in the community, man. Support vendors.

Just a word to the wise, though: keep it vegetarian on lot. Who knows about that meat, am I right?

24 Stroll Shakedown

The term "ground zero" describes the point on the Earth's surface directly where a nuclear bomb detonates. When Phish comes to town, and that bomb goes off, Shakedown Street is ground zero. Shakedown Street is the epicenter of Phish Tour.

The name itself comes from the eponymous 1978 Grateful Dead song and album, to which the whole scene, if you will, is native. But that doesn't get us much closer to really understanding what Shakedown Street is.

Shakedown is a marketplace, community center, shopping mall food court, playground, city center, and theme park all rolled into one parking lot. This is where everyone comes together. This is where everything is bought and sold. This is where you meet before and after the show, and this is where you end up when you have no place else to go. In simplest terms, Shakedown is an area of the parking lot of a venue where attendees and followers congregate to vend their wares, mingle, and celebrate.

The extended parking lots surrounding Shakedown often don't look much different from other concerts or sporting events: fans tailgating at their parked car. One of my favorite hobbies is to scope out the license plates in the lot: FLORIDA, PENNSYLVANIA, MARYLAND, GEORGIA, SOUTH CAROLINA, OREGON…people come from all over.

Friends and couples hanging out at their cars listening to music, chatting, enjoying some drinks, the tailgaters at Phish shows tend to skew more…open to meeting new people? They're sharing and exchanging stories, sharing and exchanging drinks—or even hugs. It's a welcoming vibe for sure and one that often feels very relaxed and easygoing. Lots of smiles, lots of high fives.

But as you come upon a row or two of vendors hawking food and just about everything else, the vibe grows a bit more serious and certainly more crowded. At the threshold of Shakedown, tailgaters leaning against cars give way to a bazaar of bona fide vendors with pop-up tents and folding tables and barbecue grills full of kebabs with thick, chalky smoke billowing into the air.

Shakedown is the ultimate, extreme tailgate party.

Shakedown Street during the day is a hodgepodge of sights and sounds and smells, with makeshift bands playing across the aisle from a team of vendors grilling cheeseburgers and veggie burgers.

"Ice cold water!" says a shirtless man maybe in his 50s— or maybe he's just a hard-living 30-year-old behind his dusty sunglasses.

A pair of men wearing patchwork pants, both terribly skinny with thick manes of dreadlocks, examine something small and precious in one's hands and then make some kind of exchange.

We're in the crowd now, a steady stream of fans making their way up and down the aisles of the parking lot-turned-Shakedown. It smells like grilled meat and sweat, and music from at least three stereos creates a cacophony of sounds, and the crowd has grown thick, almost shoulder to shoulder as everyone shuffles along, this way and that.

"Doses," someone whispers in your ear, and he's gone before you can determine who said it.

Shakedown Street is Mos Eisley Cantina. It's the Grand Bazaar. Shakedown is some kind of dusty, outdoor flea market restaurant souvenir shop where you can drink openly, smoke freely, shop for anything and everything and even buy a bootleg T-shirt to take home with you (see chapter 71).

"Heady veggie burritos!" someone yells, holding high a foil-wrapped cylinder, shining and almost blinding in the sunlight.

All manner of Phish fans and entrepreneurs and drug dealers make up Shakedown. But this isn't Burning Man. What I mean by that is not everyone has opted in. Burning Man doesn't get many tourists—curious onlookers stopping by for an hour or so. Phish Tour does and Shakedown certainly has its tourists.

And that's fine.

"Who's got my pharmies?" a girl sings aloud, using the shorthand for pharmaceutical drugs.

Tourists are welcome at Shakedown, so long as they have money. Ultimately, everyone on Shakedown has different needs and wants, but generally speaking everyone is looking to buy or sell something. Often, but not always, that something is drugs. And there are people who will sell them, no question. But there's more to it than that. Really, it's the variety of salespeople that makes Shakedown the unique place that it is.

Undoubtedly, the vendors are the matriarchs and patriarchs of Shakedown Street.

Vendors are the stalwarts of Shakedown. They're the providers, man. They're the creative ones, the entrepreneurial ones, the ones who take care of you while working to take care of themselves, too.

Shakedown *is* vendors.

They sell just about everything you could need or want: food, drinks, drugs, clothes, toys, posters, paintings, hats, socks, rocks, and even more. The food? Everything from poorly made veggie burritos to thin-crust pizza. You can find makeshift bars serving martinis from an ice-cold shaker, or you can drink lukewarm $1 cans of Bud Light.

The arts and crafts range from handmade patchwork dresses and silkscreened T-shirts to blown glass and oil paintings, and everything in between.

On Shakedown Street, I've seen games of chance, including three-card monte, and pitchmen with strange toys like head massagers and psychedelic goggles. I've seen full-on pop-up pharmacies hawking all kinds of single-use pills and medicine. Tylenol, Pepto? They've got it.

For most Shakedown vendors, their work provides a means to tour and go to the show and for them, as for other fans, it's all about the show. Vending just helps them get there, financially. But some vendors have been to so many shows that it's fine enough to hear what they can from outside the venue rather than pay to get in. Still others have no intention of going to the shows. For them, the real mission and the real prize is money. They're professional. They are there to work. Sure, selling a few cases of beer is a fun way to pass the time before the show and make a little bit of pocket money. But coming prepared to cook and sell 200 cheeseburgers at Phish show? That's serious business. (See chapter 68.)

Some vendors may be unable to earn a legitimate living. And some of them are spillover families from touring for decades with the Grateful Dead, now piggybacking on whatever traveling circus they can find since Jerry died in 1995.

Make no mistake: these are not your typical county fair food vendors or music festival merch salesmen. They don't have food-service permits or board of health certificates. Shakedown vendors are of a different ilk. It's cash only, and there are no receipts. No taxable income either. It's a livelihood and a lifestyle. They're the first to arrive, and the last to leave.

And without them, we would have no Shakedown Street. So be sure to soak it all in before the show. Arrive early, bring cash, and enjoy the eccentric bazaar. Take a stroll down Shakedown Street. Really, there's nothing else like it.

25 Hit the Road, Do a Phish Tour

Going to a Phish show is a great first step for anyone just discovering the band. Hitting all three or four nights of a run in New York for New Year's Eve or Dick's Sporting Goods Park in Colorado for Labor Day is even better, as you'll likely engage the community a bit more, hear more nuances in the jams, catch teases from nights prior, or reunite with strangers-cum-friends from Friday on Sunday. After a few shows, you begin to settle in and find comfort in the scene, in the routine.

But after a couple of weeks of Phish shows, making your way from town to town and show to show, the world of Phish becomes your home.

Quite frankly, Phish is as American as the cross-country road trip, and combining the two is the solemn duty of any red-blooded American Phan. This is your band. This is your land. Hit the road and find adventure!

"But I can't take that much time off from work," you say. "I can't afford to travel for that long," you say. "I don't have a reliable road trip car," you say.

Well, here's what I say. Sometimes in life you have to take risks; you have to throw everything to the wind and follow your bliss. Now, this is different for everyone, and I can't rightfully advise people to pack up and leave their families or make decisions that would land them destitute and homeless. But I will say this: money comes and money goes. And this band won't be around forever.

Take out a credit card. Grab a couple of friends and buy a cheap car…or a van. Sleep in Walmart parking lots. Camp! Sell bottled water or cigarettes or beer on lot. Buy groceries and stick to a daily budget.

How much you'll spend on the road depends tremendously on where you sleep, so pool your resources to find friends and friends of friends in towns along the way. Pitch a tent in a friend's backyard. Ask the hive mind on Facebook for a crash pad in Kansas City. Reserve a room at the Motel 6 just off the freeway past the venue. And cram five dudes in there.

If you play it right, you may just break even, pending any setbacks or catastrophes. And that's part of the adventure, too!

You will have car trouble. You may even run out of gas on I-90. You will end up sleeping in your car because you drank too much or there was no more room at the inn. You will get left behind at some point, forgotten at a gas station or abandoned because you missed the rendezvous.

Hopefully, you won't get in legal trouble. Be careful selling beer on lot, or selling anything for that matter. Don't speed. And don't drive under the influence. Sure, shit happens, and that's part of the adventure that is Tour. But don't be reckless. The most reckless thing you can do is drive while intoxicated. Just don't do it.

Phish Tour can be dangerous. But like most places, if you play it safe, you'll be fine. If you look for trouble, you'll find it.

Phish Tour can be a journey of self-discovery. This is your moment, your bliss. The only thing you should ever really worry about on Phish Tour is getting to the next show. You shouldn't worry about anything else.

So here's what you do when Phish announces a tour. First, as soon as the announcement is published, drop whatever you're doing and book hotel rooms. Book cheap ones, preferably, but book hotel rooms wherever you can. Rooms are the the first thing to sell out, and they're the easiest to share and easiest to cancel and get fully refunded. Consider it a backup plan if you'd like, but hey—better to have a room you can cancel than be stuck looking when every hotel in Philadelphia is sold out.

Then, do your best to get tickets. Ask friends to help out with the mail order and on sale, even if they're not into Phish or interested in going. That's even better, actually. If they have room on their credit card, or can get in front of a computer to try for Ticketmaster, that's what's up!

And good luck. It seems that demand for Phish is just increasing, while the number of shows they play each year is decreasing. In the early 1990s, Phish averaged 126 shows each year. In the late 1990s, Phish averaged 74 shows per year. In the 3.0 era, Phish is averaging 33 shows per year. And yet, in 2023, they played 47 shows.

That said, Trey Anastasio has implied that their heavy touring days may already over. In a 2016 *Wall Street Journal* article, Anastasio told Alan Paul, "I think you will see us slow down and do some different things over the next two years." And if the Summer Tour 2017 and the Baker's Dozen residency at Madison Square Garden are any indication of what's to come, perhaps we can expect shorter tours and longer residencies? Maybe so, maybe not.

I include that quote from Anastasio not to dishearten anyone who may have perhaps missed their opportunity to hit the road for Phish tour, but rather to offer encouragement for when the chance comes 'round again.

And, hey—at the end of the day, as the late, great Jack Kerouac once wrote, "All he needed was a wheel in his hand and four on the road."

26 A Picture of Nectar (1992)

This album blasts off from the opening note with Jon Fishman drumming a fierce, cymbal-laden beat. Then Trey Anastasio fires off a staccato riff for one measure before the rest of the band joins in. "Llama" is high-energy and full-on rock from moment one—though in recent years, we've had a couple of slow "Llama" performances at live shows (August 14, 2015, and June 29, 2016).

But I digress. "Llama" is a funky-fast, high-octane tune. "Taboot Taboot!"

The second track on *A Picture of Nectar* is a 90-second instrumental, one of three on the album, and serves almost as a palate cleanser before "Cavern."

A 1992 review of *A Picture of Nectar* in *Billboard* magazine reads, "The band's major-label debut should be required on all college listening lists. The songs are all over the place from whacked-out rock to bluegrass to jazz. The constant is the high quality of musicianship and spirit that runs from track to track."

Now-quintessential Phish songs on this 1992 album include "Stash," "Guelah Papyrus," "Chalkdust Torture," and, of course, "Tweezer" and "Tweezer Reprise." According to setlist.fm, "Chalkdust Torture" is Phish's fifth-most-played song. "Tweezer" comes in at No. 16 and is regarded by most as Phish's premier jam vehicle song (chapter 8). And the "Tweezer Reprise" that's nearly always paired with it? That's the Kentucky Derby of Phish, and perhaps the most exciting two minutes in all of music. You see, even Phish's studio records offer up some good, clean fun.

And perhaps it's that clean, crisp production quality that makes the album so fun and accessible? *A Picture of Nectar* was Phish's major-label debut, with Elektra Records, and they put that big company recording budget to good use.

Recorded over the summer of 1991 at White Crow Studios in Burlington, Vermont, just about a half mile down the road from Nectar's, the album would go gold 10 years later, in November 2011.

A Picture of Nectar is Phish's third official studio album. As you may have guessed, the album is dedicated to Nector Rorris, the owner of Nectar's club and bar in Burlington, Vermont, where Phish played numerous (around 50) times in 1987 and 1988 honing and refining their sound. Phish famously played three-night runs each month at Nectar's, and the album's cover art features Rorris' visage in the orange.

The album's liner notes read: "Eight and a half years ago, we played our first bar gig at Nectar's in Burlington. Nectar Rorris, the proprietor, was happy to give us a gig despite our lack of experience, organization, or a song list long enough to last two sets. The night went well enough and soon we were playing a series of monthly three night stands—three sets a night on Sunday, Monday, and Tuesday. Like countless other bands in Burlington's diverse music scene, those nights at Nectar's taught us how to play. We dedicate this album to Nectar Rorris for 16 years of bringing Burlington live music every night of the week with no cover, and the best fries this side of…France."

Timothy Monger wrote in his review at AllMusic.com, "For all of its freewheeling variety, *A Picture of Nectar* manages to be extremely cohesive, firmly establishing Phish's unique brand to a much wider audience than they'd previously enjoyed. While they would continue to grow both onstage and on record, this album captured a very vital period in their career and ranks as possibly the most essential studio album in their canon."

I'm tempted to agree. I don't believe the band has a stronger, more timeless studio album.

27 Chilling, Thrilling Ziggy Stardust

Halloween has always been a special night for Phish, particularly since the 1994 premiere of the "musical costume" album cover set. By the time we reach 2014, Phish have donned "musical costumes" at Halloween shows numerous times, but only once in Las Vegas (October 31, 1998). With the announcement of a 2014 Halloween run returning to Sin City, Phish once again raised the bar and expectations were high. But no one could have expected the über unique performance the band had in store.

On October 31, 2014, ticketholders at the MGM Arena were given a "Phishbill" upon entry showcasing the *Chilling, Thrilling Sounds of the Haunted House* album cover, the 1964 release from Walt Disney Studios. For those familiar, the revelation was absolutely exhilarating, but left questions about how Phish could possibly cover this album. For the uninitiated, *Chilling, Thrilling Sounds of the Haunted House*, the vinyl record, is a collection of horror stories on one side and spooky sound effects on the other side. This 40-year-old album may be many things to many people, but music it certainly is not.

Onstage, a theatrical setup included a giant "metal" gate with a large "P" emblem. Phish opened the first set with all Halloween-themed songs, including "Buried Alive" > "Ghost" > "Scent of a Mule." The band concluded the set with the Halloween favorite "Wolfman's Brother," and during the setbreak stagehands removed all of the band's equipment and installed headstones, building out a theatrical graveyard. Suddenly, the gate opened, revealing a large haunted house, presumably with the band inside. Once the house was positioned at the front of the stage, the show began.

With sound effects and *Chilling, Thrilling Sounds of the Haunted House* narration playing over the PA, a ghastly narrator appeared from a crypt onstage to introduce the show. Then the music started. Phish, from inside the haunted house, started with a pair of previously unheard, original, instrumental songs, named for and inspired by the stories on the album, "The Haunted House" and "The Very Long Fuse." As the band played, zombies danced and meandered through the graveyard onstage. During "Fuse," a laser slowly "cut into" the walls of the haunted house until a giant explosion sounded and the house walls collapsed to reveal the band inside wearing white tuxedos and white zombie makeup.

Using the various sound effects from the album, with narration interspliced, Phish continued the set performing 10 never-before-heard songs, their own unique interpretations of Disney's *Chilling, Thrilling Sounds of the Haunted House* record. To say the event was unprecedented is a gross understatement.

Everybody was screaming when they saw the shirt! Page McConnel delivers "Lawn Boy" in Las Vegas, 2016. (Jason Gershuny)

Here's a band, 30 years into their career, not only continuing to surprise and amaze their audience but also challenging themselves to create new and original material, and then premiering it live!

The band then, of course, returned to the stage for a third set of music, highlights including "Tweezer" and "Sand," with an encore and debut of Leonard Cohen's "Is This What You Wanted" ("And is this what you wanted / To live in a house that is haunted") followed by "Frankenstein" with Page McConnell on keytar for the first time in 100 shows.

Personally, this is one of my all-time favorite shows, if for nothing more than the ingenuity of a band aiming to make something special. Many of the *Chilling, Thrilling* songs have since been incorporated into Phish's live performances, including "Martian Monster," which has been played nearly two dozen times since its premiere.

Phish would sit out Halloween in 2015 while the Trey Anastasio Band toured briefly with a Halloween show at Brooklyn Bowl Las Vegas.

In August 2016, Phish announced a fall 2016 tour concluding with a four-night stand at the MGM Grand Garden Arena and culminating on Monday—Halloween.

For those of you playing along at home, 2016 was a difficult year for the music world. The year included the deaths of David Bowie and Prince, not to mention Phife Dawg, among others. Needless to say, the loss of these incredible musicians stirred the Phish community and many wondered if or how the band would honor them on tour.

Phish's 2016 summer tour opened in Minneapolis/St. Paul, Minnesota, the home and birthplace of Prince. But save for a few choice moments of deep purple lighting from lighting director Chris Kuroda, the band made no nod to the late, great Prince.

They would, however, honor David Bowie in the encore of their first-ever show at Chicago's storied Wrigley Field on June 24,

2016. Stepping to the microphones at the edge of the stage, Phish performed a stirring a cappella rendition of "Space Oddity" for the sellout crowd of 41,000 fans.

But still, what would Phish do for Halloween? Would they cover a classic album as they'd done so many times before, or would they do something completely new and original like their 2014 performance?

On October 24, 2016, I wrote a blog post on PhanSite.com titled "Five Reasons Why Phish Will Cover 'Ziggy Stardust' on Halloween." I had my reasons, certainly, but one such reason was a leaked 17-second clip of Phish's sound check prior to their appearance on the Jimmy Fallon show on October 10, 2016. They were riffing on "Suffragette City"! It could only mean one thing!

And sure enough, attendees at the MGM on Halloween 2016 entered and received "Phishbills" featuring the iconic Bowie cover, though in Bowie's place stood one of the four Phish band members (there were four covers). Indeed, Phish covered David Bowie's *The Rise and Fall of Ziggy Stardust and the Spiders from Mars* in its entirety on October 31, 2016.

With a string sextet and three backup singers, Phish moved through the 11-song 1972 album with style and grace, even having dressed up for the occasion.

Bowie's truly unique album received a fantastic rendition that evening. And whether Phish intended this or not, the performance allowed all of us to take a moment and perhaps find a bit of solace in the fact that despite Bowie's passing, his music lived on.

Of all of Phish's Halloween covers, this one perhaps is the truest to its original. Seldom did the band jam or extend these classic songs. For "It Ain't Easy," Anastasio took the microphone in his hand and delivered a spirited, soulful rendition. Honestly, I don't think I've heard him put so much into singing a song. Needless to say, the sounds of "Ziggy Stardust," as sung by Page McConnell, filled the arena like no other song. And with Anastasio back on lead vocals for the conclusion of "Rock 'n' Roll Suicide," belting out the lyrics atop the vocalizations from the backup singers and the tenuous sounds of the string section, well, no one in the room could deny Bowie's legacy or Phish's tender, impeccably performed homage to the Starman himself.

After the third set, including "2001" replete with "Fame" quotes from Anastasio, Phish encored with an a cappella performance of "Space Oddity" to conclude the show, the Vegas run, and their fall 2016 tour.

The band's barbershop rendition of "Space Oddity" remains stirring with each listen. Here's a band honoring a late, great artist while simultaneously remaining true to themselves. It's fun, even funny, and all the same chilling, even thrilling.

28 Great Cover Band or the Greatest Cover Band?

Sure, Phish has 16 studio albums under their belt and a full catalog of more than 300 original songs. But it doesn't stop there. According to Wikipedia, Phish has performed covers of nearly 350 different songs.

To say that Phish's band members are masterful musicians is an understatement. They can play anything. And they often do! One of the pure joys of seeing this band is the suspense of knowing that at any point they could segue into one of any hundreds or thousands of songs. And one of the most exciting aspects of any Phish show is when they do, if even for just a few notes. It's not just their talent or command of their craft, but also their extensive knowledge of and undeniable respect for the vast landscape of good, old-fashioned American rock 'n roll that sets Phish above the rest.

While some bands may shy away from the barroom cover band stigma, Phish dives in headfirst. At 2017's Baker's Dozen residency of 13 shows, Phish played 237 unique songs, including 61 covers. That's a staggering 26 percent of the total songs performed. Moreover, these covers were chosen to fit in with each night's unique theme, based on a different doughnut flavor (see chapter 13).

I'll ask again, as I have many times in this book: what band?

Hell, their Halloween tradition of donning a "musical costume" and covering an entire album by another band is an astounding feat any way you look at it (see chapters 11, 27, 83, and 90).

Mister mojo risin'. Phish performing "L.A. Woman" by The Doors for the first time in nearly 500 shows (10/30/03) at The Forum in Los Angeles on 10/24/21. (Trevor Anderson)

Phish has skillfully covered songs by The Beatles, The Who, The Doors, The Velvet Underground, Talking Heads, the Grateful Dead, The Rolling Stones, the James Gang, David Bowie, Elton John, Bob Marley, Bob Dylan, George Clinton, Dizzy Gillespie, Bruce Springsteen, Jimi Hendrix, Stevie Wonder, Frank Zappa, Prince, Pink Floyd, Led Zeppelin, Lynyrd Skynyrd, Queen, TV On The Radio, Black Sabbath, ZZ Top, and more.

And yet, what's perhaps most impressive here is not the breadth of their covers catalog but rather how they have come to absorb some of these classic tunes into their own repertoire. Phish has made some of these songs their own. "Cities" by Talking Heads; "Ya Mar" by Cyril Ferguson; "Funky Bitch" by Son Seals; "Also Sprach Zarathustra," aka "2001," by Strauss—these songs have become as much a part of Phish's live shows as the band's original songs.

But it doesn't stop there. According to Phish.net, Phish has covered "Fire" by Jimi Hendrix 138 times. "Good Times Bad Times" by Led Zeppelin? 228 times. "Hold Your Head Up" by Argent? More than 500 times!

In June 2016, Phish premiered an a cappella rendition of "Space Oddity" at Wrigley Field and followed it up just a few months later with a Halloween performance of Bowie's *The Rise and Fall of Ziggy Stardust and The Spiders from Mars*—with a six-person string section! (See chapter 27.)

Truly, with Phish you never know what they're going to play. And it may not even be a Phish song. So keep your mind open and listen closely to the clues.

Because Phish can play everything, they may play just about anything. But I suppose one question remains: Is Phish a great cover band, or the greatest cover band?

29 The Oh Kee Pa Ceremonies

Improvisation, true improvisation, is a feat that most bands playing today won't even attempt. Most bands will play the same set each and every night, perhaps changing the order of songs from gig to gig, but ultimately sticking closely to the setlist and performing each song as it was recorded.

Phish is different.

Phish has always been a force of improvisation, often journeying 20 minutes or longer on spacey, funky Type II jams. And this practice isn't to be taken lightly. Sure, Phish may make it look easy, but these musicians' ability to hear each other and tap into motifs and syncopated rhythms to build into a suddenly synchronized moment with all players dialed in perfectly...I mean, that's what we go to Phish shows to experience.

This level of skill, this improv mastery, is only honed through practice and training. And this is only part and parcel of Phish's dedication to the music and live performance.

In the late 1980s, Phish would rehearse in marathon stints, locking themselves in a room and jamming for hours and hours. Trey Anastasio called these feats of musical endurance Oh Kee Pa ceremonies.

Taking the name from the hallowed ceremonies of the Native American Mandan tribes, Anastasio had learned about these Oh Kee Pa ceremonies from the 1970 film *A Man Called Horse*.

The "O-kee-pa" or "Okipa" ceremony, which painter and pioneer George Catlin witnessed in his travels throughout the American West in 1832, was an annual event, the centermost religious event of the Mandan. During a four-day ritual of fasting and meditation, the tribe's young men would be inducted as warriors through a painful suspension ritual where they would be pierced, hung from their chests and backs, and spun in circles until rendered unconscious.

After four days of physical and mental fatigue, including the suspension, these youths would awake as warriors.

And perhaps Phish crossed a similar threshold during their own rites of passage in the late 1980s, in their own Oh Kee Pa ceremonies, moving into adulthood, listening to each other, mastering their skills, and honing their collective and independent improvisational spirits.

30 *The Simpsons* > Super Bowl

Phish fans are often torn when it comes to Phish's mainstream popularity and notoriety.

On one hand, Phish fans love that this band is an under-the-radar sensation. Phish is something their fans call their own. Phish fans have their own lingo and style, and Phish achieving this success without giant corporate sponsorship makes it all the more authentic. Phish is a true grassroots phenomenon.

On the other hand, phans want Phish to be recognized for their musical mastery. Phish fans have started petitions to get the band inducted into the Rock and Roll Hall of Fame. Phans often get frustrated when other music fans can't hear the brilliance within Phish's compositions and take offense when pop culture creates a two-dimensional caricature of the band and its fans.

Phish embodies this dichotomy in their own right. It shocks many outsiders that Phish is one of the top money-making acts in the business, raking in more money in 2016 than Sir Elton John,

Maroon 5, or Jennifer Lopez, yet have never had a major radio hit song or chart-topping album.

So whenever Phish swims into the public eye, fans are often excited, with a dash of reservation.

One classic Phish pop culture moment happened on *The Simpsons* in a 2002 episode called "A Weekend at Burnsie's." Phish played themselves performing their fan favorite "Antelope" at a medical marijuana rally, and they even snuck in a little secret-language *Simpsons* "D'oh!" (see chapter 35). Getting immortalized on *The Simpsons* is one of those pop culture measuring sticks that signals you've made it.

Phish also appear in *King of the Hill* season eight in the episode "Phish and Wildlife," where Hank and his friends take Bobby on an camping trip, only to discover that the park has been overrun by hippies.

Phish has also been referenced multiple times on the NBC hit TV show *Parks and Recreation*. Famed Phish fan and *Parks and Rec* writer and producer Harris Wittels, who also cocreated the Phish podcast *Analyze Phish* (see chapter 43), wrote Phish references into the show on multiple occasions and was often seen on screen

Phish Studies Conference

Phish in academia is growing pursuit! In 2019, Oregon State University, led by Associate Professor of Philosophy Stephanie C. Jenkins, PhD, welcomed over 50 presenting scholars and 200 attendees for the premiere three-day Phish Studies conference. The second conference is now scheduled for 2024 at OSU and will feature community panels, an exhibition fair, a poster session, a "Phishsonian" pop-up museum exhibit, a pre-conference workshop for Phans for Racial Equity and GrooveSafe, and curated art exhibits. And hey – while we may not fully understand cultural and philosophical impact of this band and its fans for years or decades to come, it's great to see a focused group of academics diving into the societal implications of the American rock band Phish.

wearing a Phish shirt. Sadly, Harris is no longer with us, but his humor and love for the band live on.

At first glance, Phish and professional sports don't seem to be a natural match, but hard dancing does require some level of athleticism, and there are many examples of Phish references within the sports world.

In the NFL, Phish's song "Wilson" and the subsequent "Wilson chant" have become a rallying cry for Seattle Seahawks quarterback Russell Wilson. The team uses the song at each home game to welcome the quarterback to the field. The NFL even filmed a short video on the subject for the 2014 Super Bowl pregame show.

Another NFL-Phish mashup happened in Super Bowl LI during introductions of the Atlanta Falcons, which featured "Tweezer Reprise" as the musical backdrop.

The NHL seems to have a hidden love affair with the Vermont four as well, and there are many examples of Phish musical snippets being played on organs at hockey arenas across the country.

ESPN's Neil Everett has often used Phish references to add some color to his highlights on *SportsCenter*. Another classic Phish sports infiltration happened when a fan who worked for the Dallas Mavericks used the song "Show of Life" in the background of a beautifully crafted 2011 NBA championship season retrospective video.

Phish had a couple of crossover moments with MTV in the 1990s, when MTV was still about the music. They were the house band for an episode of *Hangin' with MTV* in 1992. They also produced a goofy music video for their 1994 single "Down with Disease" (DWD), which was even the butt of jokes made on the classic cartoon *Beavis and Butt-Head*.

Sometimes the infiltration is overt, and other times it is much more subtle. For years the Weather Channel used Phish compositions like "Guyute" and others as the soundtrack for weather forecasts.

Recently Phish references have been found in more serious settings. On MSNBC, journalists Katy Tur and Jake Sherman have used Phish lyrics in their reporting, which has not gone unnoticed by Phish fans. According to JamBase, Katy Tur dropped 12 Phish references in one episode of *Meet the Press* following the Baker's Dozen.

In 2023, when word got out that Phish would be the second band to perform at the brand new, state-of-the-art Sphere venue in Las Vegas, it made news in channels in which Phish was not usually mentioned. Massive pop culture outlets like *People* and *Billboard* reported the news as social media erupted in confusion, with many people asking the important questions, "Who is Phish? And why are they playing Sphere?"

Sometimes the references are of the culinary nature. Phish Food is a delicious ice cream created by Ben and Jerry's, the Vermont masters of the frozen treat. They even created a special, limited-edition flavor called Freezer Reprise to commemorate Phish's Baker's Dozen residency at Madison Square Garden. The love between the Vermont success stories is not a one-way street. At the Clifford Ball in 1996, Phish welcomed Ben Cohen and Jerry Greenfield onstage to sing the bust-out of "Brother."

Even the creative team behind Facebook's emojis have dropped some subtle Phish references in their vast social media empire. Many thought that Facebook's electric guitar emoji looked eerily similar to Trey Anastasio's Languedoc guitar, and they were right. Brian Frick, one of Facebook's product designers, confirmed the guitar emoji is indeed Phish-inspired, and he added that there should be a Phish-themed llama emoji coming soon.

Phish fans in public positions love to drop a subtle nod to the band and the other fans out there. Whenever it does happen, the Phish world on the Internet practically explodes with opinions. So keep all your senses sharp, because the Phish phenomenon could soon be sneaking into a pop culture reference near you.

31 Side Projects

While Phish has always been the main focus for these musicians, the band has never been their sole creative outlet. Throughout the decades, each band member has embarked on a variety of solo and collaborative projects, producing dozens of studio albums and dozens more live performances.

In Phish's 40-year career—discounting here the forced break during COVID—they've stopped performing as a band on two occasions, which divide their history into periods 1.0, 2.0, and 3.0 (see chapter 2). The first time, what the band called a "hiatus" lasted a little more than two years (October 7, 2000–December 31, 2002). The second time was undoubtedly a breakup, including final shows; though they would eventually reunite, they would not play as Phish for nearly five years (August 15, 2004–March 6, 2009).

And yet, in both of these periods, these four talented musicians kept playing, kept recording, kept touring.

Trey Anastasio recorded a self-titled solo album released on Elektra Records in April 2002 that featured 12 songs, including some tracks developed from his highly experimental 1998 album *One Man's Trash*. Anastasio's 2002 solo effort also includes now-classic tunes "Mister Completely" and "Last Tube," among others. The album features an assortment of additional musicians and includes some orchestral elements on some compositions.

While Trey Anastasio had toured in previous years as the Trey Anastasio Band, the summer of 2002 was TAB's most prolific tour, featuring 10 musicians, including 25 shows, amd concluding with a headlining show at the Bonnaroo music festival in Tennessee.

A year later, in April 2003, Anastasio would release *Plasma*, a two-disc album of live performances from the 2002 summer and fall tours.

In 2000, Mike Gordon paired up with legendary folk guitarist Leo Kottke to record the album *Clone*. After the album's release the duo hit the road for a dozen shows. Tom Semioli writes in his review of the album at AllMusic.com, "Gordon's thick timbre and non-conformist phrasing compliment Kottke's polyrhythmic tendencies from cut to cut. The title track, as simple as it may sound on the surface, is a harmonic cornucopia of counterpoint via upper-register motifs and inverted chord voicing bolstered by reverberations and a myriad of odd sounds.... A timeless record by two artists on an organic journey."

Page McConnell recorded and toured as a trio called Vida Blue featuting Oteil Burbridge and Russell Batiste. Named for the 1970s baseball pitcher, the trio hit the road for spring and summer tours in 2002 and played a handful of additional shows in 2003 and 2004 with an Afro-Cuban sextet called the Spam Allstars.

In October 2003, Vida Blue with the Spam Allstars released their second album, *The Illustrated Band*, featuring just four tracks of Cuban fusion. Greg Heller writes in his review in *Rolling Stone*: "Vida Blue groove and roll through four ultra-loose 'movements' (the longest breaking twenty minutes), each a living breathing fusion of astral jazz and Latin beats, none remotely bound to structure. Whereas so much music this elastic sinks by the weight of ambition, *The Illustrated Band* succeeds on undeniable musicality (drummer Russell Batiste of the Funky Meters has swing for 'Days') and an obvious deep knowledge of what's being stretched."

Jon Fishman recorded with a group he called Pork Tornado. Founded in the mid 1990s, the band's core members include Lawn Boy producer Dan Archer (guitar), Joe Moore (saxophone), Aaron Hersey (bass), Phil Abair (keyboards), and Jon Fishman (drums).

Anastasio performing the world debut of "Petrichor" with the Oregon Symphony in Portland, Oregon, on September 9, 2014. (Jason Gershuny)

Pork Tornado is ultimately a cover band—a kind of eclectic country blues band, featuring funk and comedy.

While the band gigged in and around Burlington when Phish was off the road, it was during Phish's extended hiatus that Pork Tornado recorded their self-titled album and toured to support it. In a 2002 *Rolling Stone* interview, Fishman said of the Pork Tornado project, "It covers a lot more musical ground than I think any of us expected. And in more of a traditional sense. When Pork Tornado does a country tune, it really sounds like a country band. And when we do a blues tune, it really sounds like a blues band. It's kind of freakish that way. But we cover these different styles in this genuine way. We can exploit the identifying characteristics of these styles. Maybe it's being older. On one level, even though there's this humor, there's the joy of playing country music and bringing your own appreciation to it, it's not like we're making fun of the style."

When the band agreed to end the hiatus and return to gigging as Phish, they directed their focus and professional energy towards their beloved band. Of course, that wouldn't last and after just about a year and a half, Phish officially disbanded and broke up.

Similar to the hiatus, each musician returned to his various side projects.

With bassist Les Claypool, Trey Anastasio's band Oysterhead, which recorded and toured in 2001, reunited to perform at Bonnaroo in 2006.

Gordon once again played with Leo Kottke as well as the Benevento/Russo Duo, whom Anastasio then joined to tour as a four-piece. Gordon also toured with Grateful Dead drummers Bill Kreutzmann and Mickey Hart as the Rhythm Devils in 2006.

After Phish's breakup in 2004, McConnell distanced himself from the music industry for two years before reemerging with a new, self-titled album of solo material released in 2007 and head-lined California's High Sierra Music Festival that July.

Fishman continued to perform sporadically, playing with Everyone Orchestra, The Village, Yonder Mountain String Band, and The Jazz Mandolin Project.

Trey Anastasio and Mike Gordon have continued to develop their own solo projects over the years, carving out a sound and a following all their own.

Mike Gordon has recorded and toured prolifically through-out the years, releasing his first solo album, *Inside In*, in 2003 and touring that fall to support it. Since then, Mike Gordon has released a number of studio and live albums, including *Live from Bonnaroo 2005* (with the Benevento-Russo Duo). In 2008, Gordon hit the road for a 29-show summer tour to support his second solo album, *The Green Sparrow*, and he's continued to perform as the Mike Gordon Band over the years.

In 2017, Gordon released his fifth solo studio album, *OGOGO*, and toured to support with his band, including longtime col-laborator Scott Murawski, percussionist Craig Myers, organist and "synth-master" Robert Walter, and drummer John Kimock. This era of modern Mike Gordon Band has proved itself as a force of live improvisational performance separate from Phish.

More recently, in 2020, Gordon partnered once again with the acoustic guitarist Leo Kotte, recording the album *Noon*: 11 tracks recorded in both New Orleans and Vermont with music exchanged as a back and forth between the two artists. The album includes a reinterpretation of "Eight Miles High" by The Byrds as well as a cover of Prince's "Alphabet St.," one of four tracks featuring Phish drummer Jon Fishman.

Gordon also released *Flying Games* (2023) with a 14-show supporting tour. Producing the album himself, much of the writing and recording occurred during 2020's COVID lockdown, during which he worked in his makeshift Megaplum home studio.

David Goodwich reviewed *Flying Games* for *Glide* magazine in a May 2023 article, writing: "Employing a unique hybrid engineering method throughout much of the album's thirteen tracks that blends the use of live and studio-based audio beds into a single recording, as heard on the opening number "Tilting," *Flying Games* incorporates a unique sound that crackles with the energy of a live concert while maintaining the warmth of a studio environment."

Anastasio has always performed and produced music parallel to playing in Phish. Beyond the aforementioned Trey Anastasio Band (TAB) and Oysterhead, check out his free-jazz experimental band Surrender to the Air and their self-titled 1996 album. Furthermore, Anastasio has released a number of solo studio albums since his 2002 self-titled release, including the all-instrumental *Seis De Mayo* (2004), *Shine* (2005), *Bar 17* (2006), another all-instrumental album *The Horseshoe Curve* (2007), *Time Turns Elastic* (2009), *Traveler* (2012), *Paper Wheels* (2015), *Ghosts of the Forest* (2019), *Lonely Trip* (2020), and *Mercy* (2022).

Anastasio's *Lonely Trip* (2020) is in so many ways a "pandemic album," composed and recorded in isolation. The album's 15 songs span nearly an hour, concluding with the title track, with lyrics that include: "While you're on this lonely trip / Keep a watch for other ships / And if by chance our vessels pass / Perhaps we'll finally meet at last."

Trey Anastasio wrote of his recording process: "I had an electric and an acoustic guitar, a small amp, two microphones, some percussion, and two keyboards, including an old Kurzweil with

Ghosts of the Forest

2019's *Ghosts of the Forest* is the debut album by the Anastasio-led band of the same name that features Phish's Jon Fishman on drums, the now-late Tony Markellis on bass, Ray Paczkowksi on keyboards, and others. Anastasio partially conceived the project and album as a tribute to his childhood friend Chris "CCott" Cottrell, who died of adrenal cancer in January of 2018. The album is a textured lament, both methodical and heartfelt. With underlying ambience, the music is ethereal, yet intimate. Songs like "Drift While You're Sleeping," "About To Run," "Ruby Waves," and "Beneath A Sea of Stars" have all come to be included in Phish's repertoire.

Calling the album "some kind of midlife crisis on a record," Anastasio hit the road in the spring of 2019 with Ghosts of the Forest, playing their nine-track album and accompanying 11 live-only songs for nine shows across the USA.

In an October 2019 issue of *Relix* magazine, Jesse Jarnow interviews Trey Anastasio, who said: "Chris was an elk hunter, but he wouldn't get an elk most years, he just loved being high up in the Rocky Mountains. He told me that there was this Native American term, 'ghosts of the forest,' to describe elk, because they would vanish into the woods when you are tracking them."

During the recording session for *Ghosts of the Forest*, filmmaker Steven Cantor shot Anastasio and his family at home and at The Barn recording studio for what would become the film *Between Me and My Mind*, a title taken from the lyrics of the Phish song "Light." Premiering at the Tribeca Film Festival at the Beacon Theatre on April 26, 2019, the screening also featured a performance by TAB. *Variety* called the film, "A portrait of the artist as the unlikeliest—and most casually joyful—of rock stars."

very realistic drum sounds on it. Everything was recorded through a Spire 8-track."

Though Anastasio initially "released" each song from the album as Instagram posts, *Lonely Trip* officially debuted on Sirius XM's Phish Radio on July 30, 2020, along with a homemade video for the song "...And Flew Away."

Benjy Eisen reviewed the album for *Relix*, writing: "Straying from the shiny AM radio sound of some past Anastasio albums, and the joyous big band rock of classic TAB cuts, the highlights here are—appropriately—the sparsest songs: 'Lost in the Pack,' 'When the Words Go Away,' 'Lonely Trip.' These are campfire songs acutely aware that there's no campfire."

Less than two years later, Anastasio released his 12th studio album and first fully acoustic album, *Mercy*, in March 2022. Following *Lonely Trip*, this album feels very much like a continuation of Anastasio's at-home acoustic guitar explorations. He writes in the album's liner notes: "It's two years since we went into hiding. This is still going on, and it's an even lonelier trip.... Here I was, still at home, playing acoustic guitar. I thought, 'These songs just want to be one guy with a guitar, singing.'"

Donny Emerick's album review in *Acoustic Guitar*, reads: "Anastasio playing this guitar, masterfully layered upon itself and exquisitely captured by engineer Mike Fahey, is reason enough to give this album a listen. The songs are accessible (a challenge in some of Anastasio's earlier work) and rife with metaphorical references to the elements throughout his earnest lyrics: water, waves, rain, snow, light, sun."

In some ways, these albums were extensions of Anastaio's solo acoustic shows from tours in 2018 (17 shows) and 2019 (13 shows). Then in 2021 and 2022, he hit the road again for shorter runs of six shows each. These intimate shows featured Anastasio seated on a wooden chair surrounded by guitar pedals to help him adapt some stalwart Phish rockers into sometimes delicate, elegant, and experimental renditions delivered between personal, anecdotal stories both funny and somber from the Phish frontman.

The album *December*, released suddenly and surprisingly on December 24, 2020, is a 45-minute, six-song EP featuring Anastasio and McConnell offering stripped down treatments of classic Phish songs, including acoustic renditions of "If I Could," "Mountains in the Mist," and "Joy." But the real gem of this release is the 15-minute "jammed-out" rendition of "The Squirming Coil." It's a raw, almost whisper of an album that invites the listener into The Barn, where these musical masters recorded this pared down and, dare I say, pure, rendering of heartfelt ballads.

Then, they did it again! In March, 2023, McConnell and Anastasio released another striped down, guitar and keys EP titled *January*. Recorded in January 2023 at Trout Studios in Brooklyn, *January* clocks in at 30 minutes across nine tracks. "We just walked into the studio with literally an acoustic guitar and a couple of synthesizers," Trey said in an interview on SiriusXM's Phish Radio. "Songs are mysterious. They sound different. It was limiting, in a great way."

The second single off *January* was the undeniable bop that is "Life Saving Gun," which, as of early 2024, has only seen five performances from Phish. Don't sleep on the 12/30/23 performance that closes out the first set, wow. Or night one at Sphere (4/18/24).

In April 2021, Page McConnell released his third solo album, *Maybe We're The Visitors*, an ambient exploration of the landscapes of Iceland, recorded during McConnell's January 2020 visit to the land of ice and fire. Music journalist David Fricke writes in the album's liner notes: "Inevitably, music got made there. But it was unlike anything McConnell had recorded before as a solo artist, for side projects or within the collaborative energies of Phish: fully electronic pieces created on location, in response to the epic landscapes, dramatic weather, and geologic fury that he experienced in Iceland."

After 2007's eponymous album and 2013's *Unsung Cities* and *Movies Never Made*, this latest solo album by Page McConnell features no lyrics, no vocals at all, no piano or organ. Each of the nine compositions are made only with synthesizers, ranging from ethereal, windblown droning ("Moss Suite, Pt. 1") to industrial, sitar-sounding journeys ("Terra Incognita") to complex, melodic tapestries ("Set In Stone").

Listening to *Maybe We Are The Visitors* from beginning to end is very much a journey, an evolution—as the progression of song titles suggests—from exploration to colonization to the inevitable realization that, perhaps, humans are not the kind stewards of this planet as we've so conveniently convinced ourselves.

While each of these projects, and each member of Phish, is a worthwhile endeavor and supremely talented, I think we can all agree that the music they produce together as the band Phish is what we all yearn for and appreciate the most. Viva Phish!

32 Dorm Room Demos: The White Tape(s)

In full disclosure, Phish fans don't really listen to the band's studio albums. Even as authors of this book, we don't listen to the studio albums. But certainly we'd be remiss not to include them here as part of Phish's history and musical journey. That said, on with our show!

Phish's first recorded "studio" album was nothing more than a demo collection of songs the band distributed in hopes of scoring gigs. These tapes, collectively referred to as *The White Tapes*, varied in content but generally featured 90 minutes of music (45 minutes to each side of the cassette tape) and included tracks like "You Enjoy

Myself" (a cappella), "Alumni Blues," "Letter to Jimmy Page," "AC/DC Bag," "The Divided Sky," "Run Like an Antelope," and "Slave to the Traffic Light," to name just a few of the songs that have since become staples of Phish's growing repertoire.

In 1985, Phish began to circulate these tapes among friends and concert promoters. Traded, shared, and available for purchase at Phish shows, this cassette album was known simply by fans as *The White Album*. However, after the October 31, 1994, Glens Falls, New York, show where Phish covered The Beatles' (officially self-titled) *White Album*, the general consensus was to refer to this early demo as *The White Tape*, partly to eliminate any confusion regarding the Halloween 1994 show and partly to acknowledge the sole available format of this early album: cassette tape.

It would be 12 years before the album was officially released, independently through Phish Dry Goods, and thus "officially" titled *The White Tape* in 1998. Another 13 years later, Phish would release a limited edition white vinyl version of *The White Tape* at Superball IX, Phish's 2011 summer festival.

Acclaimed author and journalist Jesse Jarnow writes in his review of *The White Tape*: "The music is decidedly amateurish, but contains a certain charm that comes only with recordings made in dorm rooms and suburban basements. Pieces such as "Fluff's Travels" and the vocal-only arrangement of the future Phish standard "You Enjoy Myself" hint at the complexity the band would soon embrace and invest the album with a historical interest."

What's perhaps important to note here is that this album is not precisely a Phish album with consideration to the quartet of musicians. Of the 16 tracks on *The White Tape*, only five tracks are performed by the band Phish.

Most of the other songs are written and performed by Trey Anastasio and a roster of friends and collaborators from college and high school, including lyricist Tom Marshall and Steve Pollak aka The Dude of Life. And bassist Mike Gordon performs all instruments and vocals on the tracks "Fuck Your Face," "NO2," "He Ent to the Bog," and "Minkin."

Quite frankly, Gordon's tracks are all over the place. I describe them here as tracks because I'm hesitant to call them songs. "He Ent to the Bog," for example? At first listen you may think, *What the hell was that?* And, well, you may not even give it a second listen. A skipping record, something about a hamburger, and then a James Bond theme? Sure, why not! I guess that's Mike Gordon for ya!

Gordon's "NO2" track can only be described as a cringeworthy skit or some sort of love letter to the dentist and/or recreational use of nitrous oxide, followed by a relaxing, classical guitar composition. (It does, though, do a good job mimicking the auditory hallucinations nitrous causes.)

It's weird, this album. It's the first Phish album. And as with many firsts, it may carry more nostalgic merit than musical merit. But nevertheless, for those who heard it in the mid 1980s and through the '90s, one thing was clear: this was something different, something new, and at best a squinty glimpse of what was to come from this young band led by this young, self-taught guitarist.

This album is our first on-the-record Phish. Just a couple of young guys honing their skills and looking to play gigs. It's truly incredible that so many of these songs have become the songs we know and love at Phish shows. "YEM" has certainly come a long way, but all the better for it!

For me, *The White Tape* is raw and fun and silly and exactly the kind of album you'd expect to be recorded in a college dorm room. Does it have its moments of grandeur and glory? Certainly, but here's the thing about grand moments from college: they're only grand at the time. Over the years, those once-incredible moments now pale in comparison to truly amazing moments you've experienced as an adult.

You'll never forget your first kiss, but I'm willing to bet you've had better kisses since then.

33 Gravy Fries at Nectar's

At 188 Main Street in Burlington, Vermont, stands a three-story brick building housing the bar, restaurant, and live music club known as Nectar's.

Originally a savings and loan bank, the building was purchased and renovated to establish a two-story restaurant and lounge called the Hi-Hat that hosted live jazz on an elevated stage behind the bar. In 1975, a man named Nector Rorris bought the building with a vision to provide a home for "louder music, live music every night, with never a cover." After further renovations, Rorris opened up Nectar's on August 29, 1975, serving cafeteria-style breakfast and hosting bands from 9:30 PM into the night.

Nectar's quickly became a social and nightlife hub in Burlington. While the bar and restaurant initially occupied both floors of the building, Rorris leased the upstairs, which, through the 1980s, operated as separate "new wave" nightclubs Border and Club Metronome. Ultimately, Rorris would take over the upper level and expand Nectar's to both floors.

Over the years, hundreds of bands and DJs played Nectar's, as well as the clubs upstairs. But it's in 1984 where we set our scene.

On December 1, 1984, Phish played the first of 44 shows at Nectar's. That gig featured premieres of many Phish staples, including "Slave to the Traffic Light" and "Fluffhead." And at the gigs that followed, generally three-night runs on off nights (Sunday through Tuesday), Phish would premiere many more songs, honing their voice and developing as a band for five years.

Ultimately, Phish's popularity and fan base would outgrow the Burlington outpost, and the band moved across the street to a club called the Front (now Skirack), where it would play more than

50 times from 1998 through 1991. Unlike Nectar's, where Rorris refused to charge a cover, the Front would charge to see the band.

Since their early days in Burlington, Phish has gone on to play hundreds of venues, including abandoned airfields and massive arenas, in 15 different countries. That said, the touring band, the three-night-run jam band, the improvisational quartet, the Phish from Vermont, was truly born at Nectar's on Main Street.

Without a club like Nectar's, Phish would not exist. Without a venue at which to perform and grow and practice, Phish may have very well gone by the wayside well before the 1990s. It's important for communities to support and advocate for small, independent performance spaces to cultivate musicians and bands like Phish, which, like any band, was once just four friends looking to play some gigs.

Its was Nector Rorris who gave Phish that opportunity. And, yes, Phish's album *Picture of Nectar* is dedicated to Rorris. That's his face superimposed with the orange on the cover. And a portion of the liner notes read, "Like countless other bands in Burlington's diverse music scene, those nights at Nectar's taught us how to play. We dedicate this album to Nectar Rorris for 16 years of bringing Burlington live music every night of the week with no cover, and the best fries this side of…France."

In 2002, Rorris sold Nectar's to Damon Brink and Chris Walsh, friends and business partners, who renovated the bar with a focus to improve the club for live music with improved acoustics and better sight lines. Of course, the crystal chandelier hanging in the entryway remains from when the building was a savings and loan.

In 2008, Walsh bought out his partner, Brink, brought on a five-person consortium of investors and partners, and established Nectar's Entertainment Group to expand the brand, which included operating a satellite venue in Martha's Vineyard for several years.

And now, once again, Nectar's is up for sale. Announced in May 2017, Walsh and team are selling both the building and the NEG business. The building is listed at $2.5 million and the asking price for the business, which includes Nectar's and the upstairs Club Metronome, is $750,000.

Hopefully, the forthcoming owners will keep this now 43-year-old music venue open and operating as it has over the decades. Or perhaps some wealthy fan could develop the building into a Phish museum—still hosting live music, of course.

Whatever the fate of Nectar's, 188 Main Street in Burlington will always be the birthplace of Phish. And it's worth the pilgrimage, if only for the gravy fries.

34 *Colorado '88*

In 1988 Phish had only occasionally ventured beyond the comforts of their fan base in New England. This collection of highlights from seven shows across 10 days at small bars in Telluride and Aspen, Colorado, captures a band in transition. This music showcases Phish the bar band, ascending.

This is Phish the band touring in a van. This is Phish honing their skills weekly at their local Nectar's in Burlington, Vermont, and then somewhat spontaneously loading into a van and driving 40 hours nearly nonstop to Colorado. Listening to these recordings, one can imagine oneself as a young musician, on the road, heading west, venturing farther and further than the band had ever traveled.

Released as a three-CD set in 2006, *Colorado '88* was reviewed for *Rolling Stone* by Kevin O'Donnell, who wrote, "Long before

Phish replaced the Grateful Dead as America's greatest jam band, the foursome was one goofy-ass bar act. This three-CD set documents Phish's first trip outside their Northeast stomping ground: a 1988 seven-date tour in the Rocky Mountain state. Opting for concise compositions instead of expansive, noodly jams, Colorado '88 is a surprisingly crisp compilation that shows off the band's chops with early, by-the-numbers versions of classics like 'You Enjoy Myself' and 'Fluffhead.' There's also a mountain of rarities, including 'Harpua,' the fantastical story of a guy named Jimmy, his dog and a doomed cat called Poster Nutbag that has attained mythical status among the Phish phaithful."

The acoustics of these recordings feel intimate. You can hear the band banter and feel the crowd jokingly chided. If you close your eyes, you can almost count the people in the bar.

The July 30, 1988, show at The Roma in Telluride, Colorado, is an interesting one. Due to the absence of drummer Jon Fishman at the time of the gig, Phish played two sets of "jazz and standard Phish material" as a trio, with Trey Anastasio on drums, according to Phish.net. These opening sets are sometimes referred to as "Jazz Odyssey." Later that night, with Fishman on drums for the third set, the band played "Run Like an Antelope," during which Anastasio details what (may have) happened to Fishman in an attempt to explain his absence: "Pay no heed when your two friends each eat a hit of acid…walk over the mountain and decide you'll cut back the long way by the cabin…. Climb down towards the beautiful valley below with the pretty flowers growing everywhere. Oh, no! Realize that there's a 2,000-foot cliff in front of you. Start to shit your pants as you realize the sun's gone down! Decide it's time that you, too, should eat a hit of acid. Turn around and realize you have to climb all the way back up the mountain. Start climbing up the mountain, but wait, it's too dark you might fall…. Realize that the other three members of the band are making absolute fools of themselves playing a jazz odyssey. Finally make it to the top of the mountain and realize you've got to be back to bar in 10 minutes. And realize there's only one thing left you can do...you've got to run like an antelope out of control!"

It's this short banter that offers contemporary listeners a closer glimpse at who these musicians were at this time and place. And, well, who were they? They were four friends who were up for adventure, both hiking in the mountains with a head full of acid and improvising two sets of jazz without their drummer.

In a July 1988 *Relix* article on the Colorado '88 tour, author (and writer of this book's foreword) Mike Greenhaus quotes Page McConnell: "We were stuck together, but it was defining," McConnell laughs. "We'd never had such an intense time together and were flying by the seat of our pants."

Greenhaus' article continues, "After playing to an empty room for three nights, Lynch and others convinced the group to try their luck elsewhere. "They said, 'If you guys go across the street to the Fly Me to the Moon Saloon, everyone will see you,'" McConnell relates, referencing the cover of *Colorado '88*. "So, we carried our gear directly across the street and the shows were packed."

This move to the other club is captured perfectly in the album cover photo of Trey and Page walking their keyboard across the street with the Colorado Rockies in the background.

This is a band of young men, caught in a time and a place unknown to them, exploring the world beyond New England, beyond Nectar's, into the great unknown. This is a band coming into their own, as one may say. This is a band, as McConnell said, "Flying by the seat of our pants." And if you listen closely, you'll hear that in *Colorado '88*.

35 Secret Language

Picture this: a band you are somewhat familiar with is playing a show, and you are there having a great time. You know a couple of tunes and like what you have seen, but you are new to the scene and haven't dug deep into their immense catalog. Somewhere deep in a second set you are dancing along, having a blast, until, without warning, the band and select people all around you suddenly fall to the floor and play dead. Seconds feel like minutes as you try to figure out what is happening. Suddenly, in syncopated motion everyone gets up and continues rocking out like nothing happened. Shhh...this is one example of the Secret Language of Phish in action.

Within the Phish community, there are linguistic forms and social norms that are all our own. Dig even deeper and you will find a Secret Language, wherein the band has created musical cues that prompt fans to respond with an action. It should be noted that this language goes even deeper, and includes signals that the band members can use with each other while playing.

The best way to learn about the language is to find a recording from a show in the early 1990s where Trey Anastasio explains the concept to the audience. One of the most detailed explanations takes place at a show at the Capitol Theater in Portchester, New York, on May 14, 1992.

Trey explains, "Most of the people who come see Phish see Phish a lot. What happens is we do one of these signals. Suddenly out of the blue the whole audience does one of these things. Nobody knows what the hell is going on. There [are] 100 people out of a huge crowd that [are] just standing there dumbfounded, and then you don't say a word about it."

Writing about the Secret Language makes me feel a bit like a traitorous magician exposing the secrets of some treasured illusion. But since the band's return in 2009, the Secret Language has been mostly missing. Phish has seemingly put this language to bed, even denying the obvious *Simpsons*-inspired "D'oh!" during the doughnut-themed Baker's Dozen run.

So is it really that bad to expose the ancient mysteries of the past? Should modern magicians feel guilty about revealing the secrets of ancient Houdini tricks? Maybe so, maybe not.

According to Phish.net, there were 10 opportunities in the early '90s when Trey took the time to teach the audience about the Secret Language. Trey would often stop a song in midflow (often "Possum," "Antelope," or "David Bowie") and teach the audience the five main aspects of the Secret Language.

Like any good teacher, he would later throw out a musical pop quiz to see what the audience had learned. He added that fans should spread the word to other fans, so if you got this deep in the book, I have to assume you are a Phish fan. So my conscience is now clear.

Anyway, there is always the same initial signal to tell the audience to pay attention. Usually Trey Anastasio (although Page McConnell or Mike Gordon would do it as well) would repeat the same twinkling, high-pitched notes to grab your attention. Once the call is heard, there are five main prompts that can be thrown your way.

1. **_The Simpsons_ Theme**
   If you hear the theme from *The Simpsons'* opening, you just need to yell Homer's iconic "D'oh!" at the end of the melody.

2. **The Random Note**
   If you hear a circus theme, at the end of that melody sing a random note out loud.

3. **"Turn Turn Turn"**

   If you hear the melody of the classic Byrds tune "Turn Turn Turn," turn around and face the light board at the back of the venue and scream your head off.

4. **All Fall Down**

   ("The best one," according to Trey on May 14, 1992.) When you hear a series of four descending notes, fall down like you were struck on the head with a giant hammer.

5. **"Aww Fuck"**

   When you hear a scraping sound along the strings of the guitar, shout "Aww fuck," and raise your middle finger in the air like it was cut off in a horrible guitar-string accident.

Who knows if Phish will ever bring back the Secret Language of the 1990s, but if they do, now you'll be ready!

36 *Lawn Boy* (1990)

"The Squirming Coil of sunset..." sings Trey Anastasio over Page McConnell's gentle piano chords to open the 1990 album *Lawn Boy*. Anastasio and Page gently lead the way to the chorus, featuring all four musicians contributing, singing, "It got away...." The song continues to grow and expand as Anastasio leads the group through a composed section, giving way to a staccato riff from McConnell as Anastasio takes us through Tom Marshall's lyrics. The Squirming Coil? It got away.

At six minutes, this studio version of "The Squirming Coil" does include McConnell's emotive piano solo conclusion, though it's just a mere sampling of the majesty McConnell offers in live performances.

Lawn Boy is Phish's second official studio album. Released September 21, 1990, on the independent label Absolute A-Go-Go, the album was available on cassette, single-LP vinyl, and CD, the latter of which featured a bonus track of the song "Fee," originally released on Phish's first album *Junta*. After Phish signed to Elektra Records in 1991, *Lawn Boy* was remastered and re-released on June 30, 1992.

The nine songs on *Lawn Boy* remain in current rotation at Phish's live shows. In fact, each of the nine songs on the album was performed during the Baker's Dozen in 2017.

Lawn Boy's "Split Open and Melt" and "Bathtub Gin" each offer dozens of performances featuring Type II jams and exploratory musicianship.

The studio recording of "Split Open and Melt" is extremely textured, with a gooey consistency featuring harmonizing vocals, an additional singer, and a horn section of players who would come to be known as Giant Country Horns. With a subtle bass line and harmonized vocals, the song devolves to nearly nothing, taking the listener "among the seaweed and the slime / down, down, down..." only to ramp back up with Anastasio's powerful riffs once we're down there.

But if there's one, single darling of *Lawn Boy*, her name is "Reba." This is beloved Phish, both complex and goofy, wholly original yet somehow familiar. The song itself features multiple sections, numerous time signatures, and lyrics both brilliant and slapstick. When performed live, "Reba" jams often ascend to another level all together and many have professed their love to dear Reba after such jams. Though jamless, the studio version is what caused many fans to first fall for the Phish from Vermont.

"My Sweet One," the album's third track, is a fun bluegrass romp of a love song written by Phish drummer Jon Fishman.

Next up is "The Oh Kee Pa Ceremony," 90 seconds of Anastasio playing a joyful series of notes over McConnell's piano and a laugh track, concluding with the all-too-familiar seven-note couplet from the end of the early 1900s tune "Shave and a Haircut."

"Bathtub Gin" pairs Anastasio's composition with lyrics by his friend Susannah Goodman. And McConnell's contributions borrow heavily from "Rhapsody in Blue" by George Gershwin. This studio version features deep, dark vocalizations of the words "Bathtub Gin," overlaid with a bit of imbibed laughter.

The studio version of "Run Like an Antelope," clocking in at 10 minutes, is perhaps most closely related to its live show performances: highly upbeat, faster and faster, with all musicians in sync to bring the melody to its peak. Then, a calm moment with lyrics that almost make sense:

> "Rye, rye, Rocco / Marco Esquandolas! / Been you to have any
>   spike, mon?
> (Run run run run run run run run run run run run)
> Set the gearshift for the high gear of your soul! / You've got to
>   run like an antelope, out of control!"

The title track of the album, "Lawn Boy," lands in the eighth position, clocking in at just two and a half minutes, a far cry from the 30-minute "Lawn Boy" jam on July 25, 2017, during the Baker's Dozen. Generally, live performances of Lawn Boy feature McConnell away from his keys, sauntering around the front of stage as he sings. Mike Gordon takes a bass solo and then McConnell sings it home.

"Bouncing around the Room" is perhaps the most accessible song on the album, featuring clear, narrative lyrics and a gentle rhythm. And, according to Phish.net, "Bouncing" has been performed at about a quarter (24 percent) of all Phish shows.

The album was recorded and mixed at Archer Studios in Winooski, Vermont, in 1989 and 1990 after the band won first place at a Rock Rumble performance at a club called The Front in Burlington, Vermont. The prize? Studio time at Archer Studios.

To say that this album is cohesive would be a lie. It's all over the place. But within its eccentricity, across nine very different songs, we find a comprehensive snapshot of the band: emotional ballads, silly jaunts, compositions built for improvisation, borrowed riffs, trippy harmonies, synesthesia, moonshining, antelopes.... *Lawn Boy* has it all!

It would take 14 years for the album to sell 500,000 copies and be certified gold on July 7, 2004.

The album's cover art is a photograph of a vacuum half-buried in the lawn, while the back cover features Fishman, Mr. Lawn Boy, shirtless and painted green holding said vacuum with Anastasio, guitar in hand, over his shoulder. Outtake photographs were included in the deluxe vinyl set.

37 Weaving and Teasing

Some of my favorite Phish shows include what could perhaps best be called a musical theme, something like a riff or melody the band will continually return to throughout the night, weaving and inserting the melody into other songs. In some songs, they may just hint at the tune or tease it briefly. In other songs, they may completely segue into and out of that threaded motif.

One of the most recent examples of this occurred at the final night of the Dick's run in Colorado in 2016. Opening the second set with "Crosseyed and Painless," Phish then wove the song's main theme and chorus, "I'm still waiting…" into each of the following five songs, as well as the encore. This was perhaps meant to acknowledge that fans were left "still waiting" for Phish to spell something with their setlist, a tradition at Dick's. Tracked out as a setlist where every second-set song includes a tease of "Crosseyed and Painless," you could perhaps argue the opposite: the second set was one long version of "C&P" while the band teased the other songs! (see chapter 92).

And I would be remiss not to mention the incredible weaving and teasing at The Gorge on July 15, 2016, where Phish opened the second set with a fiery "Crosseyed and Painless" > "What's the Use?" > "No Men in No Man's Land," > only to tease and weave each of those songs in the following "Stash" > "Ghost" -> "Chalk Dust Torture." If you haven't checked out this show, now is the time.

While some fans yearn for the free-form Type II jams, this level of interplay and musical mixology is just delightful. Each tease is a gift, a secret handshake between the band and the fans.

Another 3.0-era show featuring some serious weaving and teasing is Phish's 13th appearance at Columbia, Maryland's Merriweather Post Pavilion on July 27, 2014. Opening the second set with "Wilson" > "Tweezer," the band then continued to tease and segue back and forth between "Tweezer" throughout the set. With bust-outs galore and Tweezer woven through the whole set, this "TweezerFest" show is one for the record books and a must-listen.

This is playful Phish, unpredictable and nuanced.

Of course, the era of Phish 1.0 had its own weaving and teasing. Hell, that's where it all started for the band—the original "TweezerFest" at The Bomb Factory in Dallas, Texas, on May 7,

1994. The band kicks off the second set with "Loving Cup" then "Sparkle," and then dives into what would be a 25-minute "Tweezer" woven throughout the cover-filled set, including Aerosmith's "Sweet Emotion" and The Breeders' "Cannonball." The whole set is just one big jam, showcasing the band's collaborative chops as they ride "Tweezer" and seamlessly move from song to song. The "Bomb Factory" second set concludes with Fishman singing "Purple Rain" back into "Hold Your Head Up" and finishing with, you guessed it, "Tweezer Reprise."

And then there's a show like July 11, 2000, at Deer Creek in Noblesville, Indiana. This is quality Phish like none other. This one features an absolutely stellar second set beginning with "2001" > "Down with Disease" -> Led Zeppelin's "Moby Dick," a song the band had only performed twice. That night, Phish would weave and tease "Moby Dick" numerous times throughout a jam-filled set that included Jon Fishman on the vacuum and Anastasio on drums. For the encore, Phish played "First Tube" > "Moby Dick" > "Chalk Dust Torture Reprise" to conclude one hell of a Tuesday night in Noblesville.

Perhaps one of the best Phish 1.0 examples, recently released through Live Phish as an eight-CD box set, is their February 1993 three-night stint at The Roxy in Atlanta, Georgia. Take a listen to Saturday night's show (February 20, 1993) and enjoy an incredible, tease-filled second set.

Teasing and weaving is just one of the delectable and delightful gifts this band gives us, and these examples are merely that—examples. Dig through the archives and you'll find many more of these gems!

38 Amy's Farm, August 3, 1991

In Phish lore, there are certain events that have a resonance all their own. In 1991 on Larrabee Farm, located in Maine just north of Portland, Phish threw a free thank-you party for all their fans to celebrate their eighth anniversary as a band. This was a sort of coming-out party, where the Northeast bar band was now pushing the limits of their own growth nationally.

Phish sent out an invitation to all the friends they made during the first eight years of their career. It read, "Driving along in the love van a short time ago, it suddenly dawned on us that we were only a few months away from our eighth anniversary as a band. We started thinking about all of the friends we'd met over the years and we realized that it would be great to throw a party to thank everyone for all the good times."

The invitation sent to fans described the event's host, Amy Skelton, as Phish's first fan (along with Brian Long). Having the first fan host the band's eighth-anniversary celebration seemed to make all the sense in the world.

Amy's Farm, as it is so warmly described now, was an incredibly intimate show for all those in attendance. There have always been crisp soundboard copies of the show available for fans to trade, so word of the performance spread quickly.

It was such an intimate and open party that after the first set Trey told the audience, "go wild, because nobody's going to stop you here." It was a musical coming-of-age extravaganza in which it seemed the Phish that once played in bars was retired, and the Phish of the theater circuit was born. Phish officially took the next step toward national prominence with this performance.

According to the *Maine Sun Journal,* "more than 2,000 people" showed up to this show. Musically, the show was crisp and tight with fiery playing in a mostly straight-ahead rock-and-roll kind of way. This was indicative of where Phish was at this time, when 20-plus-minute jams were not yet a part of the collective consciousness. Although much of the rest of this summer tour was accompanied by the Giant Country Horns, this run was hornless. That did not mean there were no guests joining Phish.

During the end of the third set, they brought out Jamie Janover on didgeridoo for "Buried Alive." Also, following the piano-driven "Magilla" encore, they brought out longtime friend and collaborator The Dude of Life for lead vocal duty and proceeded to run through three of his songs, including "Self," "Bitchin' Again," and "Crimes of the Mind." Page's girlfriend at the time, Sofi Dillof, added her own vocal touch to "Bitchin' Again," as well (see chapter 10).

Following this four-song encore, they thanked everyone, warned of lights left on in a car, returned a lost dog, and then returned to the stage for one final song, the essential Phish anthem "Harry Hood." This was the perfect punctuation to an ideal event celebrating everything that Phish and the Phish community had built together over these first eight years.

Interestingly enough, in 2015 Amy's Farm itself went up for sale, so if you want to own a special piece of music history, and you are some sort of financial mogul or impresario, please look into this, and maybe you can host Phish's 38th-anniversary festival back at that magic farm.

39 Paul Languedoc

Phish has a sound that is uniquely their own. And while part of that is a result of the musicians' interplay and mastery of their instruments, part is a result of the instruments themselves and the live soundboard mix during their shows. The man responsible for this is named Languedoc, a moniker that has perhaps transcended the man himself and come to mean a sound and feel in itself.

Paul Languedoc (b. 1958) was Phish's soundman from the very beginning through the band's breakup in 2004.

He also worked as the band's chief sound engineer and live house mixer, responsible for recording and mixing 1995's *A Live One* as well as the original series of 20 Live Phish releases.

But perhaps most important is that Languedoc was and still is Phish's custom luthier, having custom-built numerous guitars and basses for Trey Anastasio and Mike Gordon.

In March 2009, when Phish returned to the road, Garry Brown, who had been working sound for the Trey Anastasio Band, took over at the soundboard while Languedoc continued to build and repair beautiful custom guitars. As detailed on his website, the Languedoc custom-built guitar waitlist is currently full.

Can you imagine the band without Anastasio's truly unique guitar sounds? Even still, each of Anastasio's Languedoc guitars has a tone and feel all its own.

Trey Anastasio's first Phish guitar is commonly known as "Blonde No. 1." Built by Paul Languedoc in 1987, the headstock features an inlaid illustration of Anastasio's dearly departed dog Marley, aka "Mar-Mar," with a thought bubble that reads, Who's the Mar-Mar?

A second guitar, built by Languedoc in 1991, is called "I'm the Mar-Mar!" and also features Marley, this time chasing a cat.

Anastasios' go-to axe for Phish 3.0, the "Koa 1," was built in 1996 with Paul Languedoc's signature inlaid on the headstock. Anastasio played this guitar almost exclusively during The Baker's Dozen, save for "Izabella," "Cinnamon Girl," and "The Wind Cries Mary," for which he played Languedoc "Koa 2."

Then there's "Koa 3," aka Ocelot, aka Ocedoc, which premiered in 2010 to awe and praise from the fans. Mr. Miner wrote in August 2010 on his site PhishThoughts.com, "Without dominating pieces with overwhelming solos or responding to his band mates with copious pitch-bending, The Ocedoc's responsiveness allowed Trey to contribute with both passion and finesse to the most exquisite jams we've heard in years. From "Rebas" to "Hoods" and from "Lights" to "Tweezers," the difference made by The Ocedoc in Phish music became staggering. Like a kid at play with the coolest toy he's ever had, Trey took the stage night after night, slaying everything in his path."

For more on Anastasio's custom-built Languedoc guitars, including his pedals, amplifier, and signal chain, visit TreysGuitarRig.com.

Furthermore, Mike Gordon's website, Mike-Gordon.com, offers details on his instruments, though it doesn't mention much about the electric drill he employs from time to time.

Page McConnell's stage presence is that of a captain at the helm of a spaceship, surrounded by keyboards, synths, organs, and a baby grand piano, all of which is outlined on his site, PageMcConnell.com.

Fishman's drum kit is the kit dreams are made of. With more than half a dozen drums and a dozen cymbals, not to mention woodblocks and a cowbell, well, it's enough to make contemporary drummers salivate with envy.

Oh, and sometimes Fishman plays the vacuum, a mid 60s baby-blue Electrolux. Yes, it's true, but you knew that already!

40 *Rift* (1993)

Recorded in 1992 and released in 1993, *Rift* is Phish's fourth studio album, a concept album masterpiece that tells a singular story throughout its 15 songs. Produced by Barry Beckett at White Crow Studios in Vermont, this album was distributed through Elektra Records, achieved gold-record status in 1997, and is considered by many fans as the gold standard for Phish albums.

As Trey describes on the *Rift* promotional video, *Rift* is focused around a person who "is experiencing a rift in a relationship." The album's protagonist "is consciously thinking of his situation, and there is a segue and he starts to drift off to sleep. Through the night he goes through different cycles of sleep."

Those cycles are reflected in the songs and the expansive range of emotions the protagonist feels. At one point he is seemingly looking back at the relationship fondly ("The Wedge"); at another point there is a more foreboding view toward the future ("Mound"). There are moments of nightmarish fear ("Maze"), and even feelings of deep sadness and anger ("Horn").

Ultimately, the album ends with "Silent in the Morning" and leaves the listener wondering if this restless night of subconscious pondering has led to the demise or the salvation of the relationship.

The beauty of Tom Marshall's lyrics is that they are ambiguous enough to be left open to interpretation. This allows the listener to personalize each song's meaning.

There is more to *Rift* beyond the 15 connected songs of this dream. The album cover itself is iconic. Created by longtime Phish artistic collaborator David Welker, this album cover contains images that encapsulate 14 of the 15 tracks. Missing from the cover is a reference to "The Horse," which, interestingly enough, was the focal image on Phish's 1994 follow up album, *Hoist*.

Outside the cohesive nature of the album's story, *Rift* is a perfect sample of classic Phish songs with which any fan should be well-versed. Songs like "Maze," "My Friend My Friend," and "It's Ice" have been 20-plus-year staples of Phish's live repertoire.

If you want to learn more, there is a highly entertaining promotional video that Elektra released about *Rift* floating around the Internet. It is a great snapshot of Phish's blossoming infancy, or maybe more accurately, their toddlerhood. *Rift* came about at a pivotal time, and having a mini documentary with fans and the band gives us all an opportunity to step back in time for a moment to experience early-'90s Phish.

41 NYE 1991–1994

Phish in the early 1990s was a band growing into itself. They were very quickly gaining momentum, growing their fan base, and playing larger venues. And perhaps the best testaments to this growth are Phish's early-1990s New Year's Eve shows.

December 31, 1991, would be only the third New Year's Eve show of Phish's career, and playing at The New Aud, now known as The Worcester Memorial Auditorium, with a 4,000-person capacity, would also be their largest to date.

Billed as the band's first three-set show, tickets were just $16.50 and quickly sold out. And it was this show that established the three-set structure as a standing characteristic of New Year's Eve shows to come.

Strange highlights of the show include Trey Anastasio experimenting with a novelty voice box keychain called The Final Word that he had been given as a Christmas present and spoke curse words on demand. And just before the encore, Anastasio referenced the debut of "The Minkin," an eight-panel painting on Plexiglas by bassist Mike Gordon's mother that the band used as a backdrop, replacing her original canvas painting. Other highlights include jams in "Stash" and "Llama," and third-set performances of "Tweezer" and "Mike's Song."

Upon the 2011 release of the show's soundboard and audience recording matrix through Live Phish to celebrate the show's 20th anniversary, Phish archivist Kevin Shapiro wrote, "The first-ever New Year's Eve set III started with Fish's kick drum and Trey's Final Word commentary about the evil King of Prussia. This was years before fans began chanting "Wilson" and the spellbound spectators cheered with anticipation as the band dipped into "The Squirming Coil." Trey joined Page's piano outro near the end to set up the show's improvisational highlight—a ground-breaking, earth-shattering "Tweezer" complete with primal vocalizations and a ferocious jam."

For the fourth New Year's Eve show on December 31, 1992, Phish chose Boston's Matthews Arena. Home to the Celtics and the Bruins, the arena held 6,300 and once again the band's New Year's Eve show would be their largest to date.

The show was recorded and broadcast live and rebroadcast the following day on Boston's largest rock station, WBCN 104.1 FM, which prompted the band to plan tricks and jokes with the live audience for the at-home listeners. As ticketholders entered the arena they were handed flyers outlining eight special signals and signs Trey Anastasio would showcase during the show, in line with the band's Secret Language, with corresponding instructions for what the audience should do in each case, such as "mass hysteria" in the middle of "Fly Famous Mockingbird" and "yay/boo" during "I

Didn't Know," all of which the audience enjoyed and participated in at the expense of the surely confused radio-listening audience.

Other highlights include touring manager Brad Sands, wearing a "mockingbird" costume, hoisted up from the light rig during "Fly Famous Mockingbird" (the band's first NYE gag?) and the first performance of "Mike's Groove" without "Hydrogen" sandwiched in the middle. Instead, "Mike's Song" led into the New Years countdown and "Auld Lang Syne" with a balloon drop followed by a jam-heavy "Weekapaug Groove."

To close the third set, Phish welcomed to the stage The Dude of Life, aka Steve Pollack, to sing vocals on their first and only performance of "Diamond Girl" by Seals and Crofts. The evening's encore featured an a cappella performance of "Carolina" without microphones followed by Jimi Hendrix's "Fire."

While 1992's venue capacity increased just a couple thousand people over 1991's capacity, Phish's 1993 New Year's Eve show would more than double their previous audiences at the Worcester Centrum, a hockey arena with a capacity of 14,700.

1993's New Year's Eve show is the show that pretty much kicked off the tradition of New Year's gags in the form of theatrical productions. The entire stage had been built out to look like an aquarium, leaving everyone guessing as to what would go down. And after two solid sets of music, including a second-set-opening "Tweezer" and fiery performances of "It's Ice" and "Possum," the band played "You Enjoy Myself" to conclude the second set, at the end of which all four members donned wetsuits and walked offstage. What would come of this aquarium scene as our players went scuba diving?

To begin the third set, with the band's voices audible over the PA, four men in diving suits were lowered from the ceiling to the stage. The giant clam at the center back of the stage started counting down to midnight in a deep, dark voice, at which point the band took to their instruments and played "Auld Lang Syne" > "Down

The Hot Dog

Phish would "reprise" the four-seat hotdog in 1999 at their Big Cypress New Year's Eve Festival to the tune of "Meatstick," flying over the crowd at the turn of the millennium. Afterward, in January 2000, the hot dog (and fries and soda cup), designed by artist Chris McGregor and built by the scenery company Rocket Science, was installed on display at the Rock and Roll Hall of Fame in Cleveland, Ohio. But it was not retired, not yet.

Phish would fly the jumbo dog one more time, at Madison Square Garden for New Year's Eve 2010, once again to the song "Meatstick." Now 14 years from its last flight, and 30 years since its premiere, perhaps the hotdog will soon, someday, fly again....

with Disease Jam" > "Split Open and Melt" and more, concluding with "Tweezer Reprise." This was the debut of "Down with Disease."

Of course, balloons dropped during "ALS" and light shone from inside the mouth of the giant clam while fish sculptures swam around, suspended from the ceiling. Footage from the show was used for Phish's one and only music video, "Down with Disease."

And so next year they had to raise the stakes and go bigger, louder, weirder. Maybe you've heard of the giant hot dog?

On December 31, 1994, after playing two sets at the Boston Garden, the audience could hear someone over the PA notifying the band they had "five minutes, guys," but Fishman said, "I thought we had longer; I need to get something to eat."

The band's banter continued as Anastasio said they needed to go out and play and Mike Gordon futilely tried to get Fishman to eat some vegetables.

"Man, I'm sick of those vegetarian styrofoamy things that dry my mouth out," Fishman said. "I need something juicy, something that would last me."

Anastasio replied, "We could ask Brad [Sands] to order something from the concession stand and bring it to you onstage in between songs."

"Oh, yeah," Fishman said. "That would be fine. That would be fine."

"What should I tell him?" Anastasio asked.

"Well, a hot dog, get me a hot dog," Fishman said. "Get me one of those jumbo dogs, with a Coke and some fries."

"Okay, so you want me to tell Brad you want the big, jumbo hot dog, a large Coke, and large fries delivered to you onstage?" Anastasio confirmed.

"That is exactly what I want," Fishman said.

"Ok, I'll tell 'em," Anastasio said. "You guys ready to go?"

And with that, the band took the stage and opened the third set with "My Sweet One," which was interrupted in less than a minute by an announcement over the PA asking, "Excuse me, excuse me, who ordered the hot dog? Your order is ready."

As giant props of a hot dog, french fries, and a soda cup slowly descended from the ceiling, Phish played "2001," and the crowd roared ferociously with each peak.

Then, as the James Bond theme song played over the PA, all four band members made their way to the giant, 15-foot-long hot dog, equipped with four seats, and climbed in with the assistance of stage hands in white lab coats. With Page McConnell in the front seat holding a small keyboard and the other musicians with their instruments, the hot dog rose from the stage, four headlights lit up, and the band counted down to midnight as they flew above the crowd in the giant hot dog, dropping confetti and branded Ping-Pong balls and playing "Auld Lang Syne."

Then Captain Beefhart's "Tropical Hot Dog Night" played over the PA as the band flew around in their hot dog, ultimately returning to the stage and playing "Chalk Dust Torture" > "The Horse" > "Silent in the Morning," and "Suzy Greenberg" > "Slave to the Traffic Light." After a short break, Phish then encored with "Simple" and another performance of "Auld Lang Syne."

This hot dog, on the heels of the aquarium set, would cement a precedent for New Year's Eve gags that the band still honors today. Let this serve as an introduction to anyone unfamiliar with the band Phish: "They're four middle-aged white men who fly around in a giant hot dog on New Year's Eve."

42 *Bittersweet Motel*

Outside of feature-length live show Phish documentaries such as *It* or *Phish 3D*, there are a few recording session documentaries as well (*Tracking*, the *Undermind* bonus DVD, the *Rift* promo), not to mention some fan-made documentaries. But perhaps best of all is the 2000 documentary film *Bittersweet Motel*.

Directed by filmmaker Todd Phillips (*Old School, The Hangover, Joker*), *Bittersweet Motel* follows Phish through the band's 1997 summer and fall tours, and includes footage from their spring 1998 European tour, culminating with Phish's August 1997 festival The Great Went in Limestone, Maine.

On opening weekend, August 25, 2000, the film took in less than $40,000 and grossed just short of $381,000 for its theatrical run in the United States.

The 84-minute film has an 8.1 rating on IMDB. On Rotten Tomatoes, the film has a 43 percent on the Tomatometer and 93 percent audience score.

My favorite part of *Bittersweet Motel* occurs about 37 minutes into the film. The filmmaker asks a harmonica-playing, dread-locked fan, "Is it true you have to be on drugs to listen to Phish? That's what someone said."

"No," the fan says. "Someone said that?"

"Why would somebody say that?" the filmmaker asks.

"Because they like drugs?" the fan retorts. "I don't know. I like to see Phish sober. Less restrictions to that place where you need to go. For music, more or less."

"What's the place?"

"The place? It's in your soul."

"Oh..."

"*That* place. That's why I see Phish shows."

"I don't get it."

"Because they take you to a new level, that you've never experienced, of music appreciation. "

As a rockumentary, *Bittersweet* does a nice job of letting the viewer inside the world of a touring rock band. We go on the bus, back stage, and literally over the shoulders of the band members during an a cappella rendition of "Hello My Baby."

Perhaps the most cringeworthy part of the film is when Trey Anastasio is haggling with a shop owner over the price of a .357 Magnum handgun. It's clear Anastasio has no sincere interest in purchasing the gun and the back-and-forth is just for shits and giggles, but for the gun shop proprietor it's very real and sincere.

Also, there's a fair amount of drinking in this film, which, knowing now how drug and substance abuse within the band contributed to their 2004 breakup and Anastasio's subsequent DUI arrest and successful rehabilitation, makes those bits uncomfortable to watch.

But all in all, good and bad, *Bittersweet Motel* is a gem in the annals of Phish history, capturing a time and place where the band and its fans came together to celebrate something at what felt like a peak moment in time. And it was—kind of.

"We played a bad set," Anastasio says, laughing to Fishman, off camera but on mic after the first set of The Great Went. "Phish: Five sets to redeem ourselves, the new live album. Starting with just a really terrible disc one."

There are plenty of quotes you can pull from this documentary, but, like most statements, taken out of context their meaning and intent can be distorted. And so, watch for yourself! It's a great film, capturing a pivotal time and place for the Phish from Vermont.

43 Podcasts: *Analyze Phish, Helping Friendly Podcast, and Under the Scales*

By the nature of your reading this book, you're likely a Phish fan, even a phan. And like most Phish fans, I can imagine you have friends who don't like Phish or are unfamiliar with Phish. And maybe you yearn to convince them of Phish's awesomeness?

That's the basis for the podcast *Analyze Phish* that launched in August 2011. Cohosts Harris Wittels (*The Sarah Silverman Program, Eastbound & Down,* and *Parks & Recreation*), and Scott Aukerman (*Mr. Show, Comedy Bang! Bang!,* and *Between Two Ferns*) are comedians and writers, music lovers, and friends. However, Harris loved Phish and Scott did not. And so they embarked upon this journey together, through a podcast in which Harris makes an often-hilarious case for Phish with the goal to convert Scott into a phan.

Featuring a handful of special guests, every single one of the 10 episodes of *Analyze Phish* (published periodically over three years) is brilliant and hilarious, culminating with Episode 9, where Harris and Scott recap their shared experience of attending a Phish show at the Hollywood Bowl (August 5, 2013), including live recordings from the show.

If you haven't listened to this incredible podcast, I highly recommend you put this book down and start listening immediately

Phish Radio: SiriusXM and JEMP Radio

On July 14, 2019, Phish officially teamed up with SiriusXM to launch Phish Radio on channel 29. As Page McConnell said in a press release upon launch, "We're excited to make Phish Radio an extension of who we are as a band." The pairing has led to broadcasts of shows during and right after the live performances, interviews with the band, a music show hosted by Jon Fishman called *The Errant Path*, and even a daily radio show called *Crowd Control* where the fans get to play their five favorite live Phish songs. They even brought their festival radio station, The Bunny, to life outside of the festival grounds. One of the crowning achievements must be the incredibly intimate show for Sirius subscribers on 12/3/19 at the Philly Met.

There are other great options to hear Phish over the airwaves, such as the beloved JEMP Radio. Established in 2014, JEMP Radio (jempradio.com) is a not-for-profit internet radio station that has played countless hours of Phish, as well as other amazing music, with an eye toward the jamband scene. It is fully run by volunteers and is a terrific source of great music throughout the day.

to Episode 1. And I think you'll agree that it's a fun and funny way to familiarize someone with Phish.

But I must include some sad news. Between Episodes 9 and 10, Wittels attended rehab for opiate addiction, which is widely discussed in the final episode. Sadly, Wittels would die of an overdose seven months later.

Phish.net published a memoriam for Wittels written by Nathan Rabin, a Phish fan, a guest on Episode 7, and author of *You Don't Know Me But You Don't Like Me*, which details his travels and obsession with Phish. Rabin writes, "Wittels was, in my mind, the best kind of Phish fan: passionate, smart, engaged, and eager to spread the gospel of his favorite band but not in an oppressive or overbearing way."

Despite Wittel's deadly drug addiction, which now clouds the podcast, especially the "Hollywood Bowl" episode, where they take drugs at a Phish show, the podcast is incredibly funny and peppered with profound insights about the band, music, and living life to the fullest.

Another great podcast to listen to is *Helping Friendly Podcast* (hfpod.com), hosted by Brad, RJ, and Jonathan. Shout out to Brad for chatting with us as we launched *100 Things Phish* 1.0—check out episode 137—a sincere pleasure! The HFP has welcomed guests including Katy Tur, Holly Bowling, Scott Bernstein, and Phish lyricist Tom Marshall, to name a few.

Furthermore, Phish lyricist Tom Marshall has his own podcast titled *Under the Scales*, which launched in August 2016. Marshall not only shares anecdotes and personal observations but also interviews various Phish fans and collaborators, including live Phish webcast director Eli Tishberg, poster artists Jim Pollock and David Welker, and Phillip Zerbo, coeditor of the incredible *Phish Companion Volume 3*. Other guests include Steve "The Dude of Life" Pollak and Phish guitarist Trey Anastasio. If you want the inside scoop on Phish, well, head *Under the Scales*.

Another great podcast to check out is called *Inside Out with Turner & Seth*, hosted by Rob Turner and Seth Weiner. While it's not entirely dedicated to Phish, Turner and Seth interview a wide range of musicians and music industry professionals. Phish's drummer and "somewhat namesake" Jon Fishman is the guest for Episode 38, JamBase's Scott Bernstein discusses the Baker's Dozen on Episode 39, and Episode 18 features a backstage interview at the 2016 LOCKN' Festival with Phish lighting director Chris Kuroda.

Chris Kuroda also gives a lengthy interview with his associate designer and programmer Andrew "Gif" Giffin during the Baker's Dozen residency on a podcast called *The Light Side*, hosted by Dopapod lighting designer Luke Stratton, which focuses primarily on production and the technical side of live music events.

Other podcasts of note include: *No Simple Road*, covering a variety of music, often taking their show on the road; Osiris Media's *Alive Again*, an oral history of Trey Anastasio's career outside of Phish; and *Undermind,* which dives deep into the history of Phish through interviews and music analysis. Plus many more!

44 Gear Up: Essentials for Phish Shows

Going to a Phish show, like most things in life, can benefit from some planning. Plainly speaking, nothing is required of you in preparation for a Phish show, but there are some tips and tricks we've picked up along the way to help ensure you have a pleasant evening at the show.

It seems obvious, but, please: take care of your shoes! You can't dance for three hours in broken, worn-out shoes. Well, I mean, hey—you can dance barefoot all day and night if you want. But it helps to have nice, comfortable shoes. And thick socks—don't forget about the socks!

Also, in regard to the hierarchy of needs, you have to stay hydrated. Water is your friend! And the sad truth of some venues across the United States is that they won't sell you a bottle of water with the cap. (Except at the Baker's Dozen where, after a few shows, MSG did allow concertgoers to keep their water bottle caps after being pressed upon by photographer Jeff Kravitz). But you can bring in your own bottle caps! I often bring a few just to share with anyone I see carrying open bottles of water. Of course, you can also bring in full, sealed water bottles or empty Nalgene bottles and fill up at water fountains or bathroom sinks. But sometimes water fountains are scarce and bathroom sinks are gross or only pour hot water. In any case, however you can swing it, stay hydrated!

Now, for everything else.

Some people bring in a lot of, shall we say, stuff? Party supplies come in all shapes and sizes, and some items are more cumbersome than others. I can only speak to the fashion versus utility choices I've made over the years to carry and contain various items in my stash. Of course, I would be remiss to point out that while I don't condone illicit activity, most of these items would not be permitted inside a music venue. And so when considering how to smuggle goods into a venue, you basically have two fashionable options: cargo shorts or fanny pack.

And here's another small piece of advice: if you're bringing in something small, your sock is a great place to stash it.

And, yes, I can hear you. *What about booze?*, you're wondering. Well, here's the trick with bringing booze into a venue. Ready? If you want to sneak in a small half-pint or full-pint bottle of booze… just put it in your back pocket. That's right; your back pocket. Most Phish shows I've been to have had security and metal detectors that are less concerned with pot or booze and more concerned about weapons, as they should be. And so, generally speaking, if you don't make a scene about it, you'll be okay. I've had security pat me down and feel a bottle of booze or a small pipe and all I get is a flat "Enjoy the show," and I'm on my way.

Again, I don't condone smuggling or substance abuse. And I imagine if you're anything like me, you've discovered these tricks for yourself.

In that case, cheers! And, as always, imbibe with care and consideration to those around you. Don't be the obnoxious, "over-served" fan at the show.

45 Blanks and Postage

Certainly, the Grateful Dead pioneered taper culture by allowing (or giving into) and then supporting, even encouraging, fans to record their shows. Tapers brought their own audio equipment, bulky and rudimentary in the early days, and slowly built a taped catalog of live shows and a community and distribution network through which to trade and share those tapes.

While tapes exist of Grateful Dead shows in the 1960s, the band didn't sanction taping until the mid 1980s. And when they did, selling "taper section" tickets, they allocated a space near the soundboard, what is agreed to be the best area of a venue for sound quality.

Tickets immediately sold out and fans came in droves to set up their Digital Audio Tape (DAT) machines and boom-hoisted twin microphones to record the shows. What was widely prohibited, often printed on tickets No Audio Recording Permitted, was suddenly legit.

The only covenant here, the only rule, if you will, was that these taped shows were not to be sold. But you could trade them. The Grateful Dead played 2,317 shows, and Phish has played more than 2,000 shows. That's a lot of tapes!

Well, with Phish now it's almost exclusively streaming apps and membership services, though they still release live show CDs and YouTube has a good amount of shows available. Don't get me wrong; traditional tapers still set up inside the venue, there is just a lot more options and practically instant access to live show recordings. Also, with live video streaming, the hashtag #couchtour has given a new relevance and real-time access to live shows. (See chapter 55.)

Despite the seemingly instantaneous access these days, there are still people who love to record and trade live shows. But instead of trading tapes or CDs, some folks trade hard drives that contain audience copies of every show in history. We're talking terabytes, man!

Of course, the Grateful Dead pioneered the taper culture. And Phish was smart enough to continue to encourage the tradition. Both bands can ascribe much of their success to the tapers, the historians, the grassroots marketers. These bands welcomed an army of tapers to their shows who then proliferated recordings through the decades with tapes multiplying like some kind of cellular mitosis: one tape would become two tapes, which would then become four tapes, then eight tapes, introducing new fans to the music and even inspiring more tapers to join the crusade.

These days, there are plenty of websites out there where you can stream or download Phish music, most notably Etree.org or phish.in or phishtracks.com. Back in the 1980s, 1990s, even the early 2000s, before the Internet became widely used, the only way you could really get your hands on taped shows was through friends or pen pals, the latter of which was colloquially referred to as "blanks and postage." If you mailed a taper blank tapes and a self-addressed, stamped envelope requesting a specific show, said taper would copy that show onto the blank tapes you sent and return them to you shipped in your envelope. Back then, you had to seek out physical tapes and CDs of shows, some more prolific than others. Some shows, some tapes were rare and even elusive.

In the late 1990s, I sent out my fair share of blanks and postage, eagerly awaiting the treasured tapes of seminal shows like Dark Side November 2, 1998, and Paradiso, Amsterdam '97.

Back in the day, we had to walk both ways to and from the mailbox to send out BnPs for music that wouldn't return for weeks. We had to use dual cassette decks to make copies for others on Maxell XL2 cassettes, which cost around $4 per show. It certainly wasn't free, and it took time. Heaven forbid that you tried to high-speed dub those tapes!

Without blanks and postage and the kind tapers who worked to document and deliver, most of these shows just wouldn't have been heard twice.

Tapers are the archivists, the historians of this music.

I think it's safe to say that some of you first heard Phish's music playing on a stereo off a cassette tape. Maybe your older brother hit you with some tapes when you were in high school or middle school? Maybe it was "Wolfman's Brother?"

My introduction to Phish and Phish tapes was through a classmate in middle school, a hippie girl named Jennifer. We were close friends for a short time before I moved away, but I'm ever grateful for the tapes and CDs she shared with me. Thanks, Jenny!

And so, your mission, dear reader, if you choose to accept it, is to thank a taper! Send a friend one of your favorite shows... BitTorrent, mp3, CD, whatever format you prefer, but bonus points if you gift a cassette. And if you can give back or send thanks to the person who gave you that first Phish tape or CD, even better.

Share a tape or thank a taper today!

46 Visit Red Rocks

If the rarest of opportunities ever arises again, every fan needs to make a pilgrimage to see Phish at Red Rocks in Morrison, Colorado, at least once in their lifetime. Go! Don't take my word for it. Take the word of Phish's Trey Anastasio, who said during the band's first appearance at Red Rocks in 1993, "This is definitely the most incredible place I've ever played music."

Red Rocks is one of the most iconic music venues in the United States, if not the world. Built in a natural amphitheater between two 300-plus-foot red rock monoliths, this gorgeous venue has been hosting concerts and events in various genres for more than 100 years. It is an intimate venue that holds fewer than 10,000 fans.

According to the *Denver Post*, it is estimated the natural formations took more than 200 million years to form, and architect Burnham Hoyt designed the amphitheater based on the Theatre of Dionysus at the Acropolis in Athens, Greece. According to a Colorado Public Radio article, Red Rocks was opened in 1906 by John Brisben Walker and was initially named "The Garden of the Titans."

It is a glorious sight to behold, and an estimated 750,000 people visit Red Rocks each year. It is so iconic that music website Pollstar has named its annual award for the best small outdoor venue the "Red Rocks Award," just to give some other venues a chance of winning.

Since its first opening, Red Rocks Amphitheater has hosted countless concerts. One way to try to gauge the impact of this venue on the musicians who play there is to look at the bands who've released a live album based on their Red Rocks experience. This list includes U2, Neil Young, Stevie Nicks, John Tesh, Dave Matthews, The Moody Blues, Widespread Panic, Blues Traveler, and many more.

Phish have graced the stage 13 times, or what fans today would call a baker's dozen. The first show, on August 20, 1993, is legendary, and was smack-dab in the middle of the highly touted August 1993 summer tour, which is believed to be one of their best.

Right off the bat, it was clear that Red Rocks inspired the band, because they opened with a glorious "Divided Sky," which when surrounded by giant rock formations is more literal than in most venues. It was followed with the rarity "Harpua" in just the second song of the show, and the hits just kept on coming. The second set is incredibly stacked with classic Phish heavy hitters and is one of the jewels in the August '93 crown.

They followed this single show the following year with a two-night stand in 1994, with the June 11, 1994, show standing out as another Phish fan favorite. The band played two more strong shows here in 1995.

In 1996, Phish expanded their Red Rocks run to four nights, which drove up expectations and demand. These four shows had musical highlights sprinkled throughout and saw the birth of the Harry Hood chant during an epic lightning storm on August 6, 1996 (see chapter 47). These shows are also remembered for what happened outside the venue. Ticketless Phish fans and local police clashed in the tiny town of Morrison, made the local news, and led to Phish being banned from Red Rocks for 13 years.

Just because Phish was banned did not mean the individual members' projects were, as well. Trey Anastasio Band made a number of appearances at Red Rocks during the ban, as did Mike Gordon with the Leo Kottke band.

After Red Rocks' purgatory ended and Phish got back together, they made their triumphant return in 2009 for another four-night run. This time, the run was without incident, and the shows had their own mix of highlights and memorable moments. One of the major highlights of the run was on the final night. Phish welcomed out Grateful Dead drummer Bill Kreutzmann to assist on the second half of the second set.

Phish at Red Rocks is an experience not to be missed. If the opportunity ever arises again, don't hesitate; make it happen.

47 Phish Playing in the Elements

There are more than a few moments in a 40-year career when the band and the elemental forces of the universe align. When those celestial moments occur, connecting the band, the fans, the music, and nature to one another, pure magic can take place.

Some moments occur within a song, others over an entire show. One well-known incident happened during the set-closing "Taste" at Walnut Creek in North Carolina in 1997. During the first set closer, lightning literally struck the back of the venue. When watching the Walnut Creek Phish movie release from this show, you can hear the electric crackling during Page's solo. Interestingly enough, there was a lunar eclipse at Walnut Creek in 1998. Phish used the "Colonel Forbin's Ascent" narration to explain about how the Colonel's actions led to the eclipse.

Another legendary storm-related event happened at the E Center in Camden, New Jersey, on July 3, 2000. A massive thunderstorm brought inches of standing water into the concrete pavilion. When Phish played the anthemic "Bathtub Gin" and shouted "We love to take a bath!", everyone sang along and a giant splash fight broke out. Fans were both soaked and thrilled.

A more recent example took place in 2013 at the Gorge Amphitheater. But this time, the elemental force was fire instead of water. There was a visible brushfire burning behind the stage across the river during the show, which simultaneously added to the light show and took away from the air quality. Phish appropriately played Jimi Hendrix's "Fire," to the delight of those in attendance.

At Red Rocks in Morrison, Colorado, at the August 6, 1996, show, the setting, weather, and music combined to create an all-time Phish moment. During the first set, fans could see a black lightning storm slowly creeping its way from Denver toward the venue. It was slow moving, but full of raging electric fury.

When the second set began, the winds began to pick up, and the band used this ominous storm to create a uniquely spooky set of music. During the "Curtain" > "Tweezer" opening combo lightning flashed off in the distance; during "Big Black Furry Creatures from Mars," the intensity picked up from the storm. Mike screamed the lyrics "I'm running!" and Trey took this opportunity to grab his megaphone and began sprinting full speed around the stage.

As the black storm clouds settled in, lightning strikes and rain began to cover the natural amphitheater like an electric blanket. Chris Kuroda turned the purple lights from the stage up toward the storm above. In truly Phishy fashion, Phish played Prince's "Purple Rain" as lightning and swirling winds engulfed the venue. The magical moment didn't end there.

During this run, fans had handed out fliers to the audience to do surprise fan participation with the band. One of the ideas was to use the initial "Harry" lyrics of "Harry Hood" to offer a "Hood" response to the band (see chapter 84).

When "Harry Hood" started, the storm was swirling, rain was pouring, and the intensity was growing. You can still hear the audience cheer at seemingly random points in the song, when lightning lights up the sky. After the first "Harry," the audience's "Hood!" response was strong, but after each subsequent one the intensity grew exponentially until the final "Hood!" scream seemed to even rattle the venue in the midst of this thunderstorm.

These are just a taste of the many moments when the natural world and Phish seemingly collaborate to create lasting memories. Sometimes weather forces shows to end early (Northerly Island in Chicago on July 19, 2013), and other times a storm can cause the band to pause midway through a song and later return where they left off ("Mound" in Alpharetta, Georgia, on June 15, 2011).

Curveball

Phish's 11th festival, Curveball (8/11–8/13/18), was scheduled to take place at Watkins Glen, New York (where they previously held Super Ball IX in 2011 and Magnaball in 2015), but unfortunately was canceled just the day before the three-day festival was set to begin. Having sold out 40,000 tickets, many thousands of fans were already at the festival site with vendors having invested in three day's worth of food to sell. It was then that many fans learned a new vocabulary word: "turbidity," which is the cloudiness or haziness of a fluid caused by large numbers of individual particles that are generally invisible to the naked eye, similar to smoke in air.

After catastrophic flooding throughout New York state, a boil-water advisory had been issued on Thursday, August 10th, 2018 for the Village of Watkins Glen. The public reservoir had been contaminated from the flooding. And while festival organizers worked tirelessly to secure enough bottled water or water tankers for the expected attendees, it was not a viable solution. Bradley Hutton, deputy commissioner for the state Health Department's Office of Public Health told the local newspaper: "The sheer numbers of people on-site and the urgent timeframe that was needed, there was no way for the concert organizers and host location to make that happen."

At 5:19 PM on Thursday, August 10th, Phish issued a statement detailing that Curveball was forced to cancel, reading, in part: "We were about to walk onstage only moments ago for our traditional soundcheck jam for Curveball when we were told the heartbreaking news that due to the unsafe water conditions in the Village of Watkins Glen, our beloved festival is being canceled."

Needless to say, in addition to the attendees and vendors already on site, many more were in route, driving on freeways where LED traffic message boards read "CURVEBALL CANCELED." Many fans were in disbelief, hoping that somehow this was an off-tone prank from the band they loved.

Phish, of course, issued nearly immediate and automatic refunds for festival tickets, camping, and travel packages. Plus, all Curveball ticketholders received free webcasts for the Dick's run shows that Labor Day. And to help with the flood recovery across the 14 counties of New York State, Phish launched a Curveball merchandise store through which all proceeds went to flood relief.

And in recent years, it would appear that we're seeing more and more weather delays and cancellations. Four songs into the second set of Phish's 7/19/23 show in Wilmington, North Carolina, torrential rain, wind, and lightning forced the band to end the show. Reports from fans in attendance say the lightning was scary and very much a force majeure as the band's crew called for them to stop and seek shelter. With water pooling on stage and on the equipment, Fishman jested, "Ya know, Taylor Swift didn't stop!" referencing Swift's 5/20/23 show in Foxborough, Massachusetts, where heavy rain drenched the crowd and performers for the entire three and a half hour show.

Some shows have had doors and start-time delays due to evening thunderstorms, resulting in the band's performance of a single set without a break. For Phish's third visit to Boston's Fenway Park (7/6/19), a rain delay prompted the band to play for two hours and 41 minutes without a break. Similarly, bad weather forced a delayed start at the Pine Knob Music Center in Clarkston, Michigan (8/3/22), where the band played a two and a half hour set of 14 songs.

But one show certainly stands out among them all: the second night of Phish's 2022 Dick's Run (9/2/22). Not only did severe weather delay the show but the venue was also partly evacuated and doors were closed. Then, at 9:41 PM local time, Phish tweeted, "Doors have re-opened at @DSGpark and the show will begin as soon as we possibly can. There will be no setbreak tonight, just one long-ass set. Thanks for your understanding!" The show itself featured a number of great tunes ("YEM," "Ghost," "Tweezer") including an especially exciting "Carini" opener, during which Trey changed the lyrics to reference a lone streaker, with long brown hair, beard, and a pair of hiking boots, who took to the field during the weather delay and evacuation. "At least he had some boots," Trey sang, eliciting an uproar from the crowd.

The "naked guy" would come to be revealed to be a beloved Phish fan named Tim "Frenchie" Gazaille for whom Phish would later pay homage to Frenchie's Colorado antics in their New Year's Eve gag during which dozens of dancers dressed to look like the nude Frenchie climbed out of the band's 40th birthday cake (see chapter 97). Sadly, Frenchie passed away in April 2023 after a long battle with lung cancer. When Phish returned to Colorado that Labor Day weekend, Trey dedicated the opening song, "Carini," to Frenchie (8/31/23).

Embracing the unknown is an attitude widely held by Phish fans. Surrender to the flow. And severe and inclement weather is all part of the ride. Stay safe. And take it in stride.

48 *Hoist* (1994)

Acoustic guitar; finger snaps; the blues, then horns; a choir; a "Wolfman's Brother" *and* a "Dog Faced Boy;" not to mention the a cappella, harmonizing, power rock, train sounds, smelly mules, a car crash, Hebrew singing, and what would become one of Phish's most trusted jam vehicles...ladies and gentlemen, this is *Hoist*. Eleven songs clocking in at exactly 50 minutes, *Hoist*, stylized as *(Hoist)*, is Phish's fifth official studio album.

Many of these songs remain in steady rotation at Phish's live shows, including bassist Mike Gordon's "Scent of a Mule" and "Down with Disease," the latter often kicking off jam-heavy second sets with Gordon sliding up and down the bass with a spaced-out warble before dropping into the heavy groove synonymous with the song.

Recorded in October and November of 1993 at the American Recording Company in Woodland Hills, California, *Hoist* was released on March 29, 1994, by Elektra Records. The album was produced by Bob Fox, whose mid-90s production credits include *MTV Unplugged* with 10,000 Maniacs and *John Henry* by They Might Be Giants.

Back in the spring of 1994, Billboard No. 1 albums included Soundgarden's *Superunknown*, *The Sign* by Ace of Base, and Pink Floyd's *The Division Bell*. At the time of its release, *Hoist* was Phish's bestselling album to date, peaking at No. 34 on the Billboard 200 albums chart. Nine other Phish albums would later eclipse that, including 2016's *Fuego* and 1996's *Billy Breathes,* both of which peaked at No. 7.

A short documentary of the *Hoist* recording sessions, titled *Tracking*, filmed and edited by Mike Gordon, features many nuances of the working musicians' dynamic as well as a studio evacuation due to a growing 60,000-acre wildfire along the California coast. You can find the full 25-minute documentary on YouTube.

The album includes a dozen or so contributing musicians, including The Rickey Grundy Chorale with the backing vocals on "Julius," Multiple Grammy award-winner Béla Fleck on banjo for three tracks, and Jonathan Frakes, aka *Star Trek*'s Commander William T. Riker, playing trombone on "Riker's Mailbox," which is less of a song and more of a 30-second wake-up cacophony of horns and screams setting up the eponymous, power-rock refrain that is "Axilla (Part II)," which then fades into a spooky, tripped-out riff and jingle with a man talking and laughing, saying something like, "Don't shine that thing in my face, man. Get that thing out of my face, asshole."

Make sense so far?

But it's perhaps the final song on the album that is the most notable. "Demand" itself is an incredibly rare, two-minute, happy jaunt, but then we hear someone enter a car, start the engine, and

Phish's Only Music Video

"Down with Disease" is the only music video Phish has ever produced. Directed by Mike Gordon, the video depicts the band members surrealistically scuba diving in a household aquarium. The video is clearly a product of the 1990s and, at one point, features a giant clam that releases an animated Phish logo that swims away. The clam then seems to swallow the band members and transport them to a stage where they play before a live audience, filmed live at the 1993 New Year's Eve show at Worcester Centrum Centre in Worcester, Massachusetts. At that show, the band entertained an underwater theme, donning wetsuits and "diving" into the onstage aquarium with bubble noises for the third and final set.

begin driving, first listening to an ad on the radio while we hear what sounds like our driver opening a cassette tape case and inserting the tape into the tape player—a sound I imagine many younger readers may not be so familiar with. He then turns up the volume and we hear the beginnings of a live jam on "Split Open and Melt" (specifically from April 21, 1993) along with the sounds of driving and passing cars. Over the course of 10 minutes, the jam's crescendo continues to build as the car increases in speed, squealing around corners. We hear police sirens as the jam and drive continue to gain speed. And when the song furiously peaks, suddenly the car swerves and crashes, with the sound of crushing metal and breaking glass. After a brief moment of silence, we hear a cappella singing of the first verse and refrain of the Hebrew song "Yerushalayim Shel Zahav (Jerusalem of Gold)." It's intense, man.

The album cover, a photograph of a horse hoisted into the air, is rumored to reference "The Horse," which was the one song not incorporated in the album cover art for *Rift*, the band's previous album. Also worth mentioning is the undeniable similarity between the *Hoist* album cover artwork and famed Italian artist Maurizio Cattelan's piece "Novencento," which featured a taxidermied horse hung from the baroque ceiling of one of the salons at the Castello di

Rivoli in Turin in 1997, three years after *Hoist* was released. If we're gentle about it, we may say Cattelan was perhaps inspired by *Hoist*?

About three months after the album's release, Phish played their first show in West Virginia and performed the album in its entirety as their second set. The first set? A profound, must-hear performance of the Gamehendge saga (see chapter 5), prompting fans and critics to refer to this June 24, 1994 show as the "GameHoist" show. As if two of the most memorable sets in Phish history aren't enough to make this show legendary, Phish came out for a four-song encore to seal the deal. At this point it was clear to everyone: Hoist had arrived, with grandeur.

49 Hanging with the Band, aka Bedroom Jam Sessions

I ask for you to indulge me in a story that is a bit beyond belief. This may seem like a tall tale, or more accurately a Phish tale, but I promise you it is true.

My Phish tale is a tale of the unbelievable kind.

It all took place in the fall of 1999 as Phish was following their West Coast tour south from British Columbia, down the West Coast with a few stops along the way, including a weekend at the Gorge, the last time they visited Portland, Oregon (come back already!). There was a historic jaunt at Shoreline Amphitheatre which included Phil Lesh jumping on a trampoline, an epic show at Boise, and two strong shows in southern California.

As the tour began to turn east, the next stop was my college town, Tucson, Arizona. As luck would have it, jam band mainstay Leftover Salmon happened to be playing at the Rialto Theater on Phish's off night. My cousin Lauren decided to throw an intimate gathering before the show, and we figured we all would return after Leftover Salmon.

Leftover put on their typical slamgrass dance party. That all began to change when a rumor began to swirl throughout the venue that the Phish tour bus had just pulled up outside. Immediately, my first reaction was to slide on up to the stage, because if it was true, we could be in for a rare musical treat.

In the middle of the second set, Leftover Salmon's front man, Vince Herman, stopped the show to welcome Trey Anastasio to the stage. Trey strapped on a borrowed Les Paul guitar and the seven-song medley that followed was a blur of interwoven bluegrass, old time Americana, and rock and roll.

Gram Parsons' "Ooh Las Vegas" was the launching point, and the rest of the jam was bookended by Bill Monroe's "Old Kentucky." James Wayne's "Junco Partner," The Band's "Shape I'm In," and the traditional "Pig in a Pen" filled in as the meat of the medley. Trey even took the opportunity to tease Phish's "Meatstick," with some in the audience doing the accompanying dance. The story could have ended there, but this story is about what happens after the show.

Somehow, some of my Tucson friends persuaded both bands to come back to our little party. These were the pre–cell phone days, so the rest of us just went back to the house as previously planned, clueless to the additional guests who would be joining us. When both the Phish and Salmon buses pulled up and parked outside her driveway, all bets were off.

It was surreal. There we were, around 15 friends hanging out, and in walked Vince Herman, Drew Emmitt, Mike Gordon, and Jon Fishman. At one point, I was circled up with just Mike and Drew, talking about music and the universe, and thought that this must be a dream. I later found Fishman hyping the merits of the "Meatstick" dance with other friends, and how close they were to breaking the *Guinness* dance record a few months prior at Camp Oswego.

This casual hang went on for an hour or so, but changed once Trey got off the tour bus. He made a beeline for the house while grabbing my cousin's acoustic guitar along the way. Soon after, Mike found her other acoustic guitar, and then Fishman, myself, and about seven of my closest Tucson friends made our way to her bedroom.

It is hard to put into words what happened next. Trey, Mike, Fish, and the few of us blessed enough to be in that room had a group sing-along for a few hours. Trey was sitting at the end of my cousin's bed, and Mike was sitting on the ground, both of them with guitars in hand. Fishman led the rhythmic clap-along segments as he was leaning against the wall.

This was like living through an outtake from the Phish documentary *Bittersweet Motel*, but instead of ad-libbing about Page's new shirt or dudes in the front row, they were singing about a variety of keg party topics that will be left to your imagination. Yeah, it was that crazy.

They were instigating our friends to do ridiculous things in song. It was beyond hysterical. We were singing, clapping, laughing, and doing everything in our power to keep our composure.

It wasn't all comedic improvisation. They also led us through some acoustic classics like "My Long Journey Home," "Blackbird," "Nellie Kane," and "Blue and Lonesome." The musical highlight of the evening may have been "If I Could." It was less about the song and more about watching Trey try to remember how to play the notes on the fretboard.

They asked if we had any requests and I threw out my all-time-favorite song: Bob Dylan's "Tangled Up in Blue." Mike said no, because there were too many lyrics to remember. Hopefully next time!

This continued until around 4:00 AM when their road manager, Brad Sands, came into the room to wrangle up the trio. Without skipping a beat, they turned their improv barbs on Brad for ruining their good time and seamlessly busted his chops in song. All of a sudden, Trey and Jon decided to express their profound love for Mike, who was still sitting by, mutually mock-humping Mike's head from both rides in the most ridiculous act imaginable. With that, they put the guitars down, smiled, and headed out of the house toward the waiting tour bus.

We were simultaneously dumbfounded and giddy. For a few minutes, the lucky few who were in that magical bedroom just sat there in disbelief.

Did this story really happen? One hundred percent yes. Will any of you believe me? Maybe so, maybe not. This is the beauty of Phish Tales. Sometimes the story grows larger than the reality, and sometimes the reality is so incredible it is hard to believe.

50 "Auld Lang Syne" > "DWD"

Midnight on New Year's Eve is fast approaching, and somewhere deep in a jam we are brought back down to earth with a familiar countdown. "10...9...8...7...6...5...4...3...2...1...Happy New Year!" The familiar notes of Robert Burns' timeless "Auld Lang Syne" ("ALS") ring out from Trey's guitar, and everyone in the venue turns to their neighbors to share hugs, high fives, cheers, and, for some, a midnight kiss.

Thousands of balloons, or more recently the more environmentally conscious paper confetti, descend from overhead, and moments of intertwined joy, reflection, and musical anticipation

The band buried alive after it rained cats and dogs on NYE 2016.
(Jason Gershuny)

ensue. A low rumble begins to emanate from Mike's bass guitar, and that can only mean one thing. We are kicking off the New Year with another raucous rendition of "Down with Disease" ("DWD").

One experience every Phish fan should have during his or her lifetime is the pure joy of celebrating the first seconds of the New Year on the floor while the anthemic "DWD" guitar riff shreds your consciousness. Seeing an "ALS" > "DWD" New Year's Eve celebration is a Phish rite of passage that should not be missed.

This pairing is never guaranteed, but ever since "DWD" was debuted in jam form on December 31, 1993, Phish has used this combination to ring in a New Year five times—1993, 1996, 1999, 2009, and 2011. In comparison, during those same 17 total New Year's Eve shows, no other song was played directly after "Auld Lang Syne" more than once.

Trey often spends much of "DWD" as designated balloon popper, and he seems to relish that role. Tapers, on the other hand, are often seen scrambling to protect their gear from the tremendous, rubberized flying projectiles.

This clearly is one of Phish's favorite ways to ring in the New Year. A particularly notable version is 1999 Big Cypress, where instead of the typical indoor balloon drop we had a tremendous fireworks spectacular for the ages.

A couple of other New Year's Eve "Down with Disease" performances worth noting are a fiery original debut of the "DWD" jam in 1993 at Worcester Centrum Center, and the all-time (see

New Year's Eve with Phish.... A sight to behold! (Stephen Olker)

chapter 41) largest balloon drop attempt at the Boston Garden in 1996 (see chapter 63).

These days, climate consciousness around single use plastic waste may have given the band a pause on the balloon drop at New Year's Eve. On New Year's Eve 2023, the band dropped recyclable paper with printouts of lyrics and other Phish lore, perhaps representing shredded pieces of the Helping Friendly Book.

Balloons or otherwise, celebrating the stroke of midnight at a Phish show is a tremendous experience.

51 Run, O.J., Run

You may remember the day: June 7, 1994. It was the day that millions of Americans tuned in on television to watch a live low-speed police pursuit of O.J. Simpson in Los Angeles, California.

The former football star led police on a two-hour chase across southern California on I-405 in his white Ford Bronco after he was charged with killing his ex-wife Nicole Brown Simpson and her friend Ronald Goldman.

CBS, ABC, NBC, and CNN aired live coverage.

Ninety-five million Americans watched the news coverage. "Some of the coverage was watched by 67 percent of all households, or 63 million homes," David Poltrack, CBS' senior ratings analyst, told the *New York Times*.

But some folks, namely 1,500 Phish fans, were not watching the coverage. They were at a show in Milwaukee, Wisconsin, at a venue called Eagles Club. As the band took the stage, news had already broken, though no one knew exactly how much of a spectacle it would be. Still, Phish opened with "Runaway Jim."

Phish and Live Sports

During 2014's fall tour, Phish found themselves playing three nights at the Bill Graham Civic Auditorium in downtown San Francisco during the World Series games between the San Francisco Giants and the Kansas City Royals.

On the first night of the run, the Series had a travel day, so there was no game. But Phish kicked off their encore that night with a debut instrumental version of "Take Me Out to the Ball Game."

The World Series would go to seven games in 2014, with the seventh game played on the third night of Phish's stint at Bill Graham. The auditorium is across from City Hall, with a large public park where the city erected inflatable screens and projected the baseball game live from Kansas City.

With the ballgame starting at 6:07 PM PT and Phish's showtime set for 7:30 PM, some fans of both the band and the Giants stayed in the park to watch the baseball game before heading into the venue for the Phish show.

That night (October 29, 2014), Phish opened with "Stealing Time from the Faulty Plan" and then played "Moma Dance," during which the ballgame ended. The Giants were victorious. As the game ended, dozens, perhaps hundreds, of Giants/Phish fans made their way into the auditorium, prompting roars from the crowd. The Giants had won! And then Phish seamlessly transitioned from "Moma" into "We Are the Champions," McConnell and Anastasio bobbing heads and exchanging smiles. Then, just as effortlessly as they first segued, the band returned to "Moma" and the crowd howled with joy.

Phish also references live sports at some of their shows. On *Live Phish Vol. 10* at Veterans Memorial Auditorium in Columbus, Ohio, on June 22, 1994, Phish opens the second set with Anastasio announcing the score of Game 7 of the NBA championship between the Houston Rockets and the New York Knicks: "I'd like to start this set out by saying, first quarter, Houston by five." And at the very end of the show's "Cavern" encore, Anastasio gives another update: "By the way, after the third quarter, the Knicks 60, Houston 63…."

At the World Music Theatre in Tinley Park, Illinois, on August 14, 1993, during the end of "Daniel Saw the Stone," Anastasio shares the score of the Chicago Bears preseason game, saying, "Five minutes left in the third quarter, Cardinals 3, Bears 10…."

Of course, sports updates have gone by the wayside since the proliferation of smartphones.

But really, Page and Trey are baseball fans.

At that same Bill Graham show on October 29, 2014, the crowd chanted "Let's Go Giants" after "The Wedge," and Page McConnell congratulated the Giants. Anastasio then told the audience that McConnell was a Mets fan and that he "watches every Mets game streamed on his phone with many of them on the organ while the band's playing." McConnell replied, "We can't be world champions all the time." And Fish ribbed, "Or ever." Then Anastasio introduced "The Line" in honor of the losers of sports.

For both the 2014 and 2015 Philadelphia shows at The Mann Center, fans received original baseball cards with artwork featuring the band. Collect them all!

And by setbreak, the chase was on, as millions tuned in to watch. In fact, Domino's reported delivering more pizza nationwide that night than any other single day, including past Super Bowls.

When Phish returned for the second set, they came out swinging, launching right into "2001" with Trey Anastasio and Jon Fishman both saying, "Ohhhhhhh Jay…Ohhhh Jay…Go for it, O.J.," and "Whaddya say, O.J.?"

Phish would then weave shouts of "O.J." and other mentions of the fugitive chased by LAPD during the show, including "run, O.J, run!" and "Ohhhhhhhhhhh Jay!" during "Poor Heart" and more during "Mike's Groove," a performance best known as "O.J.'s Groove," complete with *Mission Impossible* theme song teases.

When you have the chance, fire up that show, June 7, 1994, in Milwaukee. It's a solid testament to our weird, wild world and Phish's talent to weave the weird into their music.

52 Phi$h, Billboard Charts, and Ticket Sales

Phish has never been a chart-topping, radio-play band. And yet, Phish had the fifth-highest concert ticket sales in the world in 2021, selling 572,626 tickets.

They've never had a top-10 single. They made only one music video (see chapter 48). And for many of us who came of age in the era of Napster and LimeWire, well, some people's best-known Phish song was a cover of Snoop Dogg's "Gin and Juice." But that wasn't even Phish. The band covering Snoop is called The Gourds, but in the days of peer-to-peer file sharing, sometimes tracks were mislabeled.

My point here is that Phish was never mainstream. And even though it seems ticket demand for their live shows is at a new high, I don't think anyone would consider Phish mainstream even today, some 40 years into their career.

Two albums share the title of peak Billboard chart toppers for Phish: 1996's *Billy Breathes* and 2014's *Fuego* both hit No. 7. *Story of the Ghost* in 1998 peaked at No. 8. In 2000, *Farmhouse* hit No. 12 and 2009's *Joy*, marking the band's return after five years, peaked at No. 13, tying 2014's *Undermind*.

The average Billboard chart position for Phish's ranking studio albums is 29.

Phish's first two sanctioned live albums, *A Live One* and *Slip Stitch and Pass*, ranked at Nos. 18 and 17, respectively. *A Live One* was the first Phish album to be certified gold and remains Phish's bestselling album.

Their only charted single is the opening track on *Billy Breathes*: "Free," which peaked at No. 11 on Billboard's Rock Chart. Rush's "Test For Echo" held the No. 1 spot when *Billy Breathes* was released, and then Van Halen's "Me Wise Magic" held the No. 1 position for six weeks.

In Richard Gehr's exhaustive *Spin* article, "All 333 Phish Songs, Ranked," he lists "Free" at No. 35, writing, "Concluding with a swirling bliss-out, this *Billy Breathes* highlight contains a Hitchcockian plot about uxoricide at sea."

And you wonder why Phish doesn't chart well? For a band who built themselves through their live shows, heavy on improvisation, why would people buy the studio albums? I suppose one may want to learn the songs before seeing them performed live? But how does that stack up?

Phish at MSG as seen from behind the stage with Chris Kuroda's dynamic light rig in full effect. (Scott Harris)

Of Phish's 13 studio albums released between 1989 and 2016, only their first album, *Junta*, has gone platinum and sold more than 1,000,000 copies. Their next five albums would go gold and sell more than 500,000 copies. *The Story of the Ghost* would ruin that streak, which continued again picking up with the band's eighth album, *Farmhouse*, going gold in 2000. In regards to live albums, *A Live One* went Platinum and *Hampton Comes Alive* went gold.

Phish's *Big Boat*, received a 5.3 out of 10 in Pitchfork and peaked at No. 19 on the Billboard charts.

Phish haven't had a gold record in 18 years. And they probably won't ever again. We've moved past the age of purchased music, purchased albums, and ranking said sales on a week-to-week basis. Now we stream. We search YouTube. We subscribe to Spotify. Wherever we may get music, we certainly don't go to Sam Goody and buy an album packaged in shrink wrap—though Billboard is incorporating streaming into its charts more and more.

The days of purchasing albums, and subsequently album charts, are gone. And still, despite lacking the mainstream ubiquity of many arena bands, Phish is one of the highest-grossing touring acts performing today. To put it bluntly, Phish is big bucks, y'all.

Live Nation, the promoter for Phish's Baker's Dozen 2017 residency at Madison Square Garden, reported that Phish grossed more than $15,000,000 in ticket sales for the residency. While Phish only sold out five of the 13 shows, total attendance was only 8,893 less than total capacity for the combined shows: 227,385 out of 236,278. Each of the 13 shows averaged a gross revenue of just about $1.6 million.

Comparatively, however, Dead and Company's CitiField Show (June 24, 2017) grossed $4,032,321 for its 27,299-capacity sellout. And Billy Joel's sold-out show at Boston's Fenway Park (August 30, 1017) grossed $4.2 million. Both acts had ticket tiers as high as $150 per ticket, twice the price of the highest ticket tier ($74) for Phish's Baker's Dozen shows.

Phish's four-night run for New Year's Eve 2011 at Madison Square Garden grossed $4.4 million, with a full sellout of the 75,707 total capacity. In 2013, Billboard's Hot Tours ranked Phish the No. 2 act in North America, grossing $18 million and selling 365,052 tickets. just behind Dave Matthews Band. In 2016, according to Pollstar, Phish ranked No. 24 in the highest-grossing music tours of the year, averaging $1.7 million per show across 42 shows in 22 cities. The top three earners were, in ascending order, Bruce Springsteen, Guns N' Roses, and Beyoncé.

According to CelebrityNetWorth.com, Phish keyboardist Page McConnell has a net worth of $55 million; bassist Mike Gordon, $60 million; drummer Jon Fishman has a net worth of $65 million; and guitarist and front man Trey Anastasio's net worth is $85 million.

53 *A Live One* (1995)

Twelve years into their career, Phish released *A Live One*, their first sanctioned live release. At this point, the band had played close to 1,000 live shows and released six albums (including the cassette *The White Tape*). Finally, 1995 would prove to be the year of *A Live One*.

Every track on this album is incredible. From the echoed chants of the crowd during "Wilson" at Phish's first Madison Square Garden performance (12/30/94) to the 30-minute (11/2/94) Bangor "Tweezer," this collection is a rare grouping of some of Phish's best performances of their best songs.

In fact, some of the songs on the album have never been given the studio treatment, including "Gumbo" and "Simple." The "song"

"Montana" isn't really a song, but rather a two-minute excerpt from the 45-minute, "Tweezer" the band played in Bozeman, Montana (11/28/94).

The "You Enjoy Myself" (12/7/94) is especially well performed, compositionally, and yet goes completely freeform with incredible results. And I must admit that I'm such a sucker for the version of "Coil" on this album; Page McConnell's solo outro will make you weep in the best way.

The band teamed up with producer Ed Thacker with his engineers in Burlington's Bearsville Studios to select the songs and mix the record. Selecting 12 songs from later 1994 performances, including the "Montana" excerpt, they arranged the album to follow the structure of a traditional performance, to feel to the listener like a two-set Phish show.

Phish fan, author, and friend Wally Holland literally wrote the book on *A Live One*, published by 33⅓ in October 2015. Each book released on 33⅓ focuses exclusively on one album. Holland's investigation into *A Live One* is the 109th release in the series.

"The album was a reward to Phish's hardcore fans," Holland said in a March 2016 interview at PhanSite.com. "But also a sample platter, this weird tapas plate, like an almanac to the band rather than a guided introduction. It's not a tutorial: it's weird and scattered and random and weirdly comprehensive, and yet missing aspects of the music, like song-to-song segues.

"We cheer for subtle shifts in dynamics in the middle of a 15-minute improvisation," Holland continues. "That's an extraordinary thing, and that's a thing all Phish fans take for granted. But a non-Phish fan has never had that experience. That's the hardest part to communicate to people who don't go to the shows and the part that I was trying like hell to bring across in the book: the wonderful sense of smallness that we experience is not from looking up at Phish and wondering how in the world did they accomplish some technical maneuver, it's being open to the emotional impulses that they're sharing on stage."

And I think it's fair to say that's what Phish was attempting with this album. For the first time, Phish tried to bottle and package their live performance, 12 songs that would hopefully help people get closer to that extraordinary experience.

"People who are not experts in music are deriving life-altering pleasure from Phish's live shows and experiencing it in this enormous range of ways and able to respond to it," Holland says. "We come to these fucking shows and do really strange things like clapping when the band syncs up in an improvised jam instead of recognizing the single. Because there is no single."

Holland is correct, yes. Phish does not have a hit single. But without a single, without a "hit," how does one introduce someone to Phish? Personally, I like to refer people to *A Live One*, the album, for all the same reasons Holland chose to write about it. Phish's *A Live One* is indeed a delicious sampler platter recorded at a pinnacle for the band and a crossroads for popular music, or at the very least a turning point for recording and publishing of music.

You can see it now, today: top-grossing musicians are making money not from selling studio albums but rather from live performances, massive national and global tours in sold-out arenas. In 1995, when *A Live One* was released, Phish was reaching an apex in their live performances and national tours. The band played 125 shows in 1994, for Christ's sake!

And we have this album, this tiny collection, as a bridge for this global transition. Some say it's Phish's answer to the Grateful Dead's *Live/Dead* album. I say it's a primer for anyone just discovering this incredible band. This is where you start. Some 20 years later, these still rank as some of the best performances of these songs.

Peaking at No. 18 on the Billboard charts, the album would go gold on November 10, 1995, just four months after its release. The album would go platinum two years later, in 1997.

Twenty years later, in October 2017, the album was released for the first time on vinyl in a limited-edition four-LP set.

To this day, *A Live One* is Phish's bestselling album and their only album to go platinum. You know, if you're into that sort of thing.

54 Deer Creek, Alpine Valley, Great Woods: The Great Barns of America

There's something to be said about seeing your favorite band in a small, bijou club—the intimacy of being close to the stage, the exclusivity of being one of just a few thousand in the room, the energy of a modest group of dedicated fans…

But there's also a case for seeing Phish in a massive, sprawling lawn or one of the great "barns" across America. Great Woods, Deer Creek, Alpine Valley… for decades, Phish has developed a storied relationship with these amphitheaters.

And frankly, I don't care what company bought the rights to name these venues. These historic barns will forever be known as Great Woods and Alpine.

Alpine Valley Music Theatre in East Troy, Wisconsin, has hosted the biggest rock bands in history: The Rolling Stones, the Grateful Dead, Metallica, and Pearl Jam, for example. Phish has performed there 17 times, including some legendary performances (see 8/9/97, 8/1/98, 7/24/99, and 6/26/04).

It is also the site where, sadly, guitarist Stevie Ray Vaughan and four others died in a helicopter crash after a performance on August 27, 1990.

The venue was built in 1977 and features a wooden roof (the "barn") that covers the 7,500-seat pavilion, and the sprawling lawn of the venue accommodates an additional 29,500 concertgoers; believe me, this place is massive.

And while some fans are vehemently opposed to lawn seats at these venues (SPAC as well), there's something to be said about seeing Phish at Alpine surrounded by tens and tens of thousands of fans and feeling the sensation of being in an open, grassy field with the vast midwestern sky above you, at once both part of something larger than yourself while feeling still quite small.

But, sadly, it seems those days are gone. Alpine Valley closed for the 2017 summer concert season, what would've been its 40th year. Live Nation purchased the venue in 1999, but now the amphitheater and its 198-acre property are currently for sale with an asking price of $8.4 million.

Deer Creek in Noblesville, Indiana, (once Verizon Wireless Music Center, then the Klipsch Music Center, now the Ruoff Home Mortgage Music Center) is located about 30 miles northeast of Indianapolis. It opened in 1989 and holds a little more than 6,000 in the barn and 18,000 on the lawn.

Phish has played Deer Creek 23 times, many of which are notable performances (see 7/24/99, 7/11/00, and 6/19/09). One such performance (8/8/96), featuring an incredibly unusual second-set "Mike's Song" > "Lifeboy" > "Weekapaug Groove" -> "Somewhere Over the Rainbow," during which McConnell plays the theremin, was later released as *Live Phish Vol.12*.

And Phish has paired gigs at both Deer Creek and Alpine Valley at least seven times in their touring career. The drive between them, about 300 miles, is one that most Phish fans can speak to. Personally, I've been stuck in Chicago traffic on that ride many times and once, somewhere in Indiana, ran out of gas and just barely, luckily rolled on fumes into a gas station.

And as for Great Woods? Well, first, Great Woods is the Tweeter Center is the Comcast Center is the Xfinity Center. About an hour southeast of Boston, Great Woods offers a similar experience for the East Coast. After expansion and renovations in 1994, Great Woods would be able to accommodate 19,000 fans.

Over the years, Great Woods has hosted bands including Aerosmith, The Allman Brothers Band, The Who, James Taylor, and the Eagles, to name a few. And Phish has played there 17 times since 1992, notably once performing a complete Gamehendge saga (7/8/94), another time opening with "Foreplay/Long Time" (7/12/99), a 310-show bust-out, and, most recently in 2016: while performing "Wolfman's Brother" early in the second set (7/8/16) the venue's PA speaker system cut out and ultimately the band just left the stage. They returned to complete the set but the sound system was only half powered, leading to the most gentle, delicate "Slave to the Traffic Light" I've ever heard.

It's moments like that (what my friend Luke would call "a once-in-a-lifetime experience"), standing just outside the shed at Great Woods with 19,000 fans collectively silent, holding their breath so we could all hear the band play solely through stage speakers, that Phish truly transcends the massive arenas and amphitheaters their fan base has grown to push them to play.

55 Couch Tour

The first live Phish webcast occurred in 1997 at the World Music Theatre in Tinley Park, Illinois, on August 8, 1997. A year later, Phish would webcast their Halloween 1998 show. But the first major webcast was Vegas 2000 (September 30, 2000). Phish was about to take their hiatus and broadcast the show through Yahoo.

"The webcast was free," Scott Bernstein of JamBase says of the Vegas 2000 livestream. "Anyone who went to music.yahoo.com could access it. And Trey used the opportunity, he said, basically told everyone, 'We'll be back, this isn't the end.'"

It would be another 10 years, until Phish New Year's Eve 2010, for the band to host and sell their own Phish webcast. And for the summer 2017 tour, Phish webcast every one of the 21 shows and offered the final night at Dick's (September 3, 2017) and Dayton's Nutter Center show (July 18, 2017) for free.

Watching these webcasts in the comfort of your own home, instead of hitting the road and touring with the band, has come to be known as "Couch Tour" among fans. I think most people, myself included, would agree that Couch Tour is a welcome, fun experience. "I'm content to watch all three Dick's shows live as they happen," Bernstein says of Couch Tour. "And I'm psyched for that experience. Perhaps not as psyched as someone who's going, but I'm pretty damn psyched. And it's cool that I still get to experience that even though I'm not going to Colorado."

"Watching from the comfort of your home..." (Andy Sinboy)

In some respects it's like cooking dinner versus dining out. And at least this way you can watch the setlist unfold in real time—no spoilers the next day!

And that's the whole gist of it, isn't it? You're still able to enjoy the show in real time even if you can't make the trip to the venue. Phish isn't shutting out anyone, to some degree. Oh, and they're getting your $26.99 for a two-show webcast, in standard definition. HD costs more, of course.

A company called Nugs.tv has revolutionized the live streaming concert industry, providing high-quality webcasts and live music downloads from acts including Phish, Pearl Jam, and Bruce Springsteen, to name a few.

However, since Phish started working with Nugs.tv it seems a lot of fan-uploaded live Phish YouTube videos have been removed and deleted due to copyright claims. A November 2016 article on LiveForLiveMusic.com seems to make a case that this is a direct result of Nugs.tv partnering with Quello Concerts to stream live shows across multiple devices.

"Eighteen months ago every webcast show was up on YouTube and now they're clearing house," Scott Bernstein says. "I'm hoping the idea there is that they're going to launch their own video repository where you can watch all these webcasts. What's the use of taking down the 2011 Alpharetta show that the band webcast if there's not a way to access it otherwise?"

An archive of Phish live show videos? Not a bad idea; not a bad idea at all…

Jump cut to March 23, 2020: A global pandemic has shut down most of the world and we're all sitting at home with nothing to do and nowhere to go. And Phish makes an announcement: "Tomorrow night (and every Tuesday for a while), Phish proudly presents *Dinner And A Movie: An Archival Video Series*. We'll be airing a full show in its entirety for free beginning at 8:30 PM ET at webcast.livephish.com or Phish's Facebook page. First up is Phish's show from August 31, 2012, at Dick's Sporting Goods Park in Commerce City, Colorado."

And, naturally, each *Dinner and a Movie* (*DaaM*) webcast also included an accompanying recipe for fans to cook "together," sharing photos of their dishes online. Plus, on *DaaM* Tuesdays, all donations made via The WaterWheel Foundation would be given to "a non-profit doing important work right now." The first non-profit was WhyHunger.

Phish's *DaaM* archival video series webcast a show nearly every week for 40 weeks, from March 2020 through the end of the year. There's too many amazing shows in *DaaM* to mention all of them—Ep. 15: 5/1/89 Northampton, MA; or Ep. 27: a triple feature of Phish's Halloween costume sets from 2014, 1996, and 2018; or Ep. 36 and 37: Thanksgiving weekend celebration of the 25th anniversary of Phish's acclaimed two-day festival, The Clifford Ball—so be sure to check out the full list at www.phish.net/page/daam. And a quick search of "phish daam episode 27," for example, will get you to the videos.

But wait, there's more! Trey Anastasio performed an eight-week virtual residency of performances streamed for free from New York City's Beacon Theatre on Friday nights from October 9 through November 27, 2020.

"Traditionally, like, a lighthouse is a beacon," Anastasio says in one of the video trailers for The Beacon Jams. "And then my head blew up when I thought, I was like, 'Oh my god, that's exactly what this is,' but sonically. Everybody's lost at sea, they're out in the fog, and it's sort of calling everybody home. So the beacon jams, they're jams that are calling everybody back home. In the best way that we can: perfectly imperfect."

Playing with their backs to the theater seating made for a super interesting backdrop of lights across the floor and balconies, the first show (10/09/20) featured Anastasio with Russ Lawton, Tony

The Ninth Cube

In lieu of a live audience performance at MSG as planned (and rescheduled for April 2022), Phish performed a live webcast "from The Ninth Cube" on 12/31/21, as part of their *Dinner and a Movie* series. If you're looking for a literal description of the facility where they played, you won't find that here (see chapter 97). This is where we're exploring the lore and mythology of The Ninth Cube...beginning on the night we all met Kasvot Växt (10/31/18, see chapter 83).

First introduced in the Phishbill distributed that night, the band Kasvot Växt came together by way of a secret government experiment known only as "Niu Teningur," which translates from Icelandic as "Nine Cubes." The Phishbill reads, quoting a lone posting from a message board dedicated to Greenlandic research installations and translated via Google: "To anyone asking about 'Nine Cubes,' good luck. You will only get denials and great confusion." That night, as Phish performed Kasvot Växt's album, *í rokk*, nine illuminated squares moved about above the stage. And the band references the "Nine Cubes" in the Kasvot song "We Are Come To Outlive Our Brains."

Now, three years later, as part of Phish's Sci-Fi Soldier performance (10/31/21), the companion comic book features Page McConnell's Sci-Fi Soldier doppelganger stating: "Each Cube is a window to a possible reality. At any given moment, time can be frozen and nine possible realities can be viewed." Do the Nine Cubes offer a connection or pathway between the worlds of 1980s Scandinavian prog group, Sci-Fi Soldiers from the year 4680, the modern American band Phish, and...Gamehendge?

In a 2021 Year in Review special on SiriusXM Phish Radio, Trey Anastasio told Ari Fink, "The Ninth Cube was actually the Rhombus, it just bent in transport. It came from the future. All of this is gonna lead to that eventually. You're almost there. Were you paying attention to my "Harpua" story? (10/30/21, see chapter 77) The math theorem I was expounding on?"

Whether all of this is part of one epic, unfolding story that transcends time and space, with "messages from beyond" about doughnuts touching turtles and turtles touching doughnuts, you know, "the very stuff of the universe," we can only postulate. Who knows what secrets are left to be revealed? And how perhaps Icculus, the author of *The Helping Friendly Book*, may fit into all of this? Maybe we'll find the answers if we read Icculus? Maybe so, maybe not.

Markellis, Cyro Baptista, and Ray Paczkowski. Jeff Tanksi joined on piano for "Stash" and "The Inlaw Josie Wales."

The eight shows of The Beacon Jams are inarguably special and unique, featuring a number of debut songs, the full Trey Anastasio Band (TAB) lineup, and the Rescue Squad string section among others, an album release, accompanying video projects, and more. The fifth show of the residency featured a Ghosts of the Forest lineup and set with Phish drummer Jon Fishman and others.

The performances also took advantage of the livestreaming production in the Beacon Theatre, as the final show (11/27/20) opened with the debut of "Just a Touch" with Anastasio playing acoustic guitar accompanied by TAB vocalists in a stairwell before they made their way to the stage. The show then concluded with Trey walking through the lobby of the Beacon with dancers as he handed out facemasks to people while exiting the theater.

As part of the shows, Trey would read live comments posted by viewers on the Twitch livestream platform. And on the penultimate performance (11/20/2020) he read aloud: "Heather McDougal, a nurse in Maine" and then paused so he and the rest of the band could applaud her. He continued to read: "Thank you, this has gotten me through these weeks, you people keep killing it and I'll keep saving it." Reacting with joy, Trey and the band then improvised "Heather McDougal Song."

A short documentary about The Beacon Jams, *What Calls You Home*, features behind the scenes shots and interviews with Anastasio at the Beacon Theatre.

The Beacon Jams album, a compilation of 18 live tracks from the eight performances, clocks in at 145 minutes and was released in November 2022, on the second anniversary of the last performance in the residency.

And lastly, The Beacon Jams also included a short film, *43 Weeks Later*, directed and edited by Trey Kerr, that aired before the fourth show (10/30/22). The film spoofs *28 Days Later*, with TAB playing the opening theme of the film "In the House—In a Heartbeat" and shows Trey finally escaping from his midair platform from Phish's New Year's Eve 2019 show and making his way to the Beacon Theatre while referencing a number of Phish memes and jokes.

The Beacon Jams, *Dinner and a Movie*, and The Ninth Cube New Year's Eve show have all brought new meaning and depth to the expanding world of "Couch Tour." Of course, we would all prefer to attend live shows in person, but it's with a hat tip and a slow clap that we acknowledge and applaud Phish for continuing to deliver creative, heartfelt performances—be them live webcasts or archival videos—for their fans to enjoy from the safety and comfort of our homes.

56 Phish and Politics

Throughout the decades, Phish have proactively supported various nonprofits, encouraged voter registration and local political involvement, and even hosted fundraisers.

In fact, in 1995, Phish played a benefit show for Voters for Choice. The event's host, Gloria Steinem, introduced Phish, promising to the concertgoers that they would hear more new music in one night than ever before. And Phish delivered, debuting nearly a dozen songs, including "Theme from the Bottom" and "Free." They encored with "Gloria."

But perhaps no one in the Phish camp has so overtly supported a single politician as drummer Jon Fishman did during Phish's 2016 summer tour.

Jon Fishman has traditionally worn a dress to all of Phish's gigs. This dress is a muumuu, solid blue with a pattern of red circles or doughnuts. Needless to say, this pattern has come to be a motif for the band, adorning official and unofficial merchandise alike. Fishman's doughnuts pattern is now available on shirts and shoe-laces, hats and socks, hoodies and sweatbands. Short of the original Phish logo, with "Phish" written inside a fish blowing bubbles, the red doughnuts on blue is the most iconic Phish emblem.

This is why it's worth noting that Fishman, a fervent supporter of 2016 presidential candidate Senator Bernie Sanders, altered his iconic muumuu, replacing the red circles with red circular outlines of Bernie's unmistakable balding head and glasses. Fishman wore the so-called Bernie dress for all of Phish's summer 2016 tour. Furthermore, Fishman travelled across the country that summer speaking at rallies and performing at political benefits like "Get Out and Vote for Bernie" at Brooklyn's MP Hall featuring Kung Fu, Oteil Burbridge, and more.

In fact, Bernie Sanders, speaking at a rally in Portland, Maine, said, "Jon [Fishman] and Phish have made New England proud. They are one of the great bands, have been one of the great bands in this country."

And now, Fishman himself is a politician. In June 2017, Fishman, a resident of Lincolnville, Maine, was elected to a three-year seat on the Lincolnville Board of Selectmen. Now part of the small group of people who make up the executive branch of local government in Lincolnville, Fishman's first orders of action were to raise $25,000 for a new Wastewater Capital Reserve Account, as well as change harbor notices, both of which voters approved.

Of course, in addition to direct political involvement, there are active charity organizations surrounding the band, including Phish's WaterWheel Foundation, Phish.net's The Mockingbird Foundation, and the Mimi Fishman Foundation, all of which joined forces to host an online auction in the fall of 2016.

Another strong political connection within the Phish world is the band's relationship with the nonpartisan/nonprofit HeadCount.

HeadCount and Phish Collaborations

HeadCount's first benefit was also the first Mike Gordon/Russo Benevento show (June 7, 2004).

The 2004 HeadCount Summer Tour poster was the first poster ever licensed featuring both the Grateful Dead and Phish.

Trey Anastasio filmed a public service announcement for HeadCount with Dave Matthews in 2004 that aired on both TNT and TBS and then appeared in the HeadCount documentary *A Call to Action*.

Phish has welcomed HeadCount on Phish tour for every presidential election cycle since 2004.

Phish's charitable arm, WaterWheel, has awarded multiple grants to HeadCount.

HeadCount is a national voter registration organization, started by music fans for music fans. In the 13-plus years since HeadCount launched, they have registered nearly half a million people at more than 5,000 concerts.

From HeadCount's launch in 2004, Phish immediately embraced the nonprofit and invited HeadCount to set up voter registration tables and booths at shows. One of the cofounders of HeadCount, Andy Bernstein, believes Phish's continued support of HeadCount is a "position of great honor." Bernstein, who also was one of the original authors of *The Pharmer's Almanac*, adds, "Everything we know about grassroots marketing, we learned in the Phish parking lot."

Furthermore, HeadCount is an organization founded by jam band fans, catering specifically to the community of jam band fans. Bernstein estimates that of HeadCount's 20,000 volunteers, more than half are avid Phish fans, including this book's coauthor Jason Gershuny, one of the original team leaders in 2004.

57 Analog, Print Phish: *Doniac Schvice* and Beyond

The Internet has been an invaluable resource for Phish stats and news over the decades, growing in scale and scope in synchronicity with the band itself. As the Internet became ubiquitous, so too did the websites and resources for Phish setlists and more. But it wasn't always this way.

Early in Phish's career, they communicated with their fan base as most bands and celebrities did: through a snail-mail newsletter. Phish's official newsletter was called the *Doniac Schvice*, a typically Phish nonsensical title, though Fishman reportedly once answered fan mail asking what it meant and he wrote, "Doniac Schvice is the feeling you have when someone is chasing you and you have reached your locked door and you are panicked and cannot seem to get the correct key in the door." Take that for what it's worth.

Published and delivered from 1996 through 2000, the *Schvice* offered tour dates, band updates, and articles written by the band members themselves ("Mike's Corner"). It included full-color photos, answered fan mail questions, and, most importantly, offered an order form for tickets by mail.

Similarly to the Grateful Dead, offering their dedicated fans access to tickets through a newsletter mail-order before general sale has always set Phish apart from the pack.

These days, you can find at least on Phish-focused publication on lot.

The free, fan-produced *Surrender to the Flow* published its first issue in 1998. Look for them at shows! Across dozens of pages colorful artwork and articles cover Phish tour, history, reviews, and more, all of which are written by the fans themselves. Based in

Denver, Colorado, *Surrender to the Flow* welcomes contributions. Visit SurrenderToTheFlow.com for details.

A number of books have been written about Phish over the years, some sanctioned, some not so much. This book you're reading right now is an updated edition of an initial 2018 publication. Hopefully, you're enjoying it! And we're certainly not the first in this arena. *The Pharmer's Almanac*, initially published in 1995, attempted to capture and collect the deep well of Phish folklore, setlists, and history and printed updated editions through 2000.

Additionally, Phish.net and the Mockingbird Foundation published *The Phish Companion: A Guide to the Band and their Music* in 2000. Very much a comprehensive guide to the band and their music, this is the Phish encyclopedia. The third edition, published in 2016, is a 698-page hardcover tome of colorful photos, original illustrations, year-by-year histories, setlists, song histories, and more.

Next time you're at a show, be sure to seek out a copy of *Surrender to the Flow*. And every Phish fan should own a copy of *The Phish Companion*, though you may have to wait until the potential fourth edition, as 2016's is currently sold out.

The world of analog Phish content may have had its heyday in the 1990s, but it's still an important element of our contemporary, Internet-archived study and appreciation of Phish.

Hey, who doesn't love Phish books—am I right?

58 Choose a Side: Mike Side, Page Side

In theatre, we have stage right and stage left. In the theatre of Phish, we have Mike Side and Page Side. Mike Side, Right Side. Page Side, Rage Side.

And before all you musical theatre majors get fussy, yes, Mike Gordon positions himself stage left from the perspective of performing auteurs. Let that be noted.

But really, the language is nothing more than a position map for fans to find each other before a show or at setbreak. "I'm Mike Side, about 20 feet from the soundboard."

Although it's also a philosophy, is it not? To stay "right" or to "rage" at a show?

Though I wouldn't think too much of it. Or should you?

Maybe so, maybe not!

59 The Great Went (1997)

Phish's August 16 and 17, 1997, festival, The Great Went, in Limestone, Maine, was the sequel to The Clifford Ball festival the year prior. While The Great Went was not the first Phish festival, in many ways it was more profound. At the very least, it demonstrated that the first festival wasn't a total fluke.

The success of The Great Went proved that Phish was not just doing something unique with these festivals, but doing it successfully. They were actually pulling it off. According to Wikipedia, 75,000 people attended The Great Went.

The band kicked off the weekend of shows with a wink and a nudge, performing "Makisupa Policeman" promptly at the scheduled 4:20 PM start time. The second song performed at The Great Went, "Harpua," picked right up where the unfinished Clifford Ball "Harpua" left off, a full year later, the longest gap to reprise in Phish history.

After the first set of the weekend, the documentary *Bittersweet Motel* (chapter 42) captures Anastasio complaining to Jon Fishman about the "shitty" first set. Then, perhaps in response to their self-criticism, Phish delivered a second set for the ages, critically acclaimed for the band's fluid improvisation and transitions, including "The Wolfman's Brother" and a minimalist jam leading into "Slave to the Traffic Light," perhaps a nod to the traffic jam festival attendees slogged through leading to the Air Force base festival site, with some reports saying it stretched over 60 miles.

During "Julius," Anastasio tells the audience that they will "definitely play a third set and be right back with a lot more strange and weird music for you." He continues bantering, adding, "And don't forgot to go to the disco tonight."

The third set of August 16, 1997, opened with "Halley's Comet," which the band extended into a jam that segued into an exceptional "Cities," then transitioned into "Llama," followed by "Lawn Boy" and a stellar version of "Limb By Limb," and ending with "Funky Bitch." Phish encored with Mike Gordon's cute and sweet "Contact" followed by a cover of "The Loving Cup" to conclude the first day of the festival.

Or did it? After all, there was the disco to attend!

Throughout the day, attendees discovered copies of a random flyer promoting a "Disco" at 1:00 AM at a location to be determined, featuring MC Neoncellgap, Groomed Ink, DJ Lemore Lalip, and DJ Heavy P, the first two names being anagrams for Page McConnell and Mike Gordon. Sure enough, at 1:00 AM attendees were treated to a rare and strange "DJ set" from Phish, with each band member seated on the back of an 18-wheeler playing keyboards and synthesizers with some vocal jamming to conclude the days' festivities.

On Sunday morning, photographer Spencer Tunick invited volunteers to participate in one of his famous all-nude crowd photographs. Eleven hundred Phish fans showed up, completely naked, for the photo.

Also on Sunday, the Bangor Symphony Orchestra performed in the afternoon as a glider pilot flew above the audience performing aerial feats synchronized to the classical compositions performed by the orchestra.

Throughout the weekend, festival attendees were invited to paint various pieces of wood that were then assembled and attached to an art tower. The members of Phish contributed their own art pieces to the tower, painting their portions onstage during the second set of Sunday's show. With each band member taking turns, Page McConnell and Jon Fishman painted during "Down with Disease," while Mike Gordon and Trey Anastasio painted during "2001." During the Art Jam, the band passed their collaborative contribution to the Art Tower to the crowd, who carried it from person to person back to where it was added to the tower.

As published at Phish.net, each song of Sunday's six-song set (excluding "Pigpen" and "Art Jam") features an exceptional and noteworthy jam. But it is "Hood" that is perhaps the most magical

What's with the Name, Though?

It's commonly agreed that name of the The Great Went festival comes from the 1992 David Lynch film *Twin Peaks: Fire Walk with Me*. In the film, there is a scene referred to as the Pink Room scene, in which Jacques Renault, drunk, surrounded by inebriated, half-dressed women in a clublike environment, refers to himself as "The Great Went."

moment of The Great Went, as it produced the very first Glow Stick War (see chapter 61).

After a third set of music, featuring a standout "Scent of a Mule," among others, Phish returned to the stage to encore with "When the Circus Comes" and "Tweezer Reprise," during which the climactic burning of the Art Tower occurred, lit by a giant matchstick.

At the time—1997—the Burning Man festival, after being held for six years at the Black Rock desert, had 10,000 attendees. That night, in Limestone, Maine, at a Phish festival, a crowd of 75,000 people watched the art tower, engulfed in flames, glow brightly against the night sky.

60 *Billy Breathes* (1996)

When talking about *Billy Breathes,* I think it's safe to say this is one of Phish's most poppy, accessible albums. But the album cover art—a weird, black-and-white, fisheye photograph of bassist Mike Gordon's big face? Who thought *that* was a good idea?

Well, Trey Anastasio detailed the artwork decision, or lack thereof, in a 1997 interview in *Sno Magazine*, a publication of the American Skiing Company. "We've kind of had a bad habit of reacting [laughs] when I look back at our albums more than our concerts. I see them all as a reaction against the one before! Like, I really thought *Hoist* was a good album, but I didn't like the cover. I felt it wasn't us. We had hired this graphic designer, which is what bands do. [The design] always rubbed me the wrong way. So we finished *Billy Breathes* and our manager kept saying, "What are you going to do about the cover?" So, finally, it was the *last* day, and it was, like, three in the morning. They [management] said, "We *need* a cover tomorrow." You know all those pictures on the back? We cut them out and stuck them on with scotch tape. Mike [was] on the cover [because] he just shot a picture of himself. The whole thing took, like, five minutes! It's funny, because in retrospect, it was a reaction to the (album) before it."

Phish lyricist Tom Marshall would go on the record in a 2007 *Relix* magazine interview, detailing his opinions of the album's cover. "Trey's frustration with almost every studio album in different ways, like the need to sabotage the album in a way, I'm not sure if this is his analysis a lot later looking back or if it was immediate but, like, that picture of Mike on *Billy Breathes*, he thought just ruined it, ruined the whole album. You pick it up and say, "What the fuck is that?" It doesn't belong there."

Marshall continues: "There was a musical peak right around the time; they were getting huge, they were at Bearsville [Studio] with this amazing producer and everyone was smiling the whole time. You're right. If I'm looking back, it should have been the big album and they shouldn't have put that picture on the front."

But enough about the artwork; what about the music?

Richard Gehr writes in his review of *Billy Breathes* in *Rolling Stone*: "Phish take a well-deserved breather, so to speak, on *Billy Breathes*, shedding much of the sophisticated trickery that has been their musical trademark. *Billy Breathes*, the group's first studio release in two years, is a quiet gem of an album, and it confirms that guitarist Trey Anastasio, drummer Jon Fishman, bassist Mike Gordon, and keyboard player Page McConnell are much more than a jam band from Burlington, Vermont, with a swelling fan base. As rustic as the New England countryside, *Billy Breathes* is a warm declaration of optimism packaged in concise, radio-attractive songs."

The first track, "Free," would go on to be Phish's most successful single, peaking at No. 11 on Billboard's Rock Chart.

Prince "Magna" Caspian

"Prince Caspian," named for the C.S. Lewis children's fantasy novel in the *Chronicles of Narnia* series, has been played prolifically over the years, at one out of every 12 Phish shows since its debut, according to Phish.net. However, this oft-performed song has never much thrilled Phish fans. That is, until recently.

During the second set of August 22, 2015, at Phish's Magnaball Festival in New York, the band kicked off "Tweezer" and the jam that ensued is one for the record books. But then the band made a sharp left, segueing into "Prince Caspian," but oh, man, were we pleasantly surprised by this epic jam performance!

Now heralded as "The Tweezpian," coined by Kevin Shapiro on the following day's *From the Archives* radio show, this performance is not just one of the best performances of the song but perhaps one of Phish's best performances of late! 20 years later, Prince Caspian had finally proved himself.

Phish's sixth studio album, *Billy Breathes* would peak at No. 7 on the Billboard 200 in November 1996 behind albums by Kenny G, Celine Dion, Counting Crows, Korn, No Doubt, and Alanis Morissette. The album was certified gold by RIAA in January 1999.

Produced by Steve Lillywhite and Phish, the album was recorded and mixed at Bearsville Studios, just outside of Woodstock, across five months in early 1996.

Lillywhite, who had never listened to Phish before joining on the *Billy Breathes* sessions, once said in a 2011 MusicRadar interview: "The band can play anything, which then raises the question: Well, what should they play? With *Billy Breathes*, it's the closest they got to making what I would say is a good stoner album. You know what I mean: you put on the CD, you fire up a big one, and you just go down that road. There hadn't been a good stoner record since *Dark Side of the Moon*. *Billy Breathes* got close."

We're lulled by gentle, sincere ballads like "Waste" and "Talk." Songs like "Cars Trucks Buses" and "Train Song" have an innate motion and rhythm to them that feels classic and timeless.

The title track swoops and sweeps across the air as Anastasio and crew harmonize on the single-line repeating chorus, "Softly sing sweet songs…." An emotive, yet restrained guitar solo ups the level of this otherwise pop-rock ballad.

"Theme from the Bottom" has proven itself to be a strong jam vehicle over the years, with Chris Kuroda, Phish's lighting director, deftly interpreting the aquatic bottom-feeder themes. And over the years, "Free" has proved to deliver standout performances.

"Character Zero" remains to be a fine first-set closer to get the crowd singing along, but nothing more.

"Swept Away" is more of a one-minute feeling than a song. It's a sensation. "Steep" also has an ethereal quality, bubbling and boiling away.

And the final track, "Prince Caspian," brings swagger-rock power chords paired with strange, unsettling lyrics for a fresh sound as the album's caboose.

Billy Breathes, clocking in at 47 minutes over 13 tracks, is kind of the perfect "stoner album." It's gentle and strange and has a movement and bounce all its own. The songs can be both background music and, at some live shows, epic jam vehicles. This is 1996 Phish: composed, yet poised for liftoff.

61 "Fight" in a Glow Stick War

Glow stick wars are one of the most unusual aspects of a Phish show. Increasingly less frequent in our post-single-use-plastic world, this is when the crowd, unprovoked except for what the band is playing, nearly simultaneously begins to throw glow sticks into the air.

Stay Safe and Safe for the Environment

These days, only the thin, skinny glow sticks are acceptable at Phish shows. Those thick tubes? Those have been shamed out of the scene. At a show, a flying tube glow stick hits like heavy battery!

And glow sticks, which are just plastic and chemicals, aren't great for the environment, so Phish asked fans not to bring them to their Riviera Maya shows on the beach. Can't fault 'em for that!

There are certain songs Phish plays that lend themselves well to a glow stick war; "Harry Hood," "YEM," and "David Bowie" are just a few.

One infamous glow stick war, critically agreed to be the first ever, occurred during The Great Went "Harry Hood" on August 17, 1997. At the six-minute mark, as the band transitioned into the improvisational part of the song, Trey Anastasio spoke into the microphone to Chris Kuroda, lighting director: "So, uh, Chris? If you wanna kill the lights, we could just look at the moon and the sculpture." The crowd roared, but no one anticipated what would happen next.

At first, a few dozen glow sticks flew through the air. Fans threw orange and green and blue glow sticks up, creating great streaks of light in the dark sky. Then dozens more, then hundreds, and as the band picked up tempo, more and more glow sticks arched across the sky as the crowd roar swelled in awe and excitement. The first glow stick war was also perhaps the most prolific, as 75,000 fans tossed and exchanged glow sticks for the 10-minute "Harry Hood" jam in Limestone, Maine, which at the time, was the largest city in the Pine Tree State.

This milestone in Phish history, The Great Went Glow Stick War, would set a precedent for future Phish shows, and without context, glow stick wars today seem to be a given—practically a certainty. But let's not forget that this experience had not occurred before August 17, 1997, showcasing a truly unique relationship, a symbiosis between the band and the audience, a new experience for everyone.

Given the opportunity, with no stage lights, the crowd reacted by throwing glow sticks, thus the band reacted by playing along with the tempo of the "war" happening before them, only further encouraging the audience to continue, culminating in a wondrous, improvised, synchronized, once-in-a-lifetime, magical Phish moment.

As Phish concluded "Harry Hood" that night, Anastasio announced, "Okay, we're going to take another break! And then we're gonna play some more! So keep throwing those things up in the air because it looks amazing, you have no idea. Go get some more of those things!"

In an interview in the short documentary *Music* by Andrew Zuckerman, Anastasio says of The Great Went "Harry Hood" glow stick war, "It was a little, teeny, mini metaphor for how it often

A war at Dick's…spectral colors in the void. (Stephen Olker)

feels. We're playing, we're listening, we're watching…and then we're reacting."

Today, glow stick wars occur at nearly every Phish show at varying magnitudes. But really, that's up to you! Bring glow sticks to Phish shows! Throw them, ideally with a gentle arch, at your favorite moments. Throw them during transitions in songs like "YEM," "Bowie," "Hood." Throw them when you're excited! Hell, you don't even have to bring your own if you make a point to collect the thrown and fallen ones from the ground around you.

Really, glow stick wars are one of the most magical things that happen at Phish shows. Other bands, other fans, just don't really have a prescribed way to participate or interact with each other. The glow stick wars were born from exactly that: fans wanting to participate in the show. Sure, Bruce Springsteen fans bring signs to request songs. But that's still putting the onus on the band.

A glow stick war is a pure, unadulterated fan contribution with no expectation put upon the band. This is just one way the fans can give back, returning and sharing some of that energy. And when it's done right, it's absolutely beautiful.

62 The Story of the Ghost (1998)

The Story of the Ghost was recorded in a unique fashion, though not entirely unique to the band. As keyboardist Page McConnell describes their recording process for the album in an October 1998 interview with David Byrne, "The book of lyrics [by Tom Marshall] we had was a couple hundred pages thick of just everything he's written for the last 10 years. And what would happen is, we would have these little bits of jams that we liked, and we would just pull one and say ok let's listen to this bit, and someone would be looking through the book and say oh this could go over that, and we'd get up to the mic and we'd sing a version of it. And that happened for about four days, ya know, we probably came up with 15 or 20 things that were lyrics on top of this jam session stuff. And we didn't know we were recording our final vocals at the time but a lot of the time these actually were the vocals that were going on the album."

This was, of course, different from their recording practice they called "The Blob" from the *Billy Breathes* sessions and not quite like the extensive Oh Kee Pa Ceremonies of jamming from the band's early years. This was something altogether different.

The result?

An instant-classic album of 14 tracks totaling 50 minutes. Cohesive, collaborative, anything but cautious, *The Story of the Ghost*, whether you like the songs or not, exemplifies an incredible success of a four-person jam band: let's head into the studio and play.

This album, more than any other studio album, includes song credits for every band member on eight of the 14 tracks. Sure, some of the album's songs started as drafts by Anastasio, but even those jelled together over a series of four-day recorded jam sessions.

With a few sessions at Bearsville Studios and Dave O's Farmhouse in the spring of 1997, another session in the fall, and then further recording and mixing sessions in the spring of 1998, *The Story of the Ghost* was told.

Spooky and spacey, serene even at times, the overall sound is somewhat funky, but less funky than funk—that is to say, it's more jazz-funk than funky-funk. It's not just about the musical notes but what's between them as well—what's not played. To me, that's *The Story of the Ghost*.

The gentle chorus of "Wading in the Velvet Sea"? That "oohhhh oh ohhhhhh" over McConnell's tender organ? "Roggae"?

The Siket Disc

The Siket Disc, released in 1999, is effectively B-sides, excerpts of the *Ghost* session jams that didn't make it on the album. But wow—a stellar collection of jams there, too! It was mixed and mastered by Page McConnell, and named for prolific mixer/engineer and Phish studio engineer many times over John Siket.

These soft-hearted songs are damn fine songs. And as most critics will gladly elaborate on, Phish isn't exactly known for writing damn fine songs.

Of course, it's also the mega songs like "Ghost," "Moma Dance," and "Birds of a Feather" that make this album in regard to live performances. In fact, Phish couldn't wait to play some of these songs, and between sessions announced a short, four-show run dubbed the Island Tour hitting Providence, Rhode Island, and Uniondale, New York, where they premiered "Birds of a Feather," "Frankie Says," and "Shafty" at Nassau Coliseum (April 2, 1998).

Rumors are that after these now-fabled Island Tour shows, Phish was so energized and inspired that they returned to the studio and set forth on completing the album. *The Story of the Ghost* would drop seven months later as the first Phish album available simultaneously both in stores and digitally online.

The album's cover art is the work of contemporary American painter George Condo, born 1957. He has exhibited prolifically in prestigious museums and galleries around the world. And aside from Phish's album, he has produced album cover art for the acclaimed pianist Martha Argerich, composer Danny Elfman, and perhaps most notably, rapper/producer Kanye West.

Released on October 27, 1998, Phish's seventh studio album kis a rhythm-heavy collection of 14 tracks obviously influenced by their historic "cow-funk" jams of the now-seminal 1997 tours.

The Story of the Ghost peaked at No. 8 on the Billboard charts.

63 NYE 1996–1998

The late 1990s are considered by many to be peak Phish. And there's many ways to argue that case: NYE 1995, the 1997 Cow Funk era, and certainly Big Cypress 1999. But there are many other milestones in the late '90s, including three great New Year's Eve runs—one in Boston and two in New York City—that make this phase of Phish stand out.

1996 was a big year for Phish. They released the album *Billy Breathes* (see chapter 60) and toured extensively, with summer tours in the US and in Europe. This was followed by a 35-show fall tour that included a Halloween show at The Omni in Atlanta where Phish covered the Talking Heads album *Remain in Light* (see chapter 11). For New Year's Eve, Phish would divide a four-night run between Philadelphia and Boston with two shows each at the CoreStates Spectrum and the FleetCenter, respectively.

Boston in late December is damn cold. And that night, New Year's Eve 1996, the high was 21 degrees. Perhaps to try and warm folks up, the band opened with the high-octane "Axilia" > Frank Zappa's "Peaches en Regalia" > "Punch You in the Eye." We were off and running! What's more, Phish closed the first set with "Tweezer Reprise" after leaving it out the night before when they played "Tweezer." The second set featured 10 songs of seamless, high-energy music starting with "Chalk Dust Torture" and ending with "Character Zero." For the third set, Phish opened with "2001," which lead into a countdown and "Auld Land Syne." And here's where we get to something truly special.

Surely, many events, particularly New Year's Eve celebrations, feature a strike-of-midnight balloon drop. And Phish's New Year's Eve shows are no exception. But the balloon drop at the FleetCenter that night was, well, exceptional. Actually, it was record-breaking. And for those in attendance, it felt like the balloons would never stop falling. Tens of thousands of balloons fell from the ceiling that night, enough to break the record set by the Democratic National Convention's 65,000-balloon drop that summer in Chicago. And then the band segued into "Down with Disease," a band favorite to follow "Auld Lang Syne" (see chapter 50).

With no true gag or prank, beyond the balloons, the Phish from Vermont did have one more trick up their sleeve. Welcoming the Boston Community Choir to the stage, they covered Queen's epic, operatic ballad, perhaps one of the greatest songs of all time, "Bohemian Rhapsody." The band and the choir then continued with "Julius" and encored with a poignant, emotive "Amazing Grace."

In 1997, Phish would have another prolific year of touring Europe and the United States in the summer and then "destroying" America in the fall. In 1997, Phish played 81 shows, which, while monumental for any band, does not compare much to their early 1990s, with each year heralding more than 100 shows, including 141 in 1990. Thier 81 shows in 1997 would be the last truly prolific year, as years since have had 50 shows or fewer.

For their 1997 New Year's Eve run, Phish returned to New York's Madison Square Garden for three shows. Both December 29, 1997, and December 30, 1997, are exceptional in their own right, with incredible improvisation from all band members. The first night's show features an ever-precious five-song second set. And the second night, well, that show has it all: extensive jams, clever teases, a few covers (most notably "I'm Gonna Be [500 Miles]," sung by Tom Marshall), a massive bust-out ("Sneakin' Sally Through the Alley," after a gap of 920 shows), a "Harpua" narration (the Pentagram) and an extended, four-song encore. Reportedly, when Phish began the encore and were informed they would be fined if they played past midnight...well, they decided that was okay, and played well past midnight. But I digress!

On New Year's Eve 1997, Phish opened with "Emotional Rescue" by The Rolling Stones > "Ya Mar" followed by a bust-out of "My Sweet One." But it was the second set that really blew the roof off The Garden. Opening with a deeply rhythmic "Timber Ho!" the band then segued into a powerhouse version of "Mike's Song," followed by a slowly boiling "Piper" > typically somber "When the Circus Comes" -> frolicking "Roses Are Free," before closing with an absolutely epic 20-minute "Weekapaug Groove" featuring intense interplay between the members, awesome tension/release jams, and expansive solos. That 'Paug, y'all—wow!

For the third set, the band doubled down on "2001" > "Auld Lang Syne" as they had played the previous year, and then performed an incredible block of music with "Tweezer" > "Maze" > "Prince Caspian" > another Rolling Stones classic, "Loving Cup."

While there wasn't much of a gag or a gimmick to the show, besides another awesome balloon drop, there was a large, bubble-shaped screen on the ceiling wrapped around the scoreboard that featured projected animations of all manner, including visual references to the "Harpua" narration from the previous night.

That night Phish encored with "New York, New York," which they reportedly learned that day, and "Tweezer Reprise," to conclude the show, the New Year's Eve run, and a year that would be forever remembered as one of Phish's best.

Which brings us to 1998, another big year for Phish. The band toured Europe again and then hit the road for a month-long summer tour in the United States, where Phish debuted a new cover song at nearly every show, including "Terrapin Station" in Virginia Beach on the third anniversary of Jerry Garcia's death (see chapter 22). And a couple weeks later, Phish would host their third weekend festival, Lemonwheel, for 60,000 people (see chapter 67).

That year, they re-released *The White Tape* album and dropped *The Story of the Ghost*. In the fall, Phish played Farm Aid and The Bridge School Benefit concerts with Neil Young and Willie Nelson, and covered *Loaded* by The Velvet Underground on Halloween in Las Vegas, followed up with Pink Floyd's *The Dark Side of the Moon* just two nights later (see chapter 70).

To conclude the year, Phish once again chose Madison Square Garden. For New Year's Eve 1998 Phish chose to play all four nights of the run at the Garden, which was the first time Phish would play four consecutive nights at the storied venue and only the band's second time playing four consecutive nights at any venue.

On the first night of the run, attendees were welcomed with a stage decorated with grass, enormous flowers, and other sculptures. The first set featured a short mini set of acoustic songs and the second set featured onstage theatrics including dancers in glow-worm costumes. Notable jams include the second-set openers "Carini" > "Wolfman's Brother" and the band encored with "Been Caught Stealing" while bouncing on mini trampolines.

For the second night, Phish opened with "Rock and Roll," performed just two months earlier as part of their *Loaded* Halloween cover set, and the crowd went wild. The band then segued into "Funky Bitch," then "Punch You in the Eye." December 29, 1998, features a solid five-song, jam-heavy second set, most notably "2001" followed by a rare encore placement of "Divided Sky."

The third night of four featured a hard and fast opening with "Chalk Dust Torture," "Big Black Furry Creature from Mars," and "Wilson," and closed with noteworthy jamming on "Reba." Another five-song second set kicked off with a killer "Down with Disease" > "Piper," and for the encore the band debuted "Grind" with Tom Marshall on vocals, followed by a roaring, crowd-pleasing "Possum."

And then came the fourth and final night, New Year's Eve 1998. The band took the stage and over the PA we could hear... something. It's half-recognizable. Then the band launched into the song, led by Page McConnell. It's Prince's "1999." Perhaps no other song would have been more fitting. Dancers joined the band onstage and at one point, both Trey and Mike played while lying on their backs onstage. The moment is forever etched into Phish history, a highly lauded "I was there" experience that proved how talented and *au fait* this band truly is. It seems obvious in hindsight that Phish would open December 31, 1998, with Prince's "1999" but at the time, those first chords from McConnell sent electric shocks through each audience member, causing a craze in the crowd that surely made the Prince proud.

For the second set, Phish delivered a stellar "Ghost" and a must-hear "Tweezer" > "Cities." For the third set, Phish opened with "Runaway Jim" -> "Auld Lang Syne" -> "Simple." During "Runaway Jim" the previous stage dancers appeared in the crowd handing out glow rings for all, leading up to the pyrotechnics that accompanied the countdown and subsequent balloon drop. Phish followed "Simple" with a lengthy "Harry Hood," then "Tweezer Reprise" and "Llama," encoring with "While My Guitar Gently Weeps."

Quite frankly, I can't imagine a better 1998-into-1999 show. The band and fans had indeed partied like it was 1999 all night. And then it was! Phish was riding a wave, hurtling toward the New Year, with the new millennium on the horizon. After first gathering momentum with New Year's Eve 1995, this band was now barreling out of the 1990s into the 2000s at breakneck speed with an immeasurable potential. No one would be able to predict the incredible NYE 1999 spectacle that would come, but at this point one thing was clear: this band could not be stopped.

64 The Phish Song Cognition Theory

In Ed Levine's 2010 book *Pizza: A Slice of Heaven*, he interviewed Sam Sifton, the *New York Times* food editor. Sifton describes what he calls the "Pizza Cognition Theory."

Sifton says, "There is a theory of cognitive development that says children learn to identify things only in opposition to other things. Only the child who has learned what is not brown, the theory holds, can discern what is 'brown.'

"Pizza naturally throws this theory into a tailspin. The first slice of pizza a child sees and tastes (and somehow appreciates on something more than a childlike, *mmmgoood*, thanks-mom level), becomes, for him, pizza. He relegates all subsequent slices, if they are different in some manner from that first triangle of dough and cheese and tomato and oil and herbs and spices, to a status that we can characterize as not pizza."

In short, your first encounter with something defines how you identify with that thing in your heart and mind.

"The first slice of pizza a child sees and tastes...becomes, for him, pizza. You cannot teach a child what pizza is, this explanation of pizza cognition asserts, by providing him with oppositional ingredients or styles. The love of pizza simply doesn't work that way. Invariably, if a child's first slice of pizza comes from a deep-dish Chicago pie or is a slick, chewy pillow of Sicilian or half-hour-guaranteed-delivery cardboard Frisbee or a frozen French-bread travesty, semolina-dusted 'Creole' or sweet pineapple and plastic ham 'Hawaiian' pie, then, well, that is pizza to him. He will defend this interpretation to the end of his life."

I would like to propose a theory for Phish based on Sifton's claim. While the first slice of pizza a child enjoys defines all other slices, the same can be said for Phish fans and their favorite songs or type of songs.

We can all agree that one's first Phish show is a special experience. No matter how many albums or live shows you may have heard, there is nothing that compares to that first live show. In many ways, you cannot teach someone what Phish is. (At best, we can only suggest 100 Things.) And like Sifton's pizza theory, I would propose that if someone's first Phish show is deep, dark, and funky, well, that's what Phish is to them. If that first show is loose, ambient, and spacey, that's their Phish.

Or perhaps this is best understood with regard to the 1.0, 2.0, and 3.0 eras. For those touring in the late 1990s, Phish may only be "cow-funk" Phish, and all other Phish is simply subpar. Whereas someone catching a bunch of 2.0 shows, well, Phish for them may be "Seven Below" and "Walls of the Cave." Our younger fans may absolutely yearn for "Fuego," while older fans will scoff it off. These youngsters are just victims to the Phish Cognition Theory: that first Phish will always be your true Phish.

Personally, if I had to choose just one favorite Phish song it would be "The Squirming Coil" from 1990's *Lawn Boy*. Now, I hadn't discovered the band until some years later and still wouldn't see Phish live until 1998. So this doesn't quite seem to prove my theory. Or does it?

Looking back at my first show, my first live Phish experience at The Gorge in 1998 (July 16, 1998), I was pleasantly surprised to discover that Phish had indeed opened with "The Squirming Coil." While I had no strong memory of this, it has clearly left an indelible mark on my psyche, and I still get chills every time I hear the band play "Coil."

And for those of you thinking, *They opened with Coil?* I hear ya.

Yes, traditionally the song closes a set or fills the encore slot. In fact, according to Phish.net, of the 368 times Phish has performed "The Squirming Coil," they have only opened a show with the song five times: once in 2010, twice in 1990, once in 1997, and once at The Gorge on that beautiful summer evening in June of 1998.

And it just so happens that "Coil" is not only my favorite Phish song, but also the very first Phish song I had heard preformed live.

Now, who wants a slice of pizza?

65 See Phish at The Gorge

There isn't a doubt in my mind that The Gorge is the best amphitheater and best concert venue in the USA. Nothing else compares! Sure, Red Rocks is great, even awe-inspiring. But while Red Rocks is wholly unique and amazing, it lacks the grandeur and magnificence of The Gorge.

Just looking at size, The Gorge's capacity is 24,000, over double The Rocks' 10,000. (Note: You should also visit Red Rocks. See chapter 46.) Though some speculate Phish is banned once again from Red Rocks.

In any case, back to The Gorge! I'm not the only one who thinks so highly of The Gorge.

The amphitheatre is a nine-time winner of *Pollstar* magazine's award for Best Outdoor Music Venue and was voted as one of the Best Outdoor Concert Venues in America by ConcertBoom.com. Both *Business Insider* and *Fodor's* name The Gorge Best Outdoor Music Venue in the United States. *Rolling Stone* gave it third place on its best amphitheatre list, behind Red Rocks and Hollywood Bowl, but what do they know?

In fair George, Washington, where we set our scene, The Gorge Amphitheatre rests nestled in a curve of the Columbia River, about 150 miles east of Seattle and 130 miles west of Spokane.

The journey to The Gorge is mostly through desert. Eastern Washington State does not have the lush evergreens and wet climate that western Washington or Oregon have. The Cascade Mountain Range separates the two worlds, and east of those mountains you'll find an arid climate.

Upon arrival to The Gorge, you'll drive through fields and grass surrounded by lush vineyards—rows and rows of gnarled grapevines as far as you can see. The dry climate, with irrigation of course, has proved to be a mecca for winemakers outside of Sonoma and Napa counties in California. The Yakima Valley is home to dozens of wineries, with dozens more in nearby Walla-Walla Valley and the Tri-Cities area, all of which make up Washington Wine Country.

In fact, it was winemaking that birthed The Gorge Amphitheatre.

Back in the late 1970s, a Seattle-based neurosurgeon named Vincent Bryan II, along with his wife, Carol, set out to purchase land in Washington State where they could cultivate grapes. After a year of searching, they found and purchased a few hundred dusty, desolate acres near the town of George, Washington. What was once cattle grazing land and alfalfa crops the Bryans tilled into a bona fide vineyard, planting in 1980 and harvesting and fermenting their first grapes in 1982. They named their vineyard and winery Champs de Brionne.

Soon thereafter, the Bryans built their tasting room and were preparing for a grand opening. But they needed a marketing strategy. As close as they were to the I-90 artery, they were prohibited from billboard advertising because promoting alcohol along the freeway was illegal at the time.

And so, as local legend tells it, the Bryans and their colleagues were taking a hike one day around the "little gorge" on their property, and as Carol and their friends descended to the cliff edge overlooking the river, Vincent remained at the top gazing across the horizon, wondering how he would be able to bring customers to his grand opening party. It was then that he noticed he could still

The Gorge at George, Washington. "'Divided Sky,' the wind blows high!"
(Stephen Olker)

very clearly hear his wife and friends chatting at the bottom some 1,000 feet below. The bowl of their "little gorge" offered incredible acoustics. Eureka!

Building a modest wooden stage and sod terraces into the hillside, the Bryans suddenly had a music venue. This stage, in a natural bowl, on the edge of a cliff overlooking the Columbia River, hosted its first performance, a brass band from Wenatchee for a crowd of 1,000, to celebrate the vineyard's grand opening.

And the Bryans didn't stop there. For many years The Champs de Brionne Summer Music Theater hosted many local and national acts, only growing in renown and recognition until 1993 when they sold the entire operation, excluding the surrounding vineyards.

The winery, Champs de Brionne, was shuttered, as was its musical theater, and The Gorge Amphitheatre was born.

Bands and musicians who have performed at The Gorge include Black Sabbath, Rod Stewart, Dave Matthews Band, and Pearl Jam, to name a few. And The Gorge has hosted numerous festivals over the years, such as Ozzfest, Lollapalooza, Sasquatch Festival, and the H.O.R.D.E. Festival.

Phish has played The Gorge 22 times since their premiere there in August 1997.

My first Phish show, as a teenager, was also my first show at The Gorge, and I think back on that day often. For those of you who have seen Phish at The Gorge, I'm sure you can relate, and likely often reminisce as well. It's a special place.

For those of you who have yet to experience The Gorge...let's imagine, shall we?

You enter the gates, and they scan your ticket, give your pockets a pat, and send you on your way down this asphalt roadway alongside a man-made pond reflecting the last of the afternoon light, those 30 minutes between day and dusk. All the concertgoers who entered with you look radiant and peaceful, some walking briskly with toothy grins, others hand in hand and one step at a time up this road that inclines steeply. When you reach the summit, all that is real or true or beautiful in this world is presented before you like an oil painting, so detailed and full of life that it seems almost more accurate than the landscape it depicts.

Under the ever-reaching bright blue sky is a rolling, thickly grassed hill that tiers into stone steps toward the bottom before the floor facing the stage that stands on the edge of a massive gorge, at the bottom of which is a shimmering cool blue ribbon that is the Columbia River. And that, dear reader, is a shameful illustration, albeit the best I can do.

Describing The Gorge is like describing heaven. Everyone's heaven looks just a little different. And my heaven isn't your heaven. But I do know this: The Gorge, hidden among the vineyards and canyons of Eastern Washington, is undoubtedly the best music venue in this country. And I strongly recommend you catch a show there. Actually, I insist.

Enjoying a show at The Gorge, hanging in the lawn, your bare feet on the grass with the band playing below as a golden sun sets behind them and a cool breeze caresses your face…there's just nothing better.

I remember once seeing Phish at The Gorge, and as they moved out of a jam, the sunset behind the canyon lit the sky bright pink and all the musicians but drummer Jon Fishman stopped playing and he drummed a slow, gentle drum roll as the sun disappeared and the pink sky darkened to navy. Then the rest of the band joined back in without missing a beat. And the crowd went wild.

Phish had performed a drumroll for the sunset.

Let me tell you, seeing Phish at The Gorge is something special.

66 Score a Miracle Ticket

Go to a show without a ticket.

Admittedly, this is a new and increasingly difficult challenge since Phish made the shift to completely digital tickets. I hate it. The community element of IRL ticket exchange will never be the same. And don't even get me started on the loss of original ticket artwork. Phish Tickets By Mail (PTBM), the presale ticket lottery the band started in 1994, has produced beautiful, often mosaic ticket art. The Phish New Year's run 2003 in Miami is one of my favorites: an incredible quadriptych illustration of a beach scene

"Who's got my extra?" "Kickdown so I can get down?" "Looking for a miracle."
(Mike Force)

with an elderly surfer and a *Miami Vice* scene bookended with the sun and moon. Hell, the Baker's Dozen full, 13-ticket PTBM package featured tickets designed as doughnuts—which came in a pink doughnut box! But I digress.

This is about miracle tickets. And, sure, it was easier to find a last-minute ticket on lot when we had physical, paper tickets. But it's not impossible! Keep the faith.

Arrive to the venue early and meander through Shakedown or the parking lot tailgaters and keep your hand held up high, with your index finger extended high, high above your head. This hand signal indicates that you're looking for one ticket.

Generally speaking, these days Phish tickets cost between $60 and $100 and often resell on secondary markets for much more, though there is a serious dislike for scalpers within the Phish fan community (see chapter 87). And so, if you were to find a fan in the lot before a show with "an extra" ticket, he or she would likely sell to you for the original cost of the ticket, or "face," the price listed on the face of the ticket.

And if you can afford it, make the deal. Buy the ticket, take the ride! You're "in the door," as they say. Buying a face-value ticket in the lot of a Phish show is far from rare. Friends bail, someone got sick and can't make it, who knows. But, generally, tickets are available. Excluding some highly anticipated holiday shows (namely New Year's Eve and Halloween), you should be able to find your ticket in the parking lot.

But a miracle ticket is something different. To be miracled is to be given a ticket to the show for free. And this exchange is perhaps one of the most unique aspects of the economy and community of Phish.

Pioneered by Grateful Dead fans who were often traveling show to show and living dollar to dollar, miracle tickets were their only way into the show. Perhaps first christened by the song "I Need a Miracle" on the Grateful Dead's 1978 album *Shakedown*

Street, it's not uncommon to see that text scrawled in black marker on a dogeared piece of cardboard held high by a hopeful fan.

You could make a simple sign for yourself, but a finger high in the air works just as well in my opinion.

But who would buy a $100 concert ticket and then gift it to a stranger in the parking lot? True fans, that's who. Fans who know it will come back to them, potentially quite literally as a ticket when they need one, or maybe in another way.

I've both given and received miracle tickets and long after the joyful hugs and high fives and applause from witnesses passing by, that special feeling stays with you. It's a kindness; it's a special generosity. And it shines. You can see it on people walking through lot.

It's a kindness that needs to be shared and engaged and continued, and ultimately I think that's why it still happens. I think that's why people still give miracles: it's special and wholly unique to this tribe of kind people. And people want to keep it going, and pay it forward, and genuinely help each other share this incredible music and wholly unique experience.

Maybe this chapter should be titled "Give a Miracle" instead? I'll let you decide.

67 Lemonwheel

Returning to Loring Air Force Base in Limestone, Maine, for the second year in a row, Phish hosted Lemonwheel, their third weekend music festival, on August 15 and 16, 1998. More than 60,000 fans attended.

Over the weekend, Phish played seven sets on the main stage, while several other bands played on a side stage, including Gordon Stone Trio, Miracle Orchestra, Manic Mule, and Keller Williams.

The concert grounds, shaped like a figure-eight, featured a Ferris wheel, an elephant (sculpture), circus performers, several beer gardens, a ceremonial pool with a lemon tree, a percussion stage, large-scale installations, a stone garden, and The Garden of Infinite Pleasantries, to name a few prominent elements.

Phish's hour-long sound check on Friday night at 11:00 PM was broadcast live on "The Badger," the official Lemonwheel radio station, 88.9 FM.

Saturday's show featured 30 songs across three sets and an encore, including notable performances of "Divided Sky," "Gumbo," "Tweezer," "Limb By Limb," and "Loving Cup." The highlight for most fans and critics may be that second-set "Gumbo" -> "Sanity" > "Tweezer." And if not, perhaps the "David Bowie" with a trippy, extended intro.

Also that night, Phish played "Cities" as part of expansive "Mike's Groove" and Trey Anastasio changed the lyrics to reference the sheer size of the festival, singing, "Build a city, build myself a city to live in," which is exactly what they had done.

For the weekend, Phish's Lemonwheel Festival was the largest city in Maine.

Throughout the day, attendees were invited at the crafts area to paint candles, all of which were gathered and organized onstage and used in lieu of stage lights for the band's fourth set on Saturday night. The hour-long "Ambient Jam," as it's now known, was lit only by candlelight and four propane-fueled flames in a stone pagoda at stage right. Some have compared the "Ambient Jam" to Brian Eno's soundscapes, a must-listen; headphones recommended.

On Sunday, Phish played another three-set show, including covers of Marvin Gaye's "Sexual Healing," "When the Circus Comes to Town" by Los Lobos, "Sabotage" by Beastie Boys,

"While My Guitar Gently Weeps" by The Beatles, and Argent's "Hold Your Head Up."

That day (August 16, 1998), Phish played four hours and forty-five minutes of music, including a notable encore of "Harry Hood" -> "Jam" during an elaborate fireworks show. But it didn't end there. Following the fireworks jam, the band lit a fuse that burned and raced all over the stage before burning off stage right and along the concert perimeter fencing until it came to a large mechanical puppet elephant. As fog or smoke rolled around the elephant's feet, a spotlight hit the animal and it raised its trunk spraying water into the air. Onstage, Fishman played the trombone to mimic elephant bellows. Cue more fireworks as Phish played a rendition of Henry Mancini's "Baby Elephant Walk" while stilt walkers and torchbearers led the elephant forward through the crowd and then out into the campsite as attendees followed.

Paul Robicheau wrote in *Rolling Stone*, "In its artistic scope and carnival-like unpredictability (the campground was a trip unto itself), Lemonwheel offered an unparalleled escape from the outside world, and a detour from today's cookie-cutter concert venues."

For the third time, Phish had successfully built a city full of infinite pleasantries for tens of thousands of dedicated fans.

68 One for $3, Two for $5, aka Shakedown Economics

143245.

In my earlier touring days as a student at Pratt Institute in Brooklyn, working as a barista, I didn't have a lot of money. So hitting the road with Phish tour, I made money selling beer and cigarettes on Shakedown Street.

Over the years, I've certainly glamorized the experience, telling and retelling stories to friends, but really, it's not a very exciting or creative activity. You buy the best beer you can at the least expensive price, and mark it up according to the supported market price of the beer on Shakedown Street. And then you hope people buy it and you hope you don't get in trouble.

Are there easier ways to make money? Perhaps. Are there more lucrative ways to make money on Shakedown? Yes, and likely more illicit as well. High risk yields high reward, ya know? You're probably not going to get in trouble for selling $1 grilled cheese sandwiches from a George Foreman grill on the trunk of your Honda Civic, but you're not going to make much money, either.

Here's the thing: everyone on lot, everyone on Shakedown, has money to spend. And while not everyone drinks beer and smokes cigarettes, I think it's safe to say those are the lowest common denominator. Most people do one or the other. And *most* people will pay $5 or $10 for cold beers or a fresh pack of smokes. In fact, in my experience, people will likely spend their last $5 or $10 on a pack of smokes or a few beers. And that's the real opportunity here.

Julia S., 38 years old, has been professionally vending on Shakedown since 2014, though she first started seeing Phish in 1998. "My first vending experience was at Big Cypress," she says, referring to Phish's 1999 NYE Festival in Florida. "We had happened on this bottled water sale on the way down and they were ringing up really cheap so we were getting, like, cases of water for 50 cents, so we bought a bunch of them and that got us gas money for the way home."

In those early days, Julia would tour and try to sell her original artwork and drawings on lot. She had always been interested in art, and often made art to relate to personal experiences. Living in Vermont, having grown up in New England, her exposure to Phish and Phish fan art only fueled her passion. "Through Deadhead friends I was familiar with the legacy of making bootleg T-shirts," she says. "And, ya know, vending food or beer on lot as a means of supporting yourself and just sort of having fun.

"Everybody has their personal history with the band and touring," she admits. "I had sort of done a bunch of it early on and then not for a really long time and then made the decision, 'Okay, I'm ready to go back and check out Phish again.' So in 2014, I found all the Facebook groups and starting making friends and actually met the man who's now my husband."

Her husband had spent years touring with Phish and The Dead and making his own merchandise to sell on lot. "We started going to shows together and he was already vending, so I just started

The Dark, the Dank, and the Dreamy—the street bazaar of Shakedown Street has it all! (Mike Force)

helping him set up," Julia says. "We did a bunch of shows in 2014 and then we did almost all the shows in 2015, and summer tour in 2016, vending most of the shows—not all of them, but most of them."

And, of course, the scene was much different than Julia remembered from the 1990s. "It was a lot less organized back then," she says. "I was just sort of floored coming back to it now and seeing all the new forms of creativity and also how it then becomes merchandise. Ya know, twenty years ago it was enough to get a T-shirt printed but now people have fabrics made and they make pins and they make all this stuff that you couldn't even have thought about getting done back then.

"We have T-shirts and pins and some hats, a disc golf imprint, a lot of our own merchandise that we make and sell and then we'll take on some merchandise that our friends make. And we always have beer," Julia says. "If you're just looking to make money, like, night to night, to supplement costs, I think beer is probably the easiest thing to sell. You just buy beer, and you sell it. You need coolers and ice and that's about it. A lot of people who sell random other things just sell beer too. Beer is probably the best thing to sell."

That's been my experience too: beer sells. It's a relatively easy, inexpensive setup, and most everyone on lot is interested in buying a beer or two. It's risky in regard to the police, but very much a sure bet otherwise. If you're smart about it, you can pay your way through tour. You just have to play by the rules. And Shakedown has its own, very particular set of rules.

Here's the thing: a cold bottle of Yuengling or Dale's Pale Ale on Shakedown costs $3; two bottles, $5. It's been this way since the 1990s. "One for $3, two for $5" is pretty much the gold standard for Shakedown. It doesn't matter if it's domestic bottles of beer or store-bought frozen chimichangas, that'll be "one for $3, two for $5."

Heady Topper

Some vendors have opted to sell nicer beers as a means to differentiate themselves and move away from the established price point. The idea here is that while someone wouldn't be able to sell swill domestic cans for more than $3 each, no one on lot would expect someone to sell two 20oz cans of rare, craft-brewed double IPA for just $5.

"I can sell 16oz craft beers for $5 and not have a problem," says Ginwright.

For Julia, it's precisely these types of locally crafted beers that she aims to sell. "If you want to talk about purely dollars," she says, "selling those super well-known, super high-end craft beers can actually be a really good racket. Heady Topper definitely funded our tour. Because that's the kind of thing that will sell immediately. And at $10 a can, that's really good money."

Heady Topper, an American Double/Imperial IPA brewed by The Alchemist in Stowe, Vermont, is only available in Vermont. And despite that, or in part because of it, this IPA has come to make a reputation for itself within the craft beer community.

"We're just lucky," Julia says. "Because it's got this sort of national mystique and you can only get it in the Northeast, and when you bring it somewhere else everybody's really, really excited for it. We brought it out to Bend, Oregon, for the start of 2015 tour, and for every one person who's like, 'What the fuck are you charging $10 a beer for?' there are five other people who are lining up to buy it, like, 'I've heard about it and wanna try it!'

But even in Vermont, it's not an easy score. Supply is limited and most stores sell out quickly.

"We spend a couple weeks before tour amassing a stock of beer," she says. "And we'll just sell all of it in the first two or three shows. If we go to lot with 10 or 15 cases, well, if you sell 15 cases of beer, that's $3,000 in two or three nights. And so then you're not stressing as much because you've got a cushion. It's always better to have a wad of money up-front because you can then keep investing it and buy some cheap beer to sell and make another couple hundred dollars a night.

"We have quite a few friends who will make trips up here, a couple hours, and come a couple times a week, just to take 10 cases of Heady Topper on tour with them. And it's not cheap, like $15 for a four-pack of cans. But if you break down the economics of it, transportation, hourly rate, ice, I can justify charging $10 per can."

Clearly, this is an exception to the one for $3, two for $5 rule. Julia is overtly targeting a specific consumer base of craft beer aficionados, moving away entirely from the range of gold standard beers and consequently taking herself out of the broader "beer economy." It's that outlier demand for something consumers can't have, paired with the higher cost of goods wholesale, that allows her to sell outside of The Golden Rule of Shakedown Street.

"Heady Topper has become lot currency," says Ben Ray Ginwright. "Those are $10 a can, ya know? No matter what. Even though they distribute more now and have a broader distribution area, they're still $10 a can. You can trade 'em for whatever, if you got 'em."

I mean, I think we'd all agree that buying or selling $10 cans of beer is a bit exceptional, just generally speaking, but if you really think about it, Julia S. is an importer/exporter. She is bringing a product to a region where it was previously unavailable. And she's successfully charging a premium for that imported product. That's Shakedown Economics!

Back in the day, even if someone was selling something for $3 or even $4 apiece, say, simple chicken tacos with salsa, if you hit them with a "two for $5?" question, they almost always acquiesced. Quoting this ratio, this rule, seemed like a secret code phrase at times, a hush-hush covenant between vendors and those in the know. Nine times out of ten, five bucks would get a pair of those chicken tacos with salsa.

"I was going to try and get a personalized license plate with the numbers 143245," says another vendor named Ben Ray Ginwright, 30. "With stickers, it's definitely one for $3, two for $5. With lighters, too. The sandwiches I make are one for $3, two for $5, beers are one for $3, two for $5."

But recently, things seem to be changing.

"One for $3, two for $5 is starting to get hard to stick with," says our vendor friend Julia. "I think people try to get a little bit more and then, ya know, if you need to drop the price, you do. But a lot of it depends on where you're at. Like, it's harder to get people to pay more for beer in the South, whereas, at SPAC [The Saratoga Performing Arts Center], people are used to paying more. I think a lot of it is showing up and trying to get what you can get, and then if you're not getting it you realize you just wanna sell it as opposed to not selling it. It also depends on what beer you're selling. If you're selling Budweiser, yeah, totally. If you're just selling your cheap water beer, that's fine.

"We all try to get on the same page," Julia says, speaking about the loose group of her neighboring lot vendors. "If we all decide that we're going to charge $4 for a beer instead of $3, then it's all okay. But inevitably somebody's like, 'Fuck it, I'm not selling any beer. I'm gonna charge $3.' And then everyone's gotta lower their price or people complain at you. That's lot economy."

Lot economy or price collusion, call it what you will. But it seems that pricing is still set by the demand—not exactly the *level* of demand, but a form of price collusion on the side of the consumers, effectively "complaining at you" or not buying until the weakest link breaks and one vendor caves and lowers her prices, forcing the other vendors to drop their prices, as well.

"Yeah, it's weird," our vendor Ginwright says. "Because if you look at the prices of different beers, you'll have Yuenglings two for $5 and you'll have Dale's Pale Ale two for $5. And you can get 12 Dale's Pale Ales for $20 and 12 Yuenglings for $12. So it's definitely a different price on the beer, but for some reason, you just can't raise the price on Dale's Pale Ale."

The truth is the laws of supply and demand are just as true on Shakedown as anywhere. But regardless, there is a ceiling for pricing. Phish fans will only pay so much, no matter how craft or delicious your beer or food.

Unless, of course, you're selling Heady Topper.

69 To Party or Not to Party

I'm guessing you picked up this book because you're a Phish fan. If you're not, perhaps you're merely curious about what some have called "America's Greatest Drug Band." Well, let me tell you this: it's not about the drugs, man. If you can't go to a Phish show sober and enjoy yourself, then you just don't get it.

Perhaps contributing to this stigma is the fact that Phish shows and the surrounding communities (whole cities that establish themselves at shows and festivals) are some of the last great truly free and welcoming places in this country. As such, Phish shows often provide an abundance of available drugs.

When I told my friend and writer Christopher Weingarten that we were writing *100 Things Phish Fans Should Know and Do Before They Die*, his comedic response was, "Are numbers one through ninety-nine simply, 'Acid?'"

No, Christopher. But speaking to that perspective, where the less familiar see Phish as a psychedelic party band, it's important to discuss the elephant in the room here.

Weed, alcohol, Molly, LSD, cocaine, mushrooms, nitrous oxide, DMT, ketamine, Xanax, and a multitude of pharmaceutical drugs can be found at Phish shows, particularly on Shakedown Street in the hours before a show.

Hey, Andy, I thought you said it's not about the drugs, man.

It's not, for most of us. However, some folks go to Phish shows only for the available drugs. And still some indulge moderately and cautiously and have a wonderful, fun experience. It's up to you how you choose to go to a Phish show. I can say confidently that most fans enjoy a few beers and a couple of joints at a show. Hell, recreational marijuana is as legal as alcohol in Washington and

"Don't eat the brown doughnuts!" (Andy Sinboy)

Colorado, perhaps adding to the popularity of Phish's Labor Day shows at Dick's these past years (see chapter 92).

But if you do choose to imbibe and perhaps experiment with drugs at a Phish show, please allow me to share some insight I've gained through my decades of going to Phish shows.

First, steer clear of powders. Quite frankly, there's just no way of knowing what it is you're taking. And I think we can all agree that taking unknown substances is a bad idea.

Similarly, buying drugs from strangers isn't a great idea, either. Hell, I wouldn't recommend buying a concert ticket on Craigslist, let alone psychedelics from a stranger.

But what if I want to trip at a Phish show? It seems like fun and a good place to do it!

Okay, fine. I get that. But experimenting with psychedelics should not be taken lightly. And perhaps a rock concert with 20,000 people is not an ideal environment for someone's first experience with psychedelic drugs. But hey, if you have a solid group of friends, or at least a wingman, and a good, reliable source, then buy the ticket and take the ride.

Just be aware that with many of these substances, there's no off switch, and coming down is a matter of time. Coffee does not help sober you up. And the most reckless, disgusting thing you can do is drive while under the influence or allow someone else to drive while intoxicated.

So I scored some trusted LSD, and the show is at 8:00 PM. When do I take it?

Okay, first, we must remind everyone that LSD is a Schedule I federal drug in the United States (along with marijuana, mushrooms, heroin, and ecstasy), and penalties for conviction of small, personal-use possession can include fines of tens of thousands of dollars and many years in prison.

That said, if the show is listed at 8:00 PM, Phish will usually take the stage a bit later, but not later than 8:30 PM. And a dose of

LSD can have lasting effects—say seven hours, sometimes longer. If you dose about an hour before the show starts, you can find your seats and otherwise get settled, and your trip will likely peak during the heavy jams in the second set. Furthermore, psilocybin mushrooms act more quickly and the effects are shorter, five hours or so, if you're debating the options.

What do I do after the show, if, ya know, I'm not quite ready to go home yet?

Most all Phish shows have their own, independent after-parties, often with live music. Or find a bar, tag along with some new friends, and enjoy the afterglow of your Phish show. Talking high-lights after the show is part and parcel of the experience.

So I shouldn't buy a balloon of nitrous oxide and huff it on the street?

No, dude. Stay away from hippie crack. The people who sell it, affectionately known as The Nitrous Mafia, are dangerous

The Phellowship

There's also a tremendous sobriety community at Phish shows. The group is called The Phellowship. While The Phellowship is an anonymous group who choose to remain drug and alcohol free, they are not affiliated with programs like Alcoholics Anonymous or Narcotics Anonymous. As stated by The Phellowship, "Our simple purpose is to provide 'phellowship,' support, and information to those who seek the comfort and camaraderie of other clean and sober people at shows. The only requirement for membership is a desire to stay substance-free at shows. Though The Phellowship consists primarily of those recovering from addiction, we are open to anyone who wishes to remain clean and sober at shows."

The Phellowship sets up a table inside the venue at most Phish shows. Just look for the yellow balloons! Often Phellowship members will wear yellow stickers, as well. And at most shows, The Phellowship will host a short meeting at setbreak for those who want to share their experiences.

people. And selling nitrous is serious, illegal business. The auditory hallucinations one experiences while huffing nitrous oxide, the "Wawawaawawaawawa" you hear in your head? That's your brain dying from lack of oxygen.

Also, it's expensive! At some shows, folks will be selling balloons for as much as $10 each! And I'm not talking ice-cold fatties; I'm talking shallow, half-full, potentially reused balloons. Yuck.

But if you insist on doing balloons, dammit, please sit down while you do it. I've seen too many people take too much and just keel right over. And that's kinda basic, you know? Like, don't fall down?

Please be safe and considerate of others, whatever your preferences may be. Take care of yourself and, dammit, take care of each other. Sharing your water with someone who could perhaps use a sip or two is probably the greatest act of kindness and camaraderie one can impart in a song break during a heavy, trippy set of jams.

Here's the thing: sometimes I party, sometimes I don't. And while the party is very much a part of the experience, once in a while we can all stand to be reminded that this whole thing, all of this, begins with the music. First and foremost, it's the music. Everything else is secondary.

With or without the substances, Phish is gonna melt your face off, man.

70 You Snooze, You Lose

In 1998, Phish kicked off their fall tour in Los Angeles followed by two nights in Las Vegas, including Halloween. For the fourth year since 1994 (skipping 1997), Phish performed in "musical costume" for the second set of their Halloween show, covering *Loaded* by The Velvet Underground (see chapter 11).

Needless to say, Phish's October 31, 1998, show is incredible, and beyond the Velvet Underground covers, includes some now-legendary jams, including the 30-minute "Wolfman's Brother" to open the third set. Still, some fans were disappointed when hopes were dashed for Phish to cover *The Dark Side of the Moon* by Pink Floyd.

That 1998 fall tour kicked off in California and would then move through the Midwest, with shows in Denver, Chicago, and Ohio, then the Carolinas, Virginia, New York, and three nights in Massachusetts to end the 22-show tour. And so most fans, if hitting the bulk of shows, starting from the beginning, may have opted to skip the out-of-the-way Utah show and head straight from Las Vegas to Denver.

For those touring with the band, the next day would be spent on the road, travelling 420 miles from Las Vegas to Phish's next stop in West Valley City, Utah. The six-hour drive takes one straight up I-15 through Fishlake National Forest and the arid landscape of Utah. Some lucky fans may have found themselves that night in Salt Lake City at The Dead Goat Saloon (now shuttered), a dive bar where Trey Anastasio and Mike Gordon performed as part of an open mic.

The following night, Monday, November 2, 1998, would go down in Phish history.

Reportedly, the show was very much undersold at the 12,000-seat E Center arena, now called The Maverick Center. But the show must go on!

Phish kicked off the show with a funky "Tube" and first-set highlights include "Jesus Just Left Chicago" and "Limb By Limb." For the second set, Phish returned to the stage and played four songs, including "You Enjoy Myself." Having performed more than two hours of music at this point, then they played "Harpua."

Anastasio's "Harpua" narration references Phish's previous performance in Las Vegas and tells the story of Jimmy, who "decides he's going to leave his house" with his cat, Poster Nutbag," and go to Las Vegas.

But when Jimmy gets to Las Vegas, "It's just too crazy, too many people, it's just too much for him," Anastasio narrates. "He

To Sphere or Not to Sphere

On November 30, 2023, Phish announced a four-night run at the brand new Las Vegas venue known simply as Sphere.

"From the moment we first heard about Sphere and its potential, we've been dreaming up ways to bring our show to this breathtaking canvas," said Phish guitarist and vocalist Trey Anastasio in a statement. "We're thrilled to present this completely unique experience to Phish fans."

Following U2's premier residency at Sphere, Phish will be only the second band to grace the stage at this 20,000-capacity, state-of-the-art venue. Equipped with a 16K-resolution wraparound LED screen and a spatial audio system of 1,600 speakers installed behind the LED panels and 300 mobile modules, Sphere offers what is undoubtedly the most high-tech concert experience in the world.

And maybe that's why the Phish ticket request was such a shit show. I think for the first time ever, Phish didn't even send out rejection emails. Rumors were that the system was completely overwhelmed with requests. Right now, the lowest listing for a four-night pass on StubHub is $2,400, or $600 per night when face value ranged from $108 to $180.

Some phans will pay hundreds of dollars per ticket. Some phans will travel to Sin City without tickets in the hopes that a finger in the air and a deep faith in community will produce a face-value ticket to what will surely be an incredible, visceral experience.

As I write this now we're about one month out from the April 18–21, 2024, shows. And many of us are still undecided: Should we stay or should we go? If we snooze, will we lose? Such is the promise, such is the curse. You could just live your life better or worse.

wants to see a concert when he's there, but it's hard to get tickets and all that stuff. And so he decides to hitch a ride with this guy who's going back to Salt Lake City. And he hitches a ride, it's like a seven-hour ride…and as they're driving this guy puts on this album and it's one of Jimmy's favorite albums. As he's driving along, ya know, it turns to night, and the sun goes down, and they get to do this beautiful long drive through the desert and as they're driving they listen to his beautiful music that they love so much…and it turns out to be an incredible drive, through the desert, listening…."

At this point, the band gently goes quiet, and rhythmic sounds come through the speakers, a heartbeat, a cash register…. On audience recordings of this show, you can hear the crowd begin to realize what's happening, applauding, roaring, and when the scream sounds, a scream that could only be the scream from "Speak to Me," the crowd goes absolutely wild and Phish launches into "Breathe." It was happening. Phish was covering Pink Floyd's seminal 1973 album *The Dark Side of the Moon*.

As detailed in Parke Puterbaugh's 2009 authorized biography of Phish, the initial idea to perform *Dark Side* came from road manager Brad Sands and crew member Eric Larson. Upon arriving to the E Center, they realized that only 3,200 people bought tickets to the show and approached Trey Anastasio with the news. As both a way to reward the loyal fans and perhaps punish those who skipped the show, Sands reportedly told Anastasio, "You've gotta hurt 'em! You've gotta get 'em good! I think it's time for *Dark Side!*"

And reportedly, with just 90 minutes before showtime, the band took a copy of the Pink Floyd album and rehearsed as best they could with the time they had.

The result of which is probably the best example of Phish surprising their audience and the biggest example of the "you snooze, you lose" aphorism.

And while this show was performed on a Monday night, I think it's fair to say the "never miss a Sunday show" adage applies here. Historically speaking, Phish's weekend runs follow a general route: Friday's for fun and hijinks, Saturday is rocking for the weekend warriors, and Sunday is reserved for the bust-outs and true rarities for the loyal fans. While some fans may opt to skip the Sunday show because of work on Monday or other obligations, Sunday shows are highly revered among die-hards and those who attend are often rewarded in one way or another.

That night in Utah, just a few thousand fans were treated to an unparalleled musical odyssey that could only be *Dark Side*, complete with Fishman scream-singing "The Great Gig in the Sky," the only song on the album previously played by Phish (July 5, 1994). McConnell and Anastasio each deliver incredible solos on "Money." Needless to say, the crowd just howls when Phish sings the album's title in the lyrics to "Brain Damage."

But Phish didn't stop there. After playing for more than three hours, Phish encored with Nirvana's "Smells Like Teen Spirit" for the first and only time in their career.

And while the Nirvana cover was perhaps not Phish's finest moment, the November 2, 1998, show, one of only seven shows Phish has played in Utah, will forever be remembered as the hidden gem of 1998, a reward for those few who made it and a regret for those who skipped it.

Never miss a Sunday show! Or, for that matter, a Monday show in Utah!

71 PTBM, Posters, and Lot Shirts

Artwork has always held a revered place in the Phish world. From limited-edition concert posters to original ticket artwork, T-shirts to hats, koozies to keychains, magnets to pins, Phish has produced a range of art and artistic products available for purchase at shows or online at Phish's Dry Goods shop. And some fans are as fanatical about the artwork as they are about the music.

Personally, I'm most impressed by Phish's ticket artwork. The Phish Tickets By Mail (PTBM) presale system is a rich tradition the band maintained for decades, going as far as to deliver round "doughnut" tickets for the Baker's Dozen residency. Designed by the Mingarro brothers at Brosmind Studios, each of the 13 BD tickets featured a unique doughnut design. And for the first time, even the Ticketmaster tickets had unique designs for each night.

Unfortunately, Phish went completely digital with ticketing in 2022. And the incredible, longstanding tradition of unique, often mosaic ticket artwork—a triptych of tickets for a three-night run, as example—had come to a close after 28 years. When you have some time, do an online image search of Phish PTBM and check out some of the beautiful and super creative artwork. One of my favorites is the 2003 New Year's Run in Miami.

Of course, there's plenty of more artwork and merchandise for tours these days than ever before. The original Phish logo has been imprinted on a vast variety of products. Commonly agreed to be designed by Trey Anastasio, the logo is the word Phish written inside a fish blowing bubbles with a rainbow gradient. For nearly 40 years, this image has served as the trademark insignia of the band.

Two of Phish's longstanding artistic collaborators include Jim Pollock and David Welker.

In the early days of Phish, visual artist Pollock created the artwork for Phish's flyers to advertise their shows. He also produced the cover art for Phish's album *Junta* (see chapter 15). And in 1995, Pollock started creating unique, limited-edition linoleum block-cut and silkscreened posters for many Phish shows. Furthermore, Pollock has designed Phish T-shirts and he is the artist behind many of Phish's beautiful mail-order tickets.

While Pollock has also created posters for other bands, such as Umphrey's McGee, Primus, Twiddle, and Greensky Bluegrass, as well as for festivals such as Bonnaroo and nonprofit organization HeadCount, his work, the unique look and feel of his prints, has

A fan showcasing his original poster artwork on Shakedown at Dick's in Colorado. (Stephen Olker)

Digital artist Jamie Lee Meyer showcasing her original posters at the PhanArt event in New York City during the Baker's Dozen. (Jason Gershuny)

become synonymous with Phish and the Phish brand. Pollock's posters for The Great Went, Phish's 1997 festival, were made on-site during the festival and limited to 100 copies. They will occasionally appear on eBay selling for thousands of dollars.

Recently, Pollock collaborated with Phish and Ben & Jerry's to create the official mascot and logo for the Baker's Dozen and corresponding release of the limited edition Freezer Reprise, including a limited-edition ice cream three-dimensional 4" pewter figurine of the logo. Pollack was also one of the eight artists to contribute limited edition posters to the Baker's Dozen residency.

In June 2016, Chicago's Galerie F held a retrospective of Pollack's work spanning 30 years and featuring more than 500 original works. And a documentary film, directed by Jay Patton, is in the works.

In fall 2017, Burlington's Flynn Center hosted an exhibition titled "Phish in the North Country," in part to celebrate the 20th anniversary of The WaterWheel Foundation. Working with Phish archivist Kevin Shapiro and WaterWheel, the Flynn Center showcased rare and early Phish concert posters and flyers, some of which were designed by the band members themselves.

Lot Shirts

Phish fans are a creative lot. Just strolling down Shakedown Street at a Phish show, you'll find original artwork ranging from illustrated posters to jewelry to wood carvings to clothing, all handmade, and most referencing the band and its music.

Phish lot shirts have been a staple of the community for decades—particularly spoof brand shirts that coyly reference Phish songs: the IBM logo redone to read *YEM*, the John Deere logo designed to reference "Run Like an Antelope," Heineken's logo reading "Hydrogen," or Tide rewritten as "Glide" are just some of the ubiquitous Phish lot T-shirt designs.

A fan showcases their original tie-dye T-shirt design on Shakedown Street.
(Malinda Fernandez)

New York City–based artist David Welker (b. 1964) is another prominent Phish collaborator, having designed a breadth of posters for the band, most recently as one of the eight Baker's Dozen artists. Welker also designed the album cover for *Rift*, featuring representations of all but one song on the concept album (see chapter 40).

But beyond Phish's official, sanctioned art, there is a sea of original, beautiful artwork. PhanArt.com, founded in 2004 by author/publisher and teacher Pete Mason, is an organization established to "preserve the legacy of the Phish community." Hosting exhibitions and events where independent artists can showcase and sell their original artwork, PhanArt.com has grown into a stalwart resource for the Phish artistic community.

Perhaps one of the most original aspects to this band is its visual identity, thoughtfully curated and consistently cutting edge. While most bands stop at T-shirts, Phish has always delivered incredible works of art in a variety of formats. And so do the fans!

Shout out to my Woo-hoo sticker dude with the Yoo-hoo chocolate drink logo redesigned to read "Woo-hoo." For so many shows of my youth, I would hear you saying "Woo hoo!" and then see you and grab a sticker. I even used you as a meet-up spot for friends on more than one occasion. ("Listen for the 'yoo hoo' and meet me there.")

72 Camp Oswego

Some shows are considered hot because of the band's ferocious playing, and others due to the sweltering heat outside, but it takes the rare combination of a smoking performance with blistering heat to elevate a show toward the top of the list of one of the hottest weekends in the history of Phish. Camp Oswego over the July 17–18 weekend of 1999 was just that hot.

Staged at the Oswego County Airport in Volney, New York, Oswego was the fourth of Phish's 10 legendary festivals. It originally was not advertised as a festival but in the end it still had the infrastructure and hijinks to make the cut. In Phish history it is an often overlooked festival, since Big Cypress was a mere five months later, but there are many aspects of this festival that make it unique in Phish lore.

One thing that made Oswego special was the nostalgic theme of attending summer camp. Summer camp is big business in the Northeast, and creating a camp theme gave many of the overgrown campers in attendance a chance to relive parts of their past. There were giant tree limbs adorned with enormous fake marshmallows sticking out of the ground, animal-themed mascots, campground areas named after different trees, canoes, log benches, and a variety of activities that riffed on other summer camp staples. It was a bit surprising that there wasn't a color war.

One of the more distinctive aspects of Oswego was the side stage, with bands such as Del McCoury Band, Ozomatli, Son Seals, and the Slip playing sets before Phish each day. Most Phish Festivals only feature Phish; this was more balanced than the other affairs. An added benefit from the side stage was that some of the musicians on the bill collaborated with Phish each night.

Musically, there were some hot moments well worth visiting. The July 17, 1999, "Tweezer" > "Have Mercy" pairing was special, especially since it was the first time the band played "Have Mercy" in five years. Seeing Son Seals play his classic "Funky Bitch" with Phish was amazing as well, as were the heavy hitters of the back end of the second set.

Another scorching day made the first set on Night 2 mellower than usual—although adding Del McCoury and his entire band for a four-song stint of bluegrass seemed really appropriate in the blistering afternoon heat. The second-set-opening, sunset-span-ning combo of "Runaway Jim" > "Free" was incredible. It seemed to be the moment when the shackles of the sun were lifted and the band and all the fans were really able to let loose. The "Meatstick" that followed included an attempt at breaking a Guinness group dancing world record. It was a good thought, but it was clear that most folks did not know or have the strength to do the dance.

The hottest musical point of the weekend came during the third set, when "Piper" launched into an all-time monstrous, fire-breathing version. This version was so good that the band used it as the basis for their studio version on *Farmhouse*.

After Trey shredded the fans' collective minds to pieces, the true Phish humor and magic took place. During a "Wilson" > "Catapult" > "Smoke on the Water" > "Icculus" combination, Trey worked in overlapping storytelling and goofiness, expos-ing that "Cat Scratch Fever" and "Smoke on the Water" are the same song, and sharing a hilarious "Icculus" lesson on the evils of TV and the benefits of reading books. This entire set is gold. Following this hilarity, "Quinn the Eskimo" seemed to be the closer, but the band was not done, and a gorgeous "Fluffhead" concluded the third set.

"Harry Hood" accompanied by fireworks capped off this incredible weekend and helped leave no doubt that these shows were hot no matter what type of thermometer you used to measure.

Phish on TV on Top of the Ed Sullivan Theater Marquee

Phish has appeared on national television in the United States and abroad many times over. What is perhaps their most memorable TV performance? Well, in 2004 Phish played atop the marquee at the Ed Sullivan Theater in midtown Manhattan, New York.

Of course, yes, The Beatles played an unannounced rooftop show atop their Apple Corps headquarters in London in 1969. And in 1987, U2 performed on the roof of a liquor store in Los Angeles to film their video for "Where the Streets Have No Name." Now Phish ranks among these bands for, well, yes, playing on a rooftop.

The show was announced just the day before, with a brief note from the band detailing the set time, set length, and best viewpoint: "on the far side of the street from the Ed Sullivan Theater." Thousands showed up, clogging the sidewalks on 53rd Street between 7th and 8th Avenues.

Touring and local fans alike would have just come off four New York shows. Phish played Keyspan Park (now MCU Park) in Coney Island, Brooklyn, on Wednesday (with Jay-Z sitting in) and Thursday, as well as Saturday and Sunday shows at Saratoga Performing Arts Center.

This marquee show was the cherry atop an already rich, indulgent run of New York shows before the tour headed west to Indiana and Wisconsin.

Phish's set included "Scents and Subtle Sounds" performed twice, with the first one airing on *The Late Show with David Letterman* that night, followed by "2001," "Wilson," "Chalk Dust Torture," "Tweezer," and "Tweezer Reprise." Of course, television viewers would only see that first "Scents," while the rest of the set was performed solely for the hundreds on-site, working New Yorkers and fans returning from Saratoga Springs.

Phish have played Letterman eight times: 1994, 1995, 1997, 1998, 2000, 2002, 2004 (marquee set), and 2014, the latter of which featured an extended set including eight songs, four from the album *Fuego*.

Here's the thing about Phish on late-night television: it's not great. They're just not suited for that format, that media cycle of releasing a new album, with a radio single, and performing said single on TV shows.

In his *Rolling Stone* review of the 2014 Letterman set, Jesse Jarnow wrote, "New albums and their attendant promotions have never been Phish's strong suit or their fans' main interest, but the lightly branded webcast was a winning compromise. Nearly each number uncoiled into efficient solos featuring Anastasio making atmospheric Echoplex loops, adjusting his custom guitar's tone and/or leaning his head back in giggling bliss."

Occasionally, they'll play to that audience, that format. In 1997, Phish debuted the song "Farmhouse" on *Late Night with Conan O'Brien*. It would be another three years before they released the song on the eponymous album. Afterward, as Conan threw it to commercial, Phish started up "Mike's Song," leading the viewing audience to wonder desperately if they had played the whole song for the studio audience. They hadn't, aborting it after about 30 seconds.

In 2000, Conan invited them back and Phish performed "Back on the Train." Conan reportedly went to see Phish on December 31, 1998, and when returning to the air she poke highly of the experience and what he called "the scene." Additionally, Conan's cue card guy is an avid fan, often the butt of jokes on air.

Also in 2000, Phish took the stage on *The Tonight Show* with Jay Leno in Burbank, California, and played a pedestrian version of "Twist" after Leno introduced them with a joke, saying, "Look at the time, ohhhh, I guess we're out of time.... No, no, no, my next guests are the great rock band from Vermont..."

More recently, Phish guested on *The Tonight Show Starring Jimmy Fallon*, performing "Waiting All Night" and "Fuego" in 2014 and "Breath and Burning" and "Blaze On" in 2016.

During ABC's 1999 New Year's Eve millennium broadcast, host Peter Jennings threw it to Phish, live at Big Cypress, for their performance of "Heavy Things." Prior to the live TV performance, Anastasio encouraged the audience to chant the word "Cheesecake" instead of applauding.

I mean, who doesn't like cheesecake?

74 *Farmhouse* (2000)

Farmhouse is Phish's eighth album release and, in some ways, was a metaphoric end-of-the-road time stamp on Phish 1.0. According to Wikipedia, *Farmhouse* was recorded in "The Barn" on Trey Anastasio's property in Vermont and was produced by Bryce Goggin and Anastasio. It was released on Elektra Records on May 16, 2000, and the majority of music was written and arranged by Trey Anastasio, with the lyrics written by Tom Marshall. Trey Anastasio Band collaborators Tony Markellis and Russ Lawton also have music writing credits, as does Scott Herman.

Phish welcomed a variety of guest musicians into the studio add their sound to the album to including Jerry Douglas (dobro), Bela Fleck (banjo), Dave Grippo (saxophone), James Harvey (trombone), Andy Moroz (trombone), Jennifer Hartswick (trumpet), John Dunlop (cello), Roy Feldman (viola), David Gusakov (violin), and Laura Markowitz (violin).

Farmhouse did achieve gold status in 2006 with 500,000 albums sold, and "First Tube" was nominated for a Grammy in the best rock instrumental category (but did not win). Metallica, Michael Kamen, and the San Francisco Symphony with "The Call of Ktulu" took home the Grammy that year.

Only five months after the album's release, Phish would break for their hiatus following their October 7, 2000, Shoreline Amphitheatre show (see chapter 75).

Interestingly enough, all of the songs included in the album had previously been introduced to the Phish faithful in concert before the album's release, and a few of the songs were debuted with Trey Anastasio's side project before being added to the Phish repertoire, which has become more and more common. There are many Phish concert staples that were included on the album, such

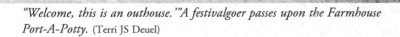

"Welcome, this is an outhouse."A festivalgoer passes upon the Farmhouse Port-A-Potty. (Terri JS Deuel)

as "Piper," "Sand," "First Tube" and "Heavy Things." Only two songs, "Sleep" and "The Inlaw Josie Wales," are not firmly embedded in the current song rotation.

A promotional video was released to radio stations to entice them to play the album, which described it as "Phish's sharpest songwriting and the most cohesive playing of their career." It also described the album as "more approachable for radio but retaining diverse flavors and rhythms of classic Phish material." Both of these are fair descriptions of *Farmhouse*, an album that represents a transitional moment in Phish's long history.

75 Breaking Up Is Hiatus to Do...

In Phish's 40-plus-year career—discounting the forced COVID break—the band stopped touring on two occasions: the two-year hiatus beginning in 2000 and the five-year breakup after the Coventry festival in 2004.

Phish's 2000 announcement was curt, to say the least. "Phish is currently on hiatus," the announcement read. And not much more was said.

Trey Anastasio took the opportunity to elaborate on the band's hiatus at Phish's September 30, 2000, Las Vegas show webcast, saying, "What we're planning on doing, so that you get the message clearly from us right here, is taking some time and writing some music and kind of getting our whole life back together before we return so that we can hopefully get another great seventeen years out of this."

As the *New York Times* reported in October 2000, "Phish has not broken up for good, the band's management says. But it is breaking up for a while…. No concerts are booked, no albums are scheduled, and band members plan to go their separate ways. 'The plan,' said the group's spokeswoman, 'is that there is no plan.'"

In the wake of Phish's 1999 Big Cypress performance, the band's manager, John Paluska, would add, "The reason for the hiatus was that everybody just hit an undefinable point of exhaustion at the same time and wanted to be with their families, especially after a year in which the band hit a new peak of popularity."

Jump cut to summer 2002. Nelly's "Hot in Herre" was the No. 1 single. The Los Angeles Lakers, led by Shaquille O'Neal, won their third straight NBA championship. And in early August, the remaining four members of the Grateful Dead reunited for a two-day festival at Alpine Valley Music Theatre for the first time since the death of Jerry Garcia.

Then, nearly two years after Phish last played together, and just 10 days after that hallowed Terrapin Station–Grateful Dead Family Reunion festival, Phish announced on Wednesday, August 14, 2002, that they were ending their hiatus.

After not playing for 26 months, Phish planned to return with a run of four shows: New Year's Eve 2002 at Madison Square Garden in New York City, followed by three shows at Hampton Coliseum in Hampton, Virginia.

The hiatus was over, and the Phish 2.0 era was scheduled to begin. Unfortunately, it wouldn't last.

Just 18 months later, Phish would play their final—definitively final—shows at a festival in Vermont. Of course, history would prove otherwise and Phish would reunite five years later, but at the time, Phish was most certainly over and done.

In a May 26, 2004, interview on PBS with Charlie Rose, Trey Anastasio sits against a black backdrop, wearing a black blazer, looking like he's pleading a case for the defense. Charlie Rose wastes no time and rattles off his introduction: "21 years, 1,100 live shows, and 11 studio albums later, the band has decided to call it quits…" he says, pausing for effect. "I'm pleased to welcome Trey to this table for the first time to talk about the Phish phenomenon and the fact that they have come to the decision to stop. Uh…can I get you to change your mind?"

And for the next 40 minutes, Rose and Anastasio discuss the band's decision to break up. And one thing we discover is that it wasn't a unanimous decision.

In a posted letter from May 24, 2004, Trey wrote, in part, "Last Friday night, I got together with Mike, Page, and Fish to talk openly about the strong feelings I've been having that Phish has run its course and that we should end it now while it's still on a high note. Once we started talking, it quickly became apparent that the other guys' feelings, while not all the same as mine, were similar in many ways—most importantly, that we all love and respect Phish and the Phish audience far too much to stand by and allow it to drag on beyond the point of vibrancy and health. We don't want to become caricatures of ourselves, or worse yet, a nostalgia act. By the end of the meeting, we realized that after almost 21 years together we were faced with the opportunity to graciously step away in unison, as a group, united in our friendship and our feelings of gratitude."

Just to be clear here, Mike said no.

But that was it; the decision seemed definitive. The announcement continued to outline the final run of shows, the last summer tour, culminating with a weekend festival in Coventry, Vermont.

Anastasio's letter continues, "For the sake of clarity, I should say that this is not like the hiatus, which was our last attempt to revitalize ourselves. We're done. It's been an amazing and incredible journey. We thank you all for the love and support that you've shown us."

In the Rose interview, Anastasio talks about how he desperately wants to pay respect to the audience, saying, "I started at 18 and now I'm 40 with two kids."

He later told *Rolling Stone,* "I'm sorry. I gotta do something new. I cannot spend my entire life going around the country playing 'You Enjoy Myself.'"

Keyboardist Page McConnell wrote and posted his own letter three days later, writing, "The pressures and schedule of this work can take its toll personally as well as creatively. As someone who has recently been through a divorce, I know how traumatic change can be. But, I also know that if you are able to let go of things and embrace change there is the potential for incredible personal (and creative) growth.

"If I sound unusually candid in this statement, I am able to do so because in my mind I've already moved on to the next phase of my life. This is a feeling I believe I share with Trey. I have a four-year-old daughter and there is nothing more important to me than being with her."

Family as a catalyst for the breakup was discussed in other interviews and articles as well, but soon other reasons and rumors surfaced, including excessive drug use, the burden of the Phish organization and payroll, the pressure of expectations from fans, and fears of devolving into a nostalgia act.

Phish's 1999 New Year's Eve Festival, Big Cypress, has often been referred to by band members as the peak of their career, and five years later, on the Charlie Rose show, Anastasio was saying it yet again. "Our millennium concert? For me it was the greatest, the pinnacle…and we looked at each other and it felt like the wave crashing into shore. We took the hiatus as an attempt to revitalize and we came back and it was different… not to say that it isn't good, but it was so good, it was so lucky, it just doesn't happen…."

And while many were saddened by the news, still some were skeptical. This couldn't be the end. To that effect, Anastasio said, "We're done. I haven't had any doubts about this. I've never been so sure about anything in my life. I know it."

That summer, 2004, Phish would play 12 more shows and a two-night festival in Coventry, Vermont (see chapter 86). Come Coventry, though, everyone knew, everyone believed, yes, this was the end of Phish. And at least for five years, it most certainly was.

In a world without Phish, a dark nothingness gripped the nation.

76 Setlists, Though: Bust-Outs, Rarities, and Debuts

Here's the thing: some Phish fans, perhaps most Phish fans, are geeks about the band's unique setlists and song histories. Many fans know exactly how many shows they've been to and what songs were played and when certain songs were last played and, in some circles, even how long said songs were jammed on. The ever-celebrated 20-minute mark is the hallmark of a good, or at least an interesting, jam. But I digress.

The only analogy I can make is baseball fans. Baseball is a game of statistics. Player statistics include stats like at-bats, RBIs, ERA, OBP, SOs, SBs, and CSs. Now, if you're a baseball fan you probably know what those acronyms mean.

Phish is also a game of statistics. And if you're a Phish fan, you'll know how long it's been since they last played "Harpua," and what songs they played in "Sunshine of Your Feeling," and how many shows they've played at Madison Square Garden and how many times they've played "Moonage Daydream."

This is all in addition to the folklore and mythology surrounding the band, as well as Anastasio's rock opera, Gamehendge, and all the characters that live there. We'll have none of that here; this is just the numbers.

And regarding numbers by the numbers, there's no place better to learn than Phish.net. And there's also David "ZZYZX" Steinberg's Phishtistics. Both sites allow you to generate your own personal Phish statistics by importing your show history. When was the last time you heard "Vultures"? Exactly how many times have you been "Zero"ed? You can find out!

Really, it's part of the fun. To love Phish is to count Phish. Sure, some have more of a penchant for studying stats than others. I tend to find that it's the ones who've been doing it longer, the ones who've been to more shows, who really get into it. And sometimes it's the ones who have been "chasing" certain songs.

Some fans heard a song once, or maybe only heard their favorite Phish song live one time, and go to every show hoping to hear that one song. And to say that doesn't contribute to the decision for people to hit many or all shows in a tour would be a lie. People chase songs for years.

And when Phish finally plays that song, that's called a bust-out. It's not inherently agreed upon within the fan base exactly how many gap shows since the last performance are required for the song to be truly considered a bust-out, though I would make the case for more than 50 shows.

During the Baker's Dozen residency (August 6, 2017), Phish played a cover of "Izabella" by Jimi Hendrix for the first time in 576 shows, since summer 1998 in Columbus, Ohio (July 31, 1998). This book's coauthor Jason was there, weeping joyfully as his baby daughter, Izabella, slept peacefully at home with her mother.

And I think it's worth noting that at the previous night's Baker's Dozen show, a small group of fans held a large pink sign with thick black lettering that read IZABELLA. Could they have been chasing that song for 19 years? Likely, yes. And hey, Phish delivered! The next night, that is.

Speaking of the Baker's Dozen, our friend Scott Bernstein, editorial director at JamBase.com, wrote a thoroughly impressive rundown titled "The Number Line: Phish Baker's Dozen Residency By The Numbers" that you just have to look up and read for yourself, but here's a taste:

237: Total number of different songs played by Phish during Baker's Dozen

176: Total number of originals played by Phish during Baker's Dozen

61: Total number of covers played by Phish during Baker's Dozen

In recent years, we've seen a few notable bust-outs: "Spock's Brain" made a return in Mexico (2/21/19) after 429 shows, "Glide II" at MSG (12/30/18) for the first time in 874 shows, "Guy Forget" at MSG (8/5/23) after 425 shows, the New Year's Eve 2022 medley, "Thunderhead" at Dick's (9/3/22) after 544

Setlist Notation
From Phish.net:

Sometimes in setlists, the difference between a > and a -> seems arbitrary or a matter of opinion. For this reason, we considered using only one type of segue notation to cover any instance where a song immediately follows another one, whether there is jamming in the transition or not. We decided to use two types of segue notations because, first, on many recordings (especially older, pre-1992 tapes), traders traditionally noted segues without distinguishing between the two types. However, differentiating fluid, improvisational transitions (the -> symbol), which are often among the highlights of a show, from routine transitions (the > symbol) gives fans a true feel for what was played, and ably communicates the significance of a transition.

shows, "Olivia's Pool" after 694 shows, and whatever else they played at Alpine Valley that night (7/14/19), and, of course, the most sought after bust-out of them all; Gamehendge (with a Harpua prelude) on 12/31/23, for the first time in nearly 30 years (see chapter 5).

The statistics go on and on. Do you know what state Phish has performed in the most? You may guess their home state of Vermont, but according to Steinberg, Vermont is second, having hosted 9 percent of all Phish shows. California comes in third with 7 percent, and New York takes gold with 15 percent.

However, Burlington does win when looking at cities, having hosted just 21 shows more than New York City.

As for top three most performed Phish songs as of January 2024?

"You Enjoy Myself:" 634
"Possum:" 568
"Mike's Song:" 547

And, yes, "Tweezer Reprise" is the No. 1 most-encored song. Would you want it any other way?

77 Jimmy, Poster Nutbag, and a Dog Named "Harpua"

"Omm pah pah, oom pah pah, oom pah pah, oom pah pahhhhhhhh-ahhhhhhhh…"

If you hear the band sing those a cappella lines, know you're in for a rare and special treat. This is the opening to "Harpua," a unique song to say the least. This song, which has never been recorded on a studio album, is a narrative journey, an improvised story about a boy named Jimmy and his cat, Poster Nutbag.

While Phish has played "Harpua" more than 80 times since its 1987 premiere, they've played it only six times in the Phish 3.0 era. As such, what was once a reliable staple at Phish shows has become a rare treat and highly sought-after performance.

With each "Harpua," Trey Anastasio narrates a new and unique story about our friend Jimmy, which often includes references to current events, recent shows, or their locations, and sets up classic cover songs the band then performs, all of which is part and parcel of the "Harpua" experience.

Recently, at the Baker's Dozen, Phish performed "Harpua" and, in a departure from the norm, read a scripted dialogue detailing how the universe is in fact a doughnut. In 2015, Phish delivered an epic encore at Dick's in Colorado (September 6, 2015) that kicked off with "Tweezer Reprise" and segued into "Harpua" with a narrative about Jimmy in Colorado listening to his favorite records (cue "After Midnight") and inhaling what he thought was oxygen ("NO2") to help battle the altitude sickness of the Rockies.

Over the years, "Harpua" has led Phish to play a variety of cover songs, including "War Pigs" by Black Sabbath (October 31, 1994), "I'm Gonna Be (500 Miles) by The Proclaimers (December 30, 1997), and Pink Floyd's album *The Dark Side of the Moon* in its entirety (November 2, 1998).

As part of almost all "Harpua" narratives, Jimmy's cat, Poster Nutbag, will meet his death. The subsequent "Harpua" dialogue onstage between Jimmy (Page McConnell) and his father (Mike Gordon) is pretty straightforward:

"Jimmy?"
"Yes, Dad?"
"Jimmy, I have bad news."

"What is it, Dad?"
"It's about your cat...Poster."
"Poster Nutbag?"
"Your cat died!"

"Poster is dead" (2x)
"Poster's so dead"
"How about a goldfish?"
"I don't want a goldfish (3x), I want a dog.... A dog..."

Famous and infamous performances of "Harpua" include the 1996 Las Vegas "Harpua" (December 6, 1996) with help from members of Primus, a pair of yodeling cowgirls, and four Elvis impersonators, as well as Chicago's 2013 "Harpua" (July 21, 2013) with members of local comedy troupe Second City.

Perhaps the most widely acclaimed, the "Pentagram Harupa," took place at Madison Square Garden in 1997, during which Anastasio bantered about the TV show *Lost in Space* and took us all on a journey into darkness from which we were saved by Tom Marshall's rendition of "I'm Gonna Be (500 Miles)" by The Proclaimers.

This author's favorite "Harpua" (July 29, 2003) took place in Burgettstown, Pennsylvania, during which Jon Fishman delivered a heartwarming interpretation of Elvin Bishop's "Fooled Around and Fell in Love."

Phish played "Harpua" in Las Vegas on the animal-themed night (10/30/21) and with the spoken narrative Trey correlated the previous number-themed show to the forthcoming Halloween show. Everything was connected! The math was deep. 4680. And so was the narrative improvisation.

As of January 2024, the most recent "Harpua" (12/31/23) was the launching point for one of the most monumental moments in Phish lore. As the Jimmy story began to unfold, we were shocked to learn that, indeed, this time we were going to hear "The real story of…Gamehendge."

At its core, "Harpua" is a love story between a young boy and his cat. It's a jukebox plotline, and Phish has a pocket of quarters ready to play anything. It's a bedtime story for all of us eager goddamn children, fawning over Uncle Anastasio.

Dare I say, "Harpua" is Phish at its most intimate?

Its performances are storied, its likelihood rare, and its potential limitless. And it continues…

Listen for that opening "Omm pah pah," and know, when you hear it, that you're now participating in an epic story, a story started in 1987, a story with a varied yet classic soundtrack, a story about a boy, his doomed cat, and a dog named "Harpua."

78 Guess the Opener and Gamble on Phish Setlists

There is a rite of passage, a badge of honor, a milestone in a Phish fan's life that is special and wholly unique. That is to correctly guess the song with which Phish will open.

Sure, there are a few songs in Phish's repertoire that are often first-set or second-set openers. But one of the reasons Phish is so great is that they can literally play anything and can and will open shows with rare, obscure covers, random a cappellas, or any one of their 300-plus original songs.

Case in point: the ice cream company Ben & Jerry's held a contest for fans who guessed the opening song of the first night of the Baker's Dozen. Reportedly more than 60,000 people entered their song guesses, and, of course, not one person correctly predicted that Phish would open with "Shake Your Coconuts," the 2003 pop song by Danish duo Junior Senior.

There have been a few times I've correctly called the opener. On couch tour: "The Curtain With" in Riviera Maya, Mexico (January 17, 2016) and "Mike's Song" in Alpharetta, Georgia (October 22, 2016). Once at a show with my dad at Wrigley Field (June 25, 2016), I whispered among our newfound friends on the field, "The Moma Dance." And when Phish opened with "Moma," our neighbors celebrated me with high fives and hugs and roars! My dad didn't really know what was going on and when I had told him I called the opener, his bewildered response was simply, "How?"

It's kind of like fishing—like, actual fishing. An experienced fisherman, someone who knows the water, knows where fish are likely to feed, knows what baits and lures work best, and is probably much more likely to catch fish than someone new to the sport or that body of water. And yet, there's still no guarantee the experienced fisherman will catch anything. The fish may elude him still. And similarly, Phish may elude us all with that obscure opening song.

Some fans take the guessing game to a whole new level in which participants will pick their choice not just for the opening song, but also the second-set opener, the encore, and a couple of "bust-out" songs that the band hasn't played in sometimes hundreds of shows. A popular contest in the Phish subgroup on Reddit asks fans to pick first- and second-set openers and closers as well as one wild-card song for each set, an encore song, and two "bonus categories" that are a bust-out and a cover song. All submissions are tracked and recorded across the entire tour, and the point system is complicated. Standard categories are worth three points each, cover songs are worth three points, bust-outs are worth five points, wild-cards are worth two points, and partial points are awarded for songs played in the alternate set that you guessed.

Of course, more casually, the subject of what song Phish will open with is a great icebreaker among fans and neighbors awaiting the band's performance. Many of us, myself included, greatly enjoy hypothesizing and discussing the many songs that could be played and what songs maybe would be played and also what songs we really want them to play.

One of the immense joys of Phish is their unpredictability. But occasionally, you can beat them at their own game. And truly, there's no greater feeling than hearing those first notes of the song you had hoped and guessed Phish would play.

79 *Round Room* (2002)

On August 14, 2002, Phish announced they would be returning from their two-year, four-month hiatus with a New Year's Eve show at Madison Square Garden in New York City followed by three shows in Hampton, Virginia. Phish was back.

The announcement also teased a new album, likely to be released in 2003.

But Phish didn't wait. Not two months after the announcement, the band hit the studio and laid down, through lengthy jam sessions during four days in October, what would become *Round Room*, Phish's ninth studio album.

Produced by Bryce Goggin, the album features 12 tracks totaling 77 minutes. With a highly anticipated winter minitour, the band announced a December 10, 2002, release date.

Round Room peaked at No. 46 on the Billboard charts. And for those first four shows returning from hiatus, Phish played two

Round Room songs each night, including encoring on the final Saturday night show with "Friday."

Rolling Stone's Tom Moon wrote in his album review, "There are five extended adventures on *Round Room,* and while they're each unique compositionally, all of them are compelling for the same reason: These guys are actually listening and responding to one another. Gone is the cruise-control comportment of their occasional bad gigs, their overreliance on a riveting groove. In its place is the collective pursuit of upheaval: After spending two years doing other things, playing music in un-Phishlike settings, the four musicians appear newly dedicated to changing the very temperature of their interactions."

Entertainment Weekly compared it to Phish's "concise songwriting" on *Farmhouse* and wrote, "*Round Room* feels informal, a chill-out session in a home studio."

Sure, it sounds rough around the edges, but maybe that's a good thing? Personally, I love hearing Trey Anastasio chuckle during "Friday." The small crowd roar at the beginning of "Mexican Cousin"? That's just great; it sounds like two people!

Phish appeared on TV twice before their official return to the stage on New Year's Eve 2002. "46 Days" was debuted live on their December 14, 2002, *Saturday Night Live* appearance, and "All of These Dreams" debuted five days later on the *Late Show with David Letterman.*

The live heavy hitters on the album include "46 Days," "Seven Below," and "Waves." Even "Walls of the Cave" has 11 Phish.net Jam Chart performances out of 72 performances. "Pebbles and Marbles" has only been performed 28 times since its premiere (January 3, 2003).

If anything, *Round Room* is a testament of Phish's 2.0 era, posthiatus but prebreakup. Here's a band returning from an extended nap with some fresh ideas and new energy. And hey, not all of it is great. But that's 2.0 for ya, no?

In so many ways, these 12 tracks—some live performances, some scripted takes, some developed out of studio jams—well, that's Phish through and through. Even Mike Gordon's two contributions, "Mock Song" and the title track, "Round Room," sound and feel like the Phish we know and love and missed in those hiatus years...with a little something different, too.

During Phish's hiatus, each band member embarked on his own journey: Anastasio recorded a solo album, Gordon recorded with guitarist Leo Kottke, Page McConnell recorded as a trio called Vida Blue, and Jon Fishman recorded with a group he called Pork Tornado (see chapter 31).

In an era of Phish that was decidedly uneasy and certainly uncertain, the band delivered an album that showcases their true and perhaps best self, if a bit uneven. *Round Room*, released four months after Phish's announced return and exactly three weeks before that first posthiatus concert, is an incredible triumph.

There isn't another band who could deliver a solid album on that schedule. And perhaps that missed context is what makes *Round Room* entirely underappreciated and overlooked.

Now, I'll be honest. "Thunderhead" is my least-favorite Phish song of all 300-plus in their catalog. I wish we could just take that one back.

But otherwise, *Round Room* is great!

Listening to "Waves" is like sitting in on a studio jam. And, really, for a Phish studio album, what's better than that?

80 Historic Guest Sit-Ins; From Jimmy Buffett to The Boss

Over the decades, Phish has welcomed a number of acclaimed musical artists to join them onstage, perhaps too many to mention. From Jay-Z to Bruce Springsteen, Kid Rock to the Merry Pranksters, Phish's esteemed guest list is enough to make any music fan blush.

In the early days, touring in support of Santana in the summer of 1992, both bands guested in each other's sets on Saturday, July 25, at the Stowe Performing Arts Center in Vermont. Four years later, in Lonigo, Italy, Phish would sit in at Santana's gig (July 2, 1996) and the next night in Trento, Italy, Carlos Santana and Karl Perazzo would sit in at Phish's gig.

Blues Traveler's John Popper joined Phish onstage about a dozen times in the 1990s, often playing harmonica during encore classics like "Good Times, Bad Times."

Both Bela Fleck and the late, great Col. Bruce Hampton guested with Phish four times each in that era, the latter perhaps most notably for a late-second-set jam featuring The Aquarium Rescue Unit, The Dude of Life, and Fishman playing the vacuum (May 5, 1993). The Aquarium Rescue Unit also guested with Phish for a few songs at a gig at Tipitina's in 1991.

Bob Weir, rhythm guitarist for the Grateful Dead, joined the band during the second set of their first night in Nashville, Tennessee (October 18, 2016). Together, they played a mix of Phish and Grateful Dead songs: "Samson and Delilah," "Twist" > "Miss You," "West L.A. Fadeaway" > "Playing in the Band." Weir also joined for the encore of Bob Dylan's "Quinn the Eskimo."

Bob Weir had once before guested with Phish, at Shoreline Amphitheatre almost exactly 16 years earlier (October 6, 2000), where he joined for an encore of "El Paso," "Chalk Dust Torture" > "West L.A. Fadeaway."

Grateful Dead bassist Phil Lesh sat in with Phish at Shoreline once in 1999 (September 17, 1999) after welcoming Trey Anastasio and Page McConnell as part of a Phil and Phriends show earlier that year. Ten years later, GD drummer Bill Kreutzmann joined Phish at Red Rocks (August 2, 2009) for the second set, including a stellar "2001."

In March 2018, The Grateful Dead's Bob Weir and Phil Lesh set out on a six-date spring tour that included two nights at NYC's Radio City Music Hall, where they welcomed Trey Anastasio to sit in for the second set of the second night. An emotional and joyful crowd was treated to "The Wheel," "Dark Star," "Eyes of the World," and "St. Stephen" before the band encored with "Ripple." (For more on the history of Phish and the Grateful Dead, see chapter 22.)

For the "welcome night" single-set show of Phish's 2020 Riviera Maya run in Mexico, the band welcomed Dave Matthews for a three-song encore of "So Damn Lucky" (debut), "The Maker" (1,001-show bust-out), and "Tweezer Reprise."

In 2023, Phish surprised fans with an end-of-summer, short-notice, two-night stint at the Saratoga Performing Arts Center (SPAC) as a flood-relief benefit that raised $3.5 million to support victims recovering from July's floods that devastated parts of Vermont and upstate New York. For the second set of the second night, Phish welcomed Derek Trucks—The Derek Trucks Band, 1999 inaugurated member of The Allman Brothers, and nephew of Allman Brother's founding drummer Butch Trucks—to perform fiery, dueling guitar versions of "Golden Age", "Everything's Right", "A Life Beyond The Dream", "First Tube", and "Possum" for the encore.

On perhaps the other end of the musical spectrum, Phish once welcomed Jay-Z to join for a couple songs at one of the band's

2004 Keyspan Park shows (June 18, 2004) at Coney Island. The Brooklyn-born rapper and percussionist Cyro Baptista joined Phish in the middle of the second set for "99 Problems" and "Big Pimpin'."

Jay-Z had released his highly acclaimed, incredibly successful *The Black Album* just six months prior. "They just reached out to me to do something," Jay-Z told *Rolling Stone* about the memorable night. "I always believe in just good music and bad music, and I want to try new things. I saw this as a great opportunity. I went out and had a great time, and I've never performed in Brooklyn like that. That was beautiful."

Over Phish's storied career, many, many musicians have sat in for a few songs to the delight of the audience. Even Mr. Margaritaville, Jimmy Buffett, once joined Phish onstage in Florida in 1995 for a performance of "Brown Eyed Girl."

At 1998's Farm Aid festival, Phish performed with Neil Young ("Down by the River," "Uncloudy Day," and "Amazing Grace") and later with Willie Nelson ("Moonlight in Vermont"). Phish even once welcomed Ken Kesey and the Merry Pranksters to jam at Darien Lake (August 14, 1997).

In 2003, B.B. King sat in with Phish in East Rutherford, New Jersey (February 24, 2003), and together they played "Every Day I Have the Blues," "The Thrill Is Gone," and "Rock Me Baby" to close out the first set.

Phish's Bonnaroo 2009 performance (June 14, 2009) included a first-set-closing triptych with The Boss himself, Bruce Springsteen, performing "Mustang Sally," "Bobby Jean" > "Glory Days."

Later that year, as part of Phish's Festival 8, soul singer Sharon Jones and members of the Dap-Kings joined Phish for their traditional Halloween "musical costume" cover of The Rolling Stones' *Exile on Main Street* (see chapter 90).

Phish has welcomed Les Claypool, Kenny Rogers, and even Kid Rock, the latter of whom performed "Walk This Way,"

"Rappers' Delight," and "You Shook Me All Night Long" in Las Vegas (September 29, 2000).

Once, award-winning actor Jim Carrey joined Phish during a private show at The Barn in Burlington, Vermont, during the production of his 2000 film *Me, Myself & Irene*. One can only imagine the atmosphere at that show. With Phish, you just never know what—or whom—you're gonna get!

81 NYE 2002–2003

Phish's 2.0 era is often overlooked in the annals of the band. Albeit short-lived, the band's 2.0 period, which spans December 31, 2002, through August 15, 2004 (63 shows total), does feature some memorable moments, including two New Year's Eve shows, the first of which kicked off the new era and heralded the band's triumphant return from their 26-month hiatus.

Phish announced their return with a one-off New Year's Eve show on a Tuesday night at Madison Square Garden, followed by a three-night run at The Mothership, Hampton Coliseum in Hampton, Virginia. While this reunion of shows wasn't exactly the kind you run home to tell Mom about, everyone can agree it was great to have The Phish from Vermont back onstage.

The band was clearly fired up, taking the stage and kicking off with a "Piper" that built into a fiery, staccato jam. After a few songs, the band paused as a clip played from the 2000 film *Castaway* starring Tom Hanks, whose character bonded with a volleyball he called "Wilson." Of course, Phish then played "Wilson," during which Trey Anastasio called Tom Hanks to the stage. Sure enough, there he was! Indeed, more than a few news outlets reported Tom Hanks' appearing onstage with Phish, but in truth it was Page McConnell's brother, who happens to look a bit like the Academy Award–winning actor.

Clearly, the band hadn't lost their sense of humor during the hiatus. Anastasio would beat this faux-intro joke to death in the following Hampton shows, "introducing" Tom Hanks again and then Al Gore the next night, though no one posed as the celebrities for those occasions.

After "Wilson," Phish busted out "Mound" for the first time since 1996. They also debuted a few songs, first "Waves" to open the second set and then "Seven Below" in the lead-up to the

A car descends upon the stage on NYE 2003 in Miami. (Marnie Morris)

New Year's countdown. During the performance, a large disco ball descended from the center of the arena and fake snow gently fell from the arena ceiling. White-clad "snow monster" dancers in masks joined the band onstage and made circles around them before descending into the crowd, where some donned stilts and continued to dance. At midnight, fireworks and explosions rang in the New Year and thousands of white balloons fell onto the crowd as the band played "Auld Lang Syne" > "Runaway Jim."

With bit of comic relief, a few new songs, some fiery jams (see also the debut, second-set closer "Walls of the Cave"), and a gentle, wintry gag, Phish was back, baby.

In 2003, Phish hit the road for a 12-show winter tour of the Northeast, followed by a 19-show summer tour with the IT festival (see chapter 82) and a four-night run to celebrate the band's 20th anniversary over Thanksgiving weekend.

Then, they hit Miami for a four-night New Year's Eve run at American Airlines Arena. The first night was pure fire: Opening with "David Bowie," the first set included "Tweezer" and "Tweezer Reprise" and an epically jammed "Frankie Says" and "Hold Your Head Up." And the second set's "Suzy Greenberg" -> "Jam" is must-hear 2.0 Phish.

And the rest of the run was no different. The second night's second set is solid and the band performed two encores that night, "Waste" then "The Squirming Coil." The third night, Phish opened with "Wilson" to honor the actor Earl Hindman, aka "Wilson" from *Home Improvement*, who had passed away earlier that day. The second set that night is an incredible, strange mix of music and jams, first summoning the spirit of the Lizard King, Jim Morrison (who was once famously arrested in Dade County, Miami), with an incredible, fun, and funky "Tube" -> "L.A. Woman" > "Birds of a Feather" > "L.A. Woman" -> which continued into "Makisupa Policeman" as Phish welcomed George Clinton and Parliament-Funkadelic onstage for a shared medley of such classics as "Give Up the Funk (Tear the Roof off the Sucker)," and "P. Funk (Wants to Get Funked Up)." Ladies and gentlemen, it was quite a show!

The following night, New Year's Eve, Wednesday, December 31, 2003, Phish once again opened with "Wilson" to complete the uncompleted song from the previous night. And Phish closed the first set with a killer "First Tube" > "Tube" to complete the previous night's abandoned > "L.A. Woman" version. Phish opened the second set with a well-jammed "Stash," then "Seven Below," perhaps nodding to NYE 2002.

With midnight approaching, Phish took the stage for the third set and debuted "Jungle Boogie," during which Jon Fishman's drum kit was moved to side stage to make room for a Mini Cooper car, lowered from the rafters. As Phish continued to play, the car doors opened and, one by one, the entire Miami Palmetto Senior High Band and Cheerleading Squad climbed out from the car to join in the jam and dance onstage. A countdown to midnight rang in the New Year as thousands of balloons dropped from the ceiling and Phish, with the marching band, played "Auld Lang Syne" > "Iron Man," a debut. The set continued with incredible nonstop music, most notably "Runaway Jim" > "Simple" then "Hold Your Head Up" with typical Fishman antics followed by a "Frankenstein" encore.

Needless to say, 2003's NYE run had some incredible, magical moments, coming in just a month after the band's celebrated 20th anniversary run. Of course, at the time, none of us had any clue that this would be Phish's last New Year's Eve show for six years.

82 It

After a nearly four-year festival hiatus, Phish returned in 2003 with It, a two-day festival at Loring Air Force Base in Limestone, Maine. This would be the band's third festival at this location, and PBS was on-site filming a documentary of the weekend.

The film *It*, directed by Mary Wharton, was released in October 2004 as a two-disc DVD. The first disc contains the full-length PBS documentary and the second disc contains a selection of complete live songs from the festival, totaling more than four hours of footage.

In an October 2004 review of the *It* DVD on JamBands.com, Benjy Eisen writes, "In addition to a stunning documentary with revealing interviews and beautiful production, the *It* DVD contains exciting and crystal-clear performance footage 150 minutes of classic Phish. Yes, I did just say 'classic Phish' to describe live versions from 2003."

According to Reuters/Billboard, *It* grossed about $8.25 million with 60,000 attendees. During that weekend, Limestone, Maine, was the largest city in the state.

And while *It* grossed double the amount previous Phish festivals did, including Clifford Ball in 1996 ($3.3 million), the Great Went in 1997 ($4.2 million), and Lemonwheel in 1998 ($4 million), it cost much more to produce. "We spent nearly twice as much as the last one we did in Maine five years ago," longtime Phish manager John Paluska told Reuters/Billboard.

To add more context, that summer's tour of 19 dates grossed nearly $14 million, averaging almost $740,000 per show. Phish's 2000 tour grossed $36 million from 54 shows, averaging $666,666 per show, according to Billboard Boxscore.

Airplane ground crew welcome festivalgoers at the gates to It in Limestone, Maine in 2003. (Brianna Leech)

But what sets It apart from other Phish shows or festivals, for that matter, is not the money spent or money earned. As always, it's the music, the jams.

Phish.net recounts It quite succinctly, highlighting the "Ya Mar" and "Birds of a Feather" from the first set. "Disease" and "Waves" are highlights of the second set, the latter a personal favorite jam moment. "Next, play the perfectly flowing fireball set three," reads Phish.net, referring to "Rock and Roll" > "Seven Below" > "Scents and Subtle Sounds" > "Seven Below" > "Spread It 'Round" > "Bug." Phish.net continues: "When you're ready, move on to the greatest 'Chalk Dust Torture' ever played," which was performed at nearly double tempo. "And the mesmerizing 30-minute "Ghost" from day two."

But the real gem of It was the first night's fourth set, performed at 2:30 AM. The "Tower Jam," as it's known, is an hour of heavy, ambient jamming from the band performing on top of the Air Force base's air traffic control tower. Lighting director Chris Kuroda controlled a spectrum of lights during the performance: lights atop the tower with the band and inside the control room of the tower, as well as exterior lights. Toward the end of the jam, aerialists suspended from ropes, performed synchronized dances against the vertical tower.

Of course, not everyone at It saw the Tower Jam. Traffic leading into the festival that morning was absolutely horrendous, and after a three-set show that night, many attendees had retired to their tents or simply passed out from exhaustion. Even still, some regret hearing what they thought was someone playing Phish from a car stereo and not venturing from their campsite.

Others could see a glowing purple tower in the distance and made their way closer for what would become one of Phish's most original moments.

And still others, perhaps some under the influence, thought it was a UFO, as Loring Air Force base had a history of encounters

Mike Says No

During the first set of the second day of It (August 3, 2003) Trey Anastasio mistakenly omitted a verse in the song "Wilson," which afterward prompted him to declare that performance the "shortest version ever," and dedicate it to Phish archivist Kevin Shapiro. Anastasio continued to banter and the audience began to chant a request for "Fluffhead! Fluffhead! Fluffhead!" Phish hadn't performed the song in nearly three years (September 29, 2000) since their return from hiatus. But Phish would yet again leave "Fluffhead" on the table as Anastasio responded, "Mike says no" as the rest of the band and audience laughed.

"Mike says no," has since come to appear on stickers, T-shirts, and memes throughout the years.

with unidentified flying objects over the years. And who knows? Maybe it was a UFO.

83 A Costume within a Costume: Kasvot Växt and Sci-Fi Soldier

Phish is known as a band that dons musical costumes on Halloween, but sometimes these pranksters feel the need to throw fans a curveball, and put a costume on top of their costume.

During Halloween of 2018 and 2021 at the MGM Grand in Las Vegas, Phish created imaginary bands with backstories, pasts and futures, and complete albums that push the envelope of creativity and deliver a deluge of new music.

On Halloween 2018 fans got their hands on the Halloween Phishbill, and found out the band was covering Kasvot Växt's *i Rokk* album. Fishman described the music as "a weird funky Norwegian dance album" by a forgotten yet impactful 1980s Scandinavian band.

In the couple hours between getting in the door and the lights going down, thousands of fans became self-deputized musical detectives. Who was Kasvot Växt?

There was some info in the Phishbill write up, and internet sleuths found corroborating websites on Kasvot's history. Even legendary radio station WFMU had an article backdated to 2005 to imbue authenticity. There were breadcrumbs of an existent yet flimsy online "paper trail" of mentions, but no music whatsoever.

The charade of Phish's imaginary Kasvot creation was convincing. Clues were there. The Phishbill started off with the line, "It is as if Kasvot Växt never existed." But a counterbalanced online presence, however scant, was enough to convince many that Kasvot was real. This was a masterclass in misdirection.

Halloween's first set had some of the spookier songs sprinkled within the set. "A Buried Alive" > "Ghost" opener was thematically apropos. This set was solid but nothing groundbreaking. The band was saving the theatrics for the second set.

As set two began, the band, the stage, and their instruments were draped in a bright white construct. Everyone wore bright white, the speaker monitors were white, the instruments were white, even Page's keys had some white faux fur to add to the Scandinavian vibe.

The connection of the venue aesthetic and the album became further illuminated during "Final Hurrah." Literal lyrics of "The shapes become unhinged" and "I am in a square, dangling in mid air", referenced giant illuminated squares that hung from the ceiling.

Faceplant into rock! On Halloween night 2018, Phish performed in musical costume covering an album by the fictitious Scandinavian 80s band Kasvot Växt titled í rokk. (Steph Port)

Lyrically and musically, the set was a fun mix of prog rock and funk that seemed to be pleasantly lost in translation. A few musical mainstays emerged from the show such as "Turtle in the Clouds," "We Are Come to Outlive Our Brains," and "Say it to Me S.A.N.T.O.S." The lyrics were strange; sometimes nonsensical and often barely coherent English. There was even some synchronized dancing from Mike and Trey during "Turtle in the Clouds."

The rest of the show had some fun moments, and a few musical call backs to some of the debuts. A big pairing of "Set Your Soul Free" > "Tweezer" opened the 3rd set. But nothing had that "must hear" value.

A couple of months later when Trey played a solo show in Boulder Colorado, he explained that the original muse behind the imaginary Kasvot album sprung from dancing drunk bridesmaids in Nashville while he was working on Ghosts of the Forest. Walking by honkey tonks he took notice of what music got people moving. Trey explains, "If it wasn't for drunken bridesmaids, there would have been no Kasvot Växt." Inspiration truly comes in many forms.

Phish had shown that they are willing to make up imaginary bands on Halloween, so all bets were off when they announced the 2021 Halloween run in Vegas, the first since Kasvot.

The excitement around a Halloween weekend is always elevated, and Phish even blew those lofty expectations out of the water, with the most complete four-night run in a decade. Some Phish runs add up to more than the sum of their parts. This particular run had all kinds of historically unique and thematic shows.

The first night (10/28/21) was the best show of the run. It was built around a mathematical theme, which seemed to come out of nowhere. The show opened with the dynamic cover duo pairing of "2001" into Prince's "1999," which blew the roof off the place.

For this show, the band decided to literally follow the title of the song, and have the setlist go "Backwards Down The Numberline."

Holy Blankenstein! On Halloween night 2021, Phish took the stage as the band Sci-Fi Soldier from the year 4680: Pat Malone (Anastasio), Clueless Wallob (McConnell), Paulie Roots (Fishman), and Half-Nelson (Gordon). Seen here, they concluded the set with Malone on acoustic guitar for the song "I Am Miami," performed with an a cappella mic set up. (Steph Port)

Starting with their largest numbered song, they progressively played smaller songs in their repertoire.

Phish busted out multiple number based rarities, debuted and shredded Hendrix's "If 6 was 9," and just played amazing versions of every tune. While the number of each song shrunk smaller, they also were keeping a mathematical sum of all songs added together. During the double encore of "Numberline" and "Grind" we found out that tonight's song titles added up to 4680, a number we would later find out had significant meaning.

The second night (10/29/21) was another flamethrower of a show. Not thematically connected like the 28th, but just as potent musically. Both sets had deep jams, and super high peaks. It is an absolute must-hear.

The third night (10/30/21) got us back to the thematic setlists. For years fans have wondered what an animal themed show would be like. This night Phish delivered a *Farmhouse* themed show chock full of creatures great and small.

This night culminated with the ultra-rare "Harpua" bust-out, which was the first one since the 2017 Baker's Dozen run. This narration called back to the mathematical vibe from the 28th, and gave us some clues as to the impending Halloween theatrics.

Entering the venue on Halloween, we were handed eye catching comic books about Sci Fi Soldiers from the year 4680 (the sum from night one), who have been sent back in time to save the world. On this night, no sleuthing was needed. Just read the (comic)book.

From "Ghost," "Bowie," and lyrical suggestions to throw pumpkins at a tree, the first set of Halloween was dripping with lyrical decor.

For the second set Phish was the conduit for a band of heroes from the future, who were here to save the galaxy from The Howling. The comic explained that the Sci-Fi soldiers used Phish as a conduit, and they were on a musical mission to save us all.

"Holy Blankenstein!" there was some serious sensory overload. Elaborate helmeted costumes, unexpected pyrotechnics, futuristic sonic effects, digital projections on rotating cubes, lit up geometric shapes of circles and squares-It was a sight to behold.

Fans were divided on this set. With all the visual effects, this set may not have translated as well for those couch touring. And admittedly the lyrics were noticeably centered around an abundance of repeating phrases and choruses.

Ultimately Phish knows how to throw down a dance party that encourages all to "Get More Down." Songs like "The Howling" will leave a lasting impact for years to come. Discerning ears may have noticed there were lyrical tie-ins to other Phish classics. In "Thanksgiving," there were references to "Guyute" and "Sleeping Monkey."

After three absolutely scorching shows leading up to Halloween, the band did seem to be running on fumes by the third set. But in totality this run was one for the ages, and the four shows should be seen as a brilliantly crafted whole.

I can't wait to see what Phish, and any other unknown alter ego from the past or the future, comes up with for the next Halloween trick and treat spectacle.

84 Fans Phucking with the Band

What is the central theme to this everlasting spoof?

Phish is a band with a sense of humor. They have a long history of pulling pranks and gags on their audience, usually to hilarious effect. Whether it is New Year's Eve "gags," Halloween costumes, using setlists to spell out messages, or using doughnut flavors to create a delicious theme to a show, Phish loves to play with the collective consciousness of their audience.

But as they say, turnabout is fair play, and there have been some classic moments where the audience has returned the favor by playing their own tricks on the band.

One of the most widely documented instances of this audience playfulness took place during the 1996 Red Rocks Amphitheater run. Before the first show began, a group of Phish.net fans handed out printouts of a list of creative ideas. One of these was to use the silent moment in "Divided Sky" as a signal for the audience to sit down and "say ahhhhhhhhhhhh" during the typical silence. Another idea was to create a new call-and-response with the band during "You Enjoy Myself (YEM)" in the "Wash Uffitzi drive me to Firenze" section where the audience repeated that line in the space between the typical lyrics. Both were done by fans in attendance, and the band seemed to love it, but neither caught on as tradition.

Another idea on that list over time has become a hallmark occurrence at Phish shows. The instruction sheet explained that during the Phish classic "Harry Hood," when the band sings "Harry!" the audience should yell a corresponding "Hood!" on the next beat. With any of these gags, no one knew whether they would even work for one night. When Phish finally played "Harry Hood," each Harry was met with a "Hood!" of increased intensity. Amazingly enough, that tradition continues 20-plus years later.

Some fans still love the chant, some abhor it, but either way, seeing a fan-inspired idea become tradition is pretty incredible.

Another moment of audience-driven antics took place at Dick's in 2014. Unlike the Red Rocks collaboration that was spread on printed paper, this one was done with the power of the Internet. *Rolling Stone* magazine was conducting a Reader's Poll: The 10 Best Phish Songs. People assumed that classics such as "Antelope" or "Tweezer" would take the cake, but that was not to be.

Before all the votes were cast, JamBase editor and longtime Phish phan Scotty Bernstein proposed a different idea on his Phish-focused YEMblog. He asked fans to use this opportunity to promote the return of the long-forgotten and minimally played "Lushington." When the votes were finally counted, the incredibly

GROUP CROWD IDEAS

SOME OF US ON PHISH.NET HAVE COME UP WITH SOME GROUP CROWD IDEAS TO GET THE CROWD, AS A WHOLE, INVOLVED IN THE FOUR RED ROCKS SHOWS. IF EVERYONE PARTICIPATES, IT WILL REALLY MAKE FOR A COOL AND DIFFERENT RUN OF SHOWS BOTH FOR US AND THE BAND.

HERE ARE THE IDEAS WE'RE TRYING TO COORDINATE:

-- If they play **DIVIDED SKY**, during the part where Trey is silent and stares at the ceiling ("The Pause"), it would be really cool if everyone were to just SIT DOWN and quietly say "ahhhhhhhhhhhh........." Imagine that; Trey would totally *LOVE IT* and it would be really great if we could pull it off.

-- If they play **YOU ENJOY MYSELF**, during the funky "Wash Uffitzi drive me to Firenze" segment, INSTEAD of singing it with them, ECHO them (sing the line over the FOLLOWING measure).   **Example:**

Band: "Wash Uffitzi drive me to Firenze...
Crowd: "...Wash Uffitzi drive me to Firenze..........etc.

-- If they play **HARRY HOOD**, when the band sings "Harry", YELL "HOOD!" on the next beat (it works perfectly with the music). **Example:**

Band: "Harry!..................Harry!....................Where do you go when the lights go out............."
Crowd:"..............HOOD!.................HOOD!...etc.

-- TO START the 2nd SET (of the first night, and every night until it works), we'll lead the whole front row (and the rest of the venue, if possible) in SINGING THE FIRST LINE from **DESTINY UNBOUND**, which is:

"Highway Bill's on a rotary still, and he can't even feel the pain"

Apparently Trey said that the only way that they'll bring that song back is if the entire front row sings that one line, so it's worth a try!

-- And, of course, **PLEASE BE QUIET** during the acoustic/accapella numbers and the quiet jams. If the person next to you is yelling during a quiet part, PLEASE tell him/her to be quiet.

PLEASE PASS THIS FLYER ON! SPREAD THE WORD! LET'S TRY TO MAKE THIS WORK!

A fan-made flyer handed out at Red Rocks. (Jason Gershuny)

obscure "Lushington" won out. Even *Rolling Stone* thought this was possibly a case of "Phish Phans Phucking with us."

To this day, Phish has only played "Lushington" eight times, four of which didn't even contain any lyrics, and they haven't played it since 1987. It is doubtful that most of the folks who voted for it in the poll would even have recognized it.

Regardless, "Lushington" surprisingly topped the *Rolling Stone* poll. It is hard not to chuckle when envisioning a new fan curious about all the Phish hoopla using this long-forgotten tune as their entry point.

Phish clearly heard the call for "Lushington" and had a trick of their own in mind. One month after the article came out, they took the opportunity at Dicks in Colorado to spell out the song title with the first letter of each song of the first set. Spelling out messages at Dick's had become an almost annual tradition, and this year was no different. Fans at the show were anticipating the bust-out following this spelling premonition. But in true prankster form, they chose to follow the final "N" in Lushington by playing "Ha Ha Ha" instead. After this fake-out, it seemed like they had a kiss-and-make-up moment when they brought out Trey Anastasio Band members Jennifer Hartswick and Natalie Cressman on horns for the final song of the set, "Suzy Greenberg."

The loving relationship between Phish and their fans has always been a two-way street. Both sides find ways to show their appreciation for one another, and quite often it is shown with a hint of humor with a splash of love. Within the Phish world, there is nothing wrong with dancing and laughing at the same time.

Also, if you missed the previous chapter, be sure to check out the '80s Norwegian prog rock band Kasvot Växt.

85 *Undermind* (2004)

Recorded primarily at The Barn, Trey Anastasio's property in Vermont, and produced by Tchad Blake, *Undermind* is Phish's 10th studio album. It was released in June 2004, one month after Phish announced they would be breaking up and two months before the final show at the final festival in Coventry, Vermont. Of course, Phish would reunite about five years later and subsequently release three more studio albums through 2017, but at the time, in the summer of 2004, *Undermind* was the final Phish studio album.

In June 2004, Mark Kemp wrote in *Rolling Stone*, "The band delivers the most commanding song of its 16-year recording career, 'The Connection.' With its blast of ringing guitars, a hummable country-rock melody and Trey Anastasio's earthy vocals and surprisingly focused lyrics, the song evokes 'Box of Rain,' one of the stronger tunes by Phish's most obvious influence, the Grateful Dead."

Despite that (or because of it), "The Connection" is certainly one of the least-played songs in Phish's repertoire, appearing in live shows only four times.

Steve LaBate wrote in a July 2004 review of *Undermind* in *Paste* magazine, "Much of the rest of *Undermind*, however, is a damn-near perfect metaphor for Phish's performances in recent years—moments of greatness sandwiched between bouts of mostly uninspired mediocrity."

I'm tempted to agree with that sentiment, but perhaps Rob Theakston wrote it best in his review at AllMusic.com: "What's important to remember is that Phish is the kind of band whose hallmark moments don't happen in the studio, but onstage where they feel most at home. That said, *Undermind* continues in the longstanding tradition of almost but not quite capturing the full band on all cylinders. It's the difference between watching an animal in its native habitat and in a caged environment: not quite as exciting, but still a curiosity to respect and observe with interest."

And so what do we have here? A strong, commanding song evoking the Grateful Dead? Slim moments of greatness amid a mediocre majority? A caged animal kept from its natural habitat?

No wonder the band broke up after recording this album!

Notwithstanding, Phish.net includes "Scents and Subtle Sounds," more than 10 times in its coveted "jam charts" list, with three performances highly recommended. And "A Song I Heard the Ocean Sing" ranks similarly with some "stand-out Type II jams," as far back as its premiere (June 17, 2004; see also June 19, 2004) and as recent as the Baker's Dozen (July 30, 2017).

The album cover seems to be a clear nod to The Beatles' *Let It Be* album cover, each featuring headshot images of the four musicians. And perhaps controversially, the album artwork seemed to be part and parcel of the cracking that lead to the band's breakup as mentioned by Trey Anastasio.

The album's digital version included an exclusive bonus track, "Tiny," which has never been performed live. Actually, harkening back to the "Montana" track on *A Live One*, which was a two-minute excerpt from a live performance of "Tweezer" in Bozeman, Montana, both *Undermind*'s "Tiny" and "Maggie's Revenge" are segments of a 45-minute improvised jam during the *Undermind* sessions that would later be released at LivePhish.com under the moniker *Headphones Jam*.

Additionally, early copies of the album included a DVD of a 25-minute making-of-the-album documentary directed by Danny Clinch titled *Specimens of Beauty*, which has a 7.1 out of 10 on IMDB.

Undermind peaked at No. 13 on the Billboard charts, and Phish did not play a single song from the album at their "final" festival in 2004.

86 Coventry: A Final Farewell?

The year 2004 was a sad one for Phish and Phish fans. In May, Trey Anastasio announced the band was breaking up and the summer tour shows, followed by the Coventry festival in Vermont, would be their final performances.

Needless to say, there was a somber (but perhaps not sober) vibe to the summer tour. In some ways it felt like the band was in hospice. Or maybe it was the fans who were in hospice. In any regard, the shows leading up to Coventry were less than stellar, and everyone felt the impending conclusion like a dark storm brewing on the horizon.

And that storm was real. In the days leading up to the August 14 and 15 weekend festival at Coventry, the region was battered by severe thunderstorms and experienced record-breaking rainfall. The festival's 600-acre farmland site was decimated. The whole scene was just one big mud pit. Thousands of attendees were driving into the festival, only to have their cars immediately sink into the mud and get stuck. Tow trucks sent in to help fell victim to the same fate. The mud made parking logistically impossible, transportation of goods and services halted to a standstill, and yet, 100,000 fans were expected.

Those few thousands who arrived early (doors to the campsites opened Thursday at noon), well, they were the lucky ones in a sense. At least they were able to get into the festival grounds.

Outside, tens of thousands were stuck in traffic on the few roads and highways leading to the remote Vermont location about 20 miles from the Canadian border.

Then on Saturday morning, state police shut down I-91 20 miles away from the festival ground and Phish bassist Mike Gordon took to the radio airwaves via "The Bunny," the festival's on-site FM station, and implored people to turn back, saying the field and venue were in a state of disaster and no more vehicles would be allowed into the venue. For some, this was especially frustrating and disparaging because onstage at the show prior, Anastasio had said to the audience that they should take their time getting to Coventry.

And then, the tens of thousands of fans stuck in standstill traffic, some waiting for more than 24 hours, did something extraordinary. They abandoned their cars, parking along the side of the road and in nearby farmland, and walked. They walked into

Phish fans walk from their abandoned cars through a field toward the festival grounds in Vermont, 2004. (Brianna Leech)

the festival, carrying only what they could, leaving tents and weekends provisions behind. Some walked as far as 20 miles. And what looked like fewer than 20,000 people on Friday swelled to 65,000 by showtime Saturday.

Saturday's show featured a number of notable jams, including "AC/DC Bag" to kick off the second set, and "Stash" and "Gotta Jibboo" and "Drowned." Overall, though, the band's playing during the show could only be described as sloppy. It was an emotional affair.

After playing "You Enjoy Myself," the band gave away their trampolines to the audience. And a few times in the show, Anastasio took the opportunity to share some personal anecdotes, talking about writing "David Bowie" and other songs while living in a cabin for the summer not far from the Coventry festival site.

Encoring with "Harry Hood," Anastasio spoke about being farther away from the crowd than usual due to the unusual stage setup as a result of the saturated grounds, and he and Mike Gordon descended from the stage and played closer to the audience.

On Sunday, the band performed what was announced and expected to be their final show ever. This was the last Phish show. While "Chalk Dust Torture," "Down with Disease," "Ghost," and "Split Open and Melt" (the latter included on *Live Bait Vol. 5*) offer some interesting jams, the show overall felt gloomy and lackluster. (One highlight was the massive glow stick war during "Ghost.")

The band's performance of "Glide" is horrendous. Anastasio, clearly emotional, completely flubbed the song. After "Glide," he and the other band members gave thanks to the crowd and each other.

"This has been a really wild ride for many many years," Mike Gordon said. "And I'm just the luckiest person in the whole world to be able to do this with these guys and all of you."

The band performed ad-libbed lyrics during "Cool Jerk" and "Dickie Scotland" to give thanks and praise to their crew and team.

Kiss and Make Up

According to Billboard, the Coventry festival grossed about $10 million, almost $2 million more than Phish's 2003 It Festival. And Phish offered a full refund to anyone who mailed in their unripped tickets. Regardless of whether you sent in your tickets to be refunded, everyone received free download codes for the shows and a signed copy of Danny Clinch's band photo book.

Furthermore, the tens of thousands of fans who were stuck waiting in gridlocked traffic to get into Coventry, some waiting for more than 24 hours, well...you can imagine the mess that was left. No trash receptacles, no restrooms, no shade, no shelter. The state of Vermont issued Phish Inc. a bill for $35,000 for cleanup, which the band's organization paid in full.

And during "Wolfman's Brother," Anastasio and Gordon invited their mothers onstage to dance.

But perhaps the realest moment during Coventry, which was broadcast live in movie theaters across the country as well as on Sirius XM radio, was the performance of "Wading in the Velvet Sea." If you've yet to visit this particular performance, well, brace yourself and grab some tissues.

Keyboardist Page McConnell can barely sing the first stanza. His voice cracks. Visibly verklempt, he tries and fails a second time before turning the microphone toward the audience. Anastasio picks up vocal duties, but he too is breaking down with emotion. Ultimately, the band makes it through their "final" performance of this emotional song with tears flowing.

Phish closed the weekend with "The Curtain With," what was then known to be Phish's final song, a forceful, swirling song Anastasio wrote in his early Vermont days, which the band premiered in August 1987. The song features the lyrics, "As he saw his life run away from him / Thousands ran along / Chanting words from a song / Please me have no regrets.'"

To say the weekend was emotional is an understatement. I think these shows, billed as the final shows, with all the feelings surrounding that, paired with the physical conditions of the festival grounds may have made for the most "had to be there" experiences. It's difficult to explain the mix of emotions. It's difficult to say goodbye. And I'm afraid that unless you were there, you won't be able to fully grasp the bittersweet atmosphere.

But crying along with Page during "Velvet Sea" is a good start.

87 CashorTrade.org and the Face-Value Ticket Crusade

Within the Phish community, selling a ticket to a show for more than face value is considered taboo. Quite frankly, scalpers are despised by Phish fans. The demand for Phish tickets has only increased over the years with particular venues, specific shows, and whole tours selling out in mere minutes.

And so, if you strike out with Phish ticket mail-order lottery, aka Phish Tickets By Mail (PTMB), and you strike out through TicketMaster, then you don't have many options for scoring tickets outside of friends and friends of friends, or the secondary marketplace with sites like StubHub. But there is another option: CashorTrade.org.

The name of the website itself refers to the often-heard request in Phish show lots of someone who's looking for a ticket: "Cash or trade for your extra!"

In 2009, when Phish announced they would be reuniting to tour again after a five-year breakup, starting with a run of shows in Hampton, Virginia, the Phish community was invigorated and thrilled, to say the least. However, this would prove to be one of the peaks of Phish ticket demand.

PTMB requests were unprecedented. TicketMaster's on-sale allotment sold out in seconds, and many hundreds, maybe thousands of Phish fans were left empty-handed as scalpers posted ads for tickets priced at thousands of dollars.

Brando Rich and his brother, Dusty, were two such fans without tickets. And they were appalled by the secondary market rates. So they decided to do something about it and founded CashorTrade.org.

For many years the site was a labor of love, a side project while Brando and Dusty ran a web design company. But in 2017, CashorTrade.org surpassed a major milestone: 100,000 users. And that year, the site facilitated more than 100,000 ticket exchange transactions. This new pinnacle gave the brothers a newfound energy and motivation to really focus on the site and give it all their energies, and Brando is now working full-time on CashorTrade.

"Our goal is to disrupt an industry and be the Airbnb of tickets," Brando says. "A fan-to-fan exchange is a fun idea among friends, but our plan is to become a real live alternative to the secondary market and compete with these billion-dollar scalper companies."

Brando and his team are currently exploring opportunities for investment and endorsement while actively expanding the site's offerings for tickets, now totaling more than 3,000 artists. But the site's preeminent band is Phish, the band around whom they first built site in 2009. And it seems the Phish ticket market is only growing, and thus the secondary Phish ticket market as well.

We sat down with Brando Rich to talk about the secondary Phish ticket market and CashorTrade.

Brando Rich: Phish is the largest ticketed artist on CashorTrade. I mean, we started in the Phish scene so it makes sense, not to mention, among the secondary ticket market, Phish is one of the most bought and sold tickets there is. It's up there on StubHub's charts as being one of the top five [highest percentage of tickets purchased by men] in 2014. And when you think of all the sports and all the tickets period, you know it's pretty impressive that Phish is one of the most sold and traded acts.

100 Things: Yeah, that's wild. I'm sure there are a lot of factors, but why do you think that is?

BR: I would say the main element is the shows sell out. So if you think of sports, there are a lot of events that aren't sold out, so there's never that same pressure, you know? But the Phish community...those kids are on it, and they want good seats, and they want floor seats, so there's a lot of focused attention.

100 Things: Yeah, but, Elton John sells out and Lady Gaga sells out, too.

BR: I'm sure those acts are up there, as well. You know, the world tour ones are pretty big. I mean, those acts are a global market, but do they have fans hitting every single show of their tour? I think, probably not.

100 Things: There does seem to be more of a conscious demand in terms of getting great seats or getting floor tickets that is really more relevant and important for Phish fans than other bands, would you agree?

BR: I would say the reason the demand is so high is it's not just the fans, but the scalpers, too. The scalpers know the demand, and know they can get more money for the tickets. When it's not just fans buying the tickets, it's going to be one of the first or quickest shows to sell out.

100 Things: So how did it all start for you guys? Back in 2009...

BR: Well, as you know, Phish was coming back after their hiatus. My brother and I were pretty upset to try and purchase tickets and be shut out, only to see them being resold for $2,000 apiece on Stubhub. Having been web designers for 15 years, at the time, Dusty and I felt something had to be done to change it. Something, finally, for fans. CashorTrade was an idea that could disrupt the secondary ticket market and offer the first alternative [to] the scalping industry. We found that no secondary reseller site gives fans what they want. CashorTrade does.

100 Things: So, let me ask you this: Were you able to get into the Hampton 2009 reunion shows at all?

BR: No. We didn't get tickets. It was February or late January when Phish announced the shows. We started building the site and launched it within a week or two after they announced them. We just kind of threw it up to see what would happen. Later that summer, we went on tour and set up the CashorTrade tent on lot. People used the tent as a spot to meet up with friends and make trades. By the end of the year, we had 5,000 registered members on the website. The site has been kind of been a side thing for a long time. We just recently sold our web design company and I am now working full-time on it. We have built a small team and are coming out swinging for this summer. As the site has reached 110,000 members, there was just no way to continue with the same success as a part-time thing. We all see the real potential it has and it is time that we give it what it deserves. We're motivated and have a lot of energy to bring it to the next level. We have begun to reach out to the investor community and are seeing what we can do to be a real competitor to these billion-dollar companies. What started out as a fun fan community is something that can really be the much bigger. CashorTrade is the Airbnb of tickets. That's our goal. The global secondary ticket market is $9 billion. StubHub has roughly

50 percent of that market. If we could obtain at least 1 percent, that's $90 million of the market. There is real potential for CashorTrade to obtain a percentage of the market while being a sustainable and conscious business model that works and supports fans rather than exploiting them. That's really it right there. Rather than having this fun, fly-by-night idea, let's make this something that can be widespread, sustain itself with growth, be a viable alternative, and carry an equal name in the secondary market.

If you're looking for an extra ticket or have an extra ticket to sell, please don't scalp the ticket. Keep it in the community, and use CashorTrade as a trusted, verified network to exchange face-value tickets.

88 "Fluffhead" Resurrection

There are certain moments in Phishtory when the stars align, the ground shakes, the band is primed, and the audience elevates. One thing every Phish fan needs to do is to listen to Phish's triumphant return from the five-year breakup with the "Fluffhead" bust-out at Hampton Coliseum in Virginia in 2009.

When Phish came back at Hampton Coliseum on March 6, 2009, the fan base couldn't have been happier. It had been nearly five years with no guarantee of their ever returning to the stage. Outside the venue, people were holding signs offering $500 to get in, and seemingly no one was tempted to sell their golden ticket.

The Hampton Coliseum itself is a major attraction. It is a general-admission indoor venue, which is a rarity. Phish even added ambience outside the venue by creating a scene of giant, smiling, cube-shaped men by the reflecting pools. Hotels are within easy walking distance, and the band has played some iconic shows there throughout their history. The 1997 and '98 runs are legendary and are immortalized in a box set live album, *Hampton Comes Alive*.

They could have played anything as their opener and the fans would have been elated, but they chose "Fluffhead." "Fluffhead" had not been played for nearly nine years, since the final tour of Phish 1.0 in Las Vegas in 2000. Coupling the triumphant return of

Sculptures outside The Mothership in Hampton, Virginia, in 2009.
(Brianna Leech)

the band with the resurrection of one of the fans' all-time favorites nearly caused "The Mothership," as the Coliseum is lovingly nicknamed, to lift from its foundation.

"Fluffhead" is one of those songs that embodies everything unique about Phish. There are extremely complicated and varied compositional sections, a concluding peaking jam, absurd lyrics, fan-favorite sing-along opportunities, and a storied history that includes the evolution of each of the sections separately as they eventually coalesced into the song we know today. Some of the lyrics were even penned by longtime Phish collaborator The Dude of Life.

"Fluffhead" may have been shelved, but it was never forgotten. The band had even added fuel to the fans' desire to hear the song when Mike reportedly said "no" to playing it at the It festival in 2003. A "Fluffhead!" chant rose up following a first-set "Wilson." Fans were hoping that chant would coerce Phish to dust off this classic, but for whatever reason, Phish did not oblige. Trey threw Mike Gordon under the proverbial bus by saying, "Mike says no," a phrase that lives on in infamy. It can still be found on many Phish memes and stickers to this day.

Those 16 minutes and 17 seconds of glorious euphoria were worth the ticket price alone. Just listen to a recording, and you can hear the fans sustaining their cheers well over a minute into the song, which was just long enough to stop cheering and start singing along with the opening lyrics.

Please find yourself 20 free minutes, a great pair of headphones, plug in, and let your imagination soar. Phish playing "Fluffhead" at Hampton Coliseum is one for the ages and is a moment in time that should not be missed by any Phish fan.

89 *Joy* (2009)

Phish returned to the stage in 2009 for the first time in five years, and shortly thereafter released their 11ᵗʰ studio album, *Joy*, thus fully bringing the Phish 3.0 era to fruition. *Joy* is Phish's first self-released studio album (JEMP Records) since *Lawn Boy* in 1990. *Joy* was recorded between April and May 2009 in New York's Chung King Studio under the guidance of Steve Lillywhite, who had last worked with Phish on their much-beloved 1996 album *Billy Breathes*.

All 10 tracks of the album have made their way into the live Phish repertoire, with only the first single off the album, the long and complicated composition "Time Turns Elastic (TTE)" being shelved from the live rotation since 2010. Even though "TTE" has not seen the light of day within Phish's touring repertoire, Trey Anastasio will often play the song with orchestral backing when opportunities arise. *Joy*'s second single, "Backward Down the Number Line," did receive some limited radio play across the nation.

Joy was warmly received by both fans and critics as a well-produced and balanced album. Many of the songs have a lyrical maturity and reflectiveness that are seen as a sign of the times for the band. According to Phish.net, the title track served dual roles as both a powerful memorial to Trey's sister Kristy, who had passed away just months before its live debut, as well as Tom Marshall's ode to the happiness shared between daughters. That lyrical ambiguity and flexibility are hallmarks of Tom Marshall's writing style and are part of why people can find personal connections to many of his songs (see chapter 10).

Alongside the new album, Phish offered a special *Joy* box set, which included the album and a second, unreleased album called

Party Time that contains other modern Phish staples, such as the album's namesake, "Party Time," and "Alaska." The *Joy* box also contained 10 miniature posters created by different visual artists, one for each of the tracks on the original *Joy* album; a DVD covering a few shows from the 2009 summer tour; and an extensive hardbound booklet.

Phish also offered up a limited-edition vinyl record version of *Joy* at Superball in 2011.

90 Exile, *Columbus*, and Phish from the Future

The Stones, Little Feat, and some weird *Wingsuit* album? Phish's 3.0 Halloween "musical costume" shows ranged from the classic to the premiere.

In 2009, returning from their five-year break, Phish would continue their Halloween tradition, and triumphantly so, if I may say. Instead of a regular venue show for Halloween, Phish chose to host their eighth major festival on Halloween weekend in Indio, California.

Leading up to the festival, Phish.com featured 100 albums that were eliminated (see chapter 94) one by one leading up to the festival. Come Saturday morning at the festival grounds, the choice was revealed. Attendees received the now-classic Phishbill programs detailing that Phish would indeed cover the 1972 double album *Exile on Main Street* by The Rolling Stones, which *Rolling Stone* magazine called "their most physically jolting album and, ultimately, their most emotionally inspiring."

To bring this album to life in the desert outside Palm Springs, California, Phish enlisted the help of Brooklyn soul singers Sharon

Dancers reveal the identity of the wombat… "It's kinda like the theme from the Fish *TV show. You know—with Abe Vigoda."* (Jason Gershuny)

Jones and Saundra Williams, and a horn section. Beginning with a video montage featuring live footage of performances by bands included in Phish's initial 100-album list, Phish took the stage, joined by Dave Guy on trumpet (a member of Jones' regular backing band the Dap-Kings), David Smith on trombone, and Tony Jarvis on saxophone, and launched into "Rocks Off."

Throughout the set, each band member took a turn on lead vocals, with singers Jones and Williams on backup vocals beginning with "Tumbling Dice," the album's fifth track. Giving this classic album the Phish treatment only enriched by this nine-piece musical group, well…it all came to a pinnacle with "Loving Cup," one of Phish's oft-played covers. This is Phish making these songs their own. And since premiering "Shine a Light" that night, Phish has since performed the song nearly two dozen times. Concluding, as the album does, with "Soul Survivor," Phish completed their "musical costume" of *Exile on Main Street*, with a set of music 30 minutes longer than the album.

In 2010, Phish announced a three-night run for Halloween weekend at Boardwalk Hall in Atlantic City, New Jersey, the final night of which was Halloween night, when Phish would once again perform in "musical costume."

Announced to attendees through the Phishbill handed out at the venue entrance, Phish would cover *Waiting on Columbus*, the 1977 premiere live album by seminal rock band Little Feat.

On the Little Feat album, between the first song and the second, recorded live in Washington, D.C., local radio personality Don "Cerphe" Colwell is heard leading the audience in a chant to spell out "F-E-A-T."

And so, prior to taking the stage for the second set, Phish played the first song from *Waiting on Columbus* ("Join the Band") over the PA system. In Phish prank tradition, the band had included instructions for the audience in that evening's Phishbill: When Colwell is heard leading the audience to chant F-E-A-T, the audience would respond instead with the letters P-H-I-S-H.

Keeping true to the album, on which Little Feat was accompanied by the Tower of Power horn section, Phish was joined by percussionist Giovanni Hidalgo and a five-person horn section (Aaron Johnson, Stuart Bogie, Ian Hendrickson-Smith, Michael Leonhart, and Eric Biondo). The set was, yet again, an awesome tribute to a classic album—intrinsically Phish but simultaneously much more with six additional musicians.

After two years without Halloween shows, Phish would return to Atlantic City's Boardwalk Hall for Halloween weekend 2013 to perform once again in musical costume. But this time, there was a twist.

Attendees were welcomed with the familiar Phishbill, though the featured musical costume was an unknown album titled

Wingsuit, whose cover art featured a man in a wingsuit gliding high above the New Jersey shore. Inside, the first and third sets were listed as "Phish" while the second set, "Wingsuit," featured a 12-song track list of an album "from the future."

That night, Phish performed their forthcoming album, *Fuego,* then known by its working title *Wingsuit,* in its entirety for the 10,000 lucky fans in attendance. While some considered it a rare privilege to hear the premiere of 12 new Phish songs, others were disappointed that Phish would not be covering a classic album as per the Halloween musical costume tradition.

Released almost eight months later, *Fuego* is almost identical to the set Phish performed on Halloween night 2013, save for moving "Winterqueen" from the first position to the last, and cutting the songs "Snow" and "Amidst the Peals of Laughter." At Boardwalk Hall, those two songs, as well as "Sing Monica," were performed acoustically.

Perhaps the highlight of the show was the performance of "Wombat," which featured a half dozen dancers performing choreography at the front of the stage, including someone in a furry wombat costume à la Disneyland characters. About halfway through the ensuing jam, the wombat grew fatigued and, in James Brown fashion, was helped offstage by a pair of the dancers. Then, referencing the song's lyrics, "It's kinda like the theme from the *Fish* TV show / You know—with Abe Vigoda," Anastasio paused the song to introduce the great actor Abe Vigoda himself as the man playing the wombat. Sure enough, to the surprise and delight of the crowd, the dancers returned to the stage with then-92-year-old Abe Vigoda wearing the wombat suit. "And he dances his ass off," Anastasio said. "In a wombat suit."

Sadly, Abe Vigoda passed away in January 2016. But his spirit lives on in the song "Wombat."

91 NYE 2009–2012

Phish's 3.0. New Year's Eve shows have kept with the gag or prank tradition in fun, unique ways, to say the least. From disco cannonballs to international "Meatstick" dances; floating, flying fans; and runaway golf carts, Phish made sure their 3.0 New Year's Eve shows kept audiences on their toes.

In 2009, Phish returned to Miami's American Airlines Arena for the first time since 2003. For the New Year's Eve show, the band had a couple of tricks in store. After what seemed like a rather uneventful show, save for a few solid bust-outs, Phish took the stage for the third set and played "Party Time" > the New Year's Eve countdown as a giant disco ball descended onto the stage into a pedestal that read 2010 as the band played "Auld Lang Syne" > "Down with Disease."

Concluding "DWD," Fishman came to join the disco ball at the front of the stage, where he donned a pair of aviator googles, opened up the disco ball, climbed inside, and closed himself in. Gordon and Anastasio, with help from stagehands, then loaded the ball into a giant cannon, decorated with flashing yellow caution lights and aimed at a massive net on the opposite side of the venue lit with an "X."

Page McConnell took his position at a detonator switch, and with Trey on the drums playing a drum roll, Page fired the cannon with an explosion and appeared to shoot the Fishman-filled disco cannonball not only through the net but straight through the arena ceiling. A spotlight shone through the ceiling "hole," seemingly from a helicopter hovering outside.

Now without a drummer, Anastasio asked the audience if anyone could play the drums, and selected a black-haired woman from the crowd. She climbed down from the seats onto the stage to occupy the drums. Of course, it wasn't the same woman who then took a seat at drums, but someone wearing the same clothes and a black wig who looked suspiciously like Fishman.

Anastasio asked her to introduce herself. "Sarah from Pittsburgh, PA, baby!" a woman said offstage as Fishman mimed. Anastasio then asked her what her favorite song was, and she replied, "Fluffhead."

And so, Phish played "Fluffhead" with Sarah from Pittsburgh, who later "reappeared" to bow with the band at the end of the show.

Afterward, in the parking lot outside the arena, concertgoers were surprised to find a white car crushed by the giant disco ball with signs stating that the car had traveled from Vermont fueled by maple syrup. Syrup seemed to spill and leak from the vehicle, which was roped off by police tape.

2010's New Year's Eve was the year of the "Meatstick" at Madison Square Garden. Opening with "Punch You in the Eye" > "AC/DC Bag," Phish launched into what would be three hours and forty minutes of music. The second set features some stellar improvisation in "Ghost," followed by "You Enjoy Myself" > "Manteca" > "You Enjoy Myself." The 1947 song co-written by Dizzy Gillespie, "Manteca," was a major bust-out for Phish, who hadn't played it in more than 300 shows (October 30, 1998), according to Phish.net.

Wasting no time, Phish opened the third set with "Meatstick," and not five minutes into the song, shortly after the band flubbed the Japanese lyrics, groups of people representing international cultures, first some African tribesmen, then a Mexican mariachi band, joined Phish onstage and sang the "Meatstick" lyrics in their own languages. A group of Hasidic Jews came next, followed by four blonde Scandinavian girls in ski outfits, and a pair of Bavarian Oktoberfest couples and tropical dancers in hula skirts, overtaking the stage with colorful representations of various international cultures. While a recording of the song played, the band members joined the dancers at the front of the stage for the "Meatstick" dance.

The dancers continued to sing and perform choreographed moves, elaborating on the song and dance. A pair of hot dog street vendors took stage left and right, but it seemed the band members had disappeared. Wait, there they were, flying high above the crowd in the large hot dog prop from New Year's Eve '94 and '99. Cruising across the arena, the band members tossed soft and squishy foam hot dogs into the crowd.

Arriving to the stage, the hot dog lowered and the band disembarked to join the global tribe to conclude "Meatstick" and count down to midnight. Happy New Year! And the whole stage sang "Auld Lang Syne" as balloons and confetti fell from the ceiling. The band then launched into "After Midnight" and performed a few more songs, concluding with "Glide" and encoring with "First Tube."

For New Year's Eve 2011, Phish returned to MSG for what will forever be known as the "Steam" gag. Phish played a solid first set, concluding with "Ocelot" > "Fluffhead," and opened the second set with an exalted version of "Party Time" > "Light," the latter of which featured Page on theremin. For the third set, approaching midnight, Phish opened with "Cavern" and then segued into "Steam."

During "Steam," not only did a foggy steam envelop the band onstage as well as the soundboard area in the crowd, but then the "steam" lifted a guitar, keyboard, and amp from the stage into the air. Then Fishman's vacuum rose up into the rafters.

Suddenly, a woman from the crowd rushed the stage, climbing over the barricade, and as security ran to stop her, the girl atop the barricade and the security guard were raised up on a scissor lift. The girl rose higher, suspended way above the stage. Suddenly, other performers, planted in the crowd, also started to rise and danced suspended in midair high above the crowd as steam billowed from their glowing backpacks. The original steam-powered flying girl then led the countdown to the New Year and Phish played "Auld Lang Syne" as balloons dropped upon the crowd.

That year, for the fifth time in history, Phish followed "Auld Lang Syne" with "Down with Disease" (see chapter 50) as the aerial dancers flew high above. During the "DWD" jam, Trey and Mike also ascended on 20-foot hydraulic pedestals and then, returning to the ground, ran circles around the stage. Phish concluded the third set with "First Tube" and encored with "Slave to the Traffic Light."

In 2012, Phish ran with a lawn-games theme, complete with the arena floor and stage covered with Astroturf. Leading up to the show, numerous performers sunbathed and played croquet and golf onstage. This "garden party" or "golfing" theme would complete the thematic acronym the band had built over the last years—"Meatstick" in 2010, "Steam" in 2011, and "Golf" in 2012. MSG.

Phish opened the show with their first and only performance of 1972's "Garden Party" by Ricky Nelson. First-set highlights included "Mike's Song" > "Walk Away" > "Weekapaug Groove." During setbreak, additional performers hit soft golf balls into the crowd. The second set featured an incredibly fantastic block of music with "Ghost" > "Piper" > "Light" > "Also Sprach Zarathustra" and concluded with "You Enjoy Myself."

To kick off the third set, Trey, Mike, and Page took the stage, and instead of manning their instruments, they merely teed up and hit soft golf balls into the crowd. Then Fishman rode onstage in his own golf cart, wearing a doughnut-themed golfing outfit complete with Scottish golf hat and argyle vest, and the full band continued to hit golf balls into the crowd before taking to their instruments and playing "Party Time" followed by the dark, spoken-word jaunt that is "Kung" with the never-more-appropriate lyrics of "We can stage a runaway golf cart marathon!" while Anastasio played his guitar with a golf club.

"Chalk Dust Torture" came next, as more carts raced across the stage and dozens of performers dressed as golfers took to the stage, dancing and hitting golf balls. After one of the little people golfers, atop a cart, led the countdown to midnight, Phish played "Auld Lang Syne," balloons dropped from the ceiling, and Ping Pong balls shot out of cannons onstage. The band then segued into "Tweezer Reprise" accompanied by backup singers including Carrie Manolakos, the Broadway actor known for her roles in *Mamma Mia!* and *Wicked*.

The rest of the set featured golf-themed songs, including "Wilson," "The Wedge," "Fly Like an Eagle," and an a cappella rendition of "Lawn Boy." For the encore, the band played "Driver" and then Page McConnell, dressed like Bob Hope in a blazer and ball cap, wished everyone a Happy New Year, before the band concluded with "Iron Man."

Personally, I'm a fan of the Miami cannonball gag. The spectacle of Fishman being shot out of a cannon straight through the roof of the venue is milked for everything it's worth. The hovering helicopter spotlight, "Sarah from Pittsburgh," the crushed car outside…Phish's 2009 NYE gag had it all!

Though a Page "Bob Hope" McConnell–led "Iron Man" is pretty sweet, too.

92 See Phish at Dick's: A 3.0 Tradition

Phish at Dick's for Labor Day weekend has become a heralded 3.0-era tradition. Every year offers a new chapter for the Phish annals, offering a unique and nuanced aspect to each show. Phish never holds back at this massive outdoor stadium.

Dick's Sporting Goods Park in Commerce City, Colorado, is a 27,000-person-capacity stadium and home to Denver's Major League Soccer team, the Colorado Rapids. And Phish has performed there every year since 2011, always on Labor Day weekend, a three-night run, with on-site camping and a Shakedown Street like no other.

The stadium opened in 2007 as part of a $130 million project that included retail and a new civic center. Close to the Stapleton International Airport and the Rocky Mountain Arsenal National Wildlife Refuge, the facility is located about 10 miles northeast of Denver, Colorado.

"Dick's," as the run of shows and venue are both commonly referred to (as in, "Are you going to Dick's this year?"), has come to signal the end of summer tour for seven years now and has offered some extraordinary shows. And we're not talking about the jams, per se.

In 2011, Phish took the stage at Dick's for the first time and opened with "Sample in a Jar," which has opened many shows. "Sparkle" followed, then "The Sloth." And then the band covered The Rolling Stones' "Sweet Virginia," which they've only played a handful of times. At this point, the audience knew something was up.

That night, Phish played 26 songs, all of which began with the letter "S," including a number of bust-out songs, such as "Sparks" by The Who, which Phish hadn't played in more than 460 shows. They even encored with "Sabotage" by Beastie Boys.

In 2012, Phish did something a little bit different. Taking the first letter of each song performed, after four songs, we had the letters F-U-C-K... Interesting... After three more songs to conclude the set, we had letters spelling F-U-C-K-Y-O-U, with a highly regarded 15-minute, Type II "Undermind" closing the set in the U slot. Nothing subtle here! But what did it mean?

A wide view of Dick's Sporting Goods Park. (Stephen Olker)

Shortly into the second set most fans had it figured out. R-F-A-C spelled out the second set, and adding an E with a bust-out cover of "Emotional Rescue" by The Rolling Stones, Phish had spelled out F-U-C-K-Y-O-U-R-F-A-C-E, the title of the Mike Gordon tune, which, of course, the band performed for just the seventh time ever to conclude the second set.

Needless to say, the crowd of nearly 30,000 fans went absolutely wild. The band then encored with "Grind" and "Meatstick," keeping the theme going.

In 2013, it seemed as if Phish had abandoned the tradition. About halfway through the first set, Phish's songs spelled G-N-I-H-T. Needless to say, fans were disappointed. But as the rest of the set rolled along, including "Esther," then "The Moma Dance," "Ocelot," and "Stash"...wait a second...G-N-I-H-T-E-M-O-S. Read backward, it spelled S-O-M-E-T-H-I-N-G. Phish continued their first set, concluding with their one and only performance of "Easy to Slip" by Little Feat.

The second set kicked off with a solid pairing of "Punch You in the Eye" > "Sand," and continued through the encore to spell out, backward of course, M-O-S-T-S-H-O-W-S-S-P-E-L-L-S-O-M-E-T-H-I-N-G. Touché, Phish. Touché.

The year after, in 2014, the band had something special in store, but it was the fans who suggested it. Or something like that. You see, that summer *Rolling Stone* magazine held an online poll to answer the question, "What is the best Phish song of all time?" And the fans answered. Led by the folks at YEMblog.com, who called for a trolling of the *Rolling Stone* poll, thousands of fans voted for an extremely obscure, obtuse song, abandoned less than a year after its 1986 premiere and performed only eight times. The song, "Lushington," is now heralded as the No. 1 Phish Song of All Time in the readers' poll. *Rolling Stone*'s editors simply stated, "We think this is Phish phans phucking with us." (See chapter 84.)

And so: Friday, August 29, 2014, two months after *Rolling Stone* published the poll, Phish took the stage at Dick's Sporting Goods Park and opened with "Llama." Then they played "Undermind." "Stash" came next. And after "Halfway to the Moon," the audience had a sense of where this was going...L-U-S-H. The show continued and an hour later, a cover of Led Zeppelin's "No Quarter" would cap the spelling of L-U-S-H-I-N-G-T-O-N, leaving the crowd breathless with anticipation for what would be only the ninth performance of the eponymous song...

But instead, Phish played "Ha Ha Ha," simultaneously an homage and a dig to their fans. Trey kept it simple when he spoke, saying, "You asked and we delivered!" And that was just the first set!

I double-dog dare you to show me a band with more crowd interaction, more engagement, more pop culture relevance, more intelligence, a more dedicated fan base, more controversy, history, and playfulness. This is Phish at Dick's.

But it doesn't stop there.

On Sunday, September 6, 2015, Phish played the final show of a three-night run in Commerce City, Colorado, that would conclude their 26-show summer tour. Having just finished a tremendous two-set show spanning nearly three hours, the band returned to the stage for their encore just minutes before the venue's curfew.

"Whataya think they're gonna do?" I asked the kid next to me in the audience.

"Whataya mean?" he replied. "'Tweezer Reprise' and that'll close the show."

"You're kidding me, right?"

"Curfew is 11:45, so they don't have time to play anything else."

He was right about that: curfew was just a few minutes away. And having played "Tweezer" late in the second set, Phish was assuredly going to encore with "Tweezer Reprise."

But that just wouldn't be enough, in my opinion.

"No fuckin' way," I said. "There's no fuckin' way they're gonna come back out, play 'Tweezer Reprise,' say good night, and go home. No fuckin' way. Not after this show, this whole weekend, this summer tour. Are you kidding me? No fuckin' way. They've got something in store for us…. Just wait. There's no way, no way."

With the band at their instruments, Trey on guitar began the first notes of "Tweezer Reprise."

The crowd roared and the stadium came alive.

"Told ya," the kid said.

"Dude," I said. "Just wait."

And after a rockin' three-minute "Tweezer Reprise," with the crowd roaring and applauding, the band members shuffled their feet, looked to each other, leaned into their microphones, and sang, "Om-pa-pa oom-pa-pa oom-pa-pa oom-pa-paaaaa!"

I howled with excitement! It was "Harpua!" High fiving the crowd around me, I knew we were in for something special now.

"Hell yeah," I said to the kid. "Here we go!"

"Harpua" is a rare song in Phish's repertoire. Often played in the late 1980s and early 1990s, "Harpua" has only been played eight times since the band reunited in 2009 (see chapter 77).

What's more is that each performance of the song is unique. Each "Harpua" includes a story, narrated by Trey, about a boy named Jimmy and his cat, Poster Nutbag. But each telling of the story is different. Jimmy and Poster are consistent characters but each plot is unique and often incorporates nuances calling back to performances from the tour or references to towns and venues played. To me, "Harpua" always feels something like a bedtime story. Trey ambles through a sweet story, likely making it up as he goes, about a pair of familiar characters whom we've all come to know. And like the best bedtime stories, this one also includes musical tangents, transitions, and punctuations.

With this particular performance, approaching the venue's midnight curfew, Trey detailed a story of Jimmy at home enjoying some of Denver's special treats "when he decides to put on a record," Trey said, stepping back from the microphone as the band began to perform a cover of J.J. Cale's "After Midnight." It was precisely 12:02 AM.

Now, bear with me here. Following "After Midnight," the band picked back up on the story of Jimmy and, traditionally, that would be tracked and written as such: "Harpua" > "After Midnight" > "Harpua." However, at this performance, Trey said, "If you're tracking this, only put down 'Harpua' once." A clue!

That night, Phish played a 35-minute encore of eight songs: "Tweezer Reprise," "Harpua" > "After Midnight" > "NO2" > "Keyboard Army" > "Your Pet Cat" > "Once in a Lifetime" > "United We Stand."

And if you take the first letters of each of those songs, it spells out T-H-A-N-K-Y-O-U.

What band does something like that? What band would play a 29-show summer tour, then a three-day festival in New York, then a three-night run in Colorado, performing at or near their peak musicianship throughout, only to conclude with an extended, curfew-breaking encore that spells out "Thank You?"

Best. Band. Ever.

And that brings us to Dick's 2016.

What would the band do? What would they spell? For arguably the first year at Dick's, tickets were difficult to come by. Fans showed up. People came to see what Phish would do.

The first night went off without spelling anything, which already bucked tradition but fans were hopeful. Saturday came and went as well. And Sunday's first set? Nothing was spelled. But Phish being Phish, they couldn't leave it open and came out for Sunday's second set with "Crosseyed and Painless," the Talking Heads song with the refrain "I'm still waiting…I'm still waiting… I'm still waiting…."

Indeed, all of us were still waiting for the band to spell something with their song choices, and it was a clever ribbing from Phish to play "Crosseyed and Painless." They would not be spelling anything at this run (potentially ending the tradition altogether) and would instead leave all of us still waiting. Instead, Phish wove the "C&P" riff and refrain into every song they played that set, including the encore. Every song had 30,000 fans "still waiting" for that spelled-out set that would never come.

The following year, 2017, Phish would again return to Dick's to conclude the summer tour that included, of course, the Baker's

Dozen run. The three-night Labor Day weekend run sold out in advance for the first time ever. Anticipation was palpable.

Dick's 2017 went off mostly without incident. Phish performed a solid run of originals (excluding "2001"), which is notable only because the 13 shows prior featured more than 60 covers. Highlights include the first night's second set, the second night's first set, and the final night's "Disease" > "Light."

Even though Phish have seemed to move on from spelling out setlists, Dick's has continued to stack memorable runs as the years roll by. From prairie dogs carrying the plague in the campgrounds in 2019 to Frenchie dancing naked on the floor during the weather evacuation of 2022—and then getting memorialized with a huge "Carini" dedication in 2023—to a wild six-song encore in 2023, there is always something amazing happening in that soccer stadium.

A Labor Day run at Dick's offers more than the chance to catch a set where Phish spells something.

Colorado is beautiful. Marijuana is legal. Dick's offers general-admission seating in two tiers: field and stands. The whole vibe of Phish at Dick's is very special, relaxed, fun, and absolutely massive. You can camp on-site for just $30 per person per night. And then join 30,000 of your closest friends on Shakedown Street, featuring dozens and dozens of food vendors, artists, musicians—just a massive lot of fans enjoying themselves.

Really though, Dick's is a special place and a unique experience, whether Phish spells something or not. Visit Denver, see the city, see the zoo! Catch a couple of Phish shows too!

Step into the Freezer: Tahoe "Tweezer" and Other Ebenezers

As of January, 2024, Phish has played "Tweezer" many, many times—445 times, according to Phish.net, since the song's 1990 premiere.

And of those performances, there are some widely agreed-upon standout jams that rise above the rest. As you know, "Tweezer" is Phish's No. 1 jam vehicle (see chapter 8), and they've taken the song into Type II territory like none other.

In recent years, there was the Tahoe "Tweezer" of 2013 (July 31, 2013) at Lake Tahoe Outdoor Arena at Harvey's in Stateline, Nevada. Some would argue this is the best "Tweezer" of all time. In many ways it has everything: sustained, progressive jamming; crisp collaboration; crowd participation—if nothing else, perhaps this "Tweezer" serves as the winning defense of crowd "Woos!" during performances. YouTube clips of this performance have upwards of 500,000 views.

Kicking off the second set of Phish's two-night run in Stateline, this 36-minute "Tweezer" never falters, never wavers. Dark at times, light at others, loud and powerful, then quiet and gentle, this is top-notch, must-listen Phish.

The day after the show, David Calarco, aka Mr. Miner, wrote on his site PhishThoughts.com, "The reason I see Phish is in pursuit of what happened last night. Not only was it the best jam of the band's career, it was 'Tweezer'—my favorite jam by—oh—about infinity miles. 'Tweezer' is Phish. The Freezer is our home. And home has never felt as special as right now. Anyone who has ever doubted that Phish would be back and better than before—put that in your pipe and smoke it. Sculpting a piece of music far beyond anything they've ever done, the band wielded powers greater than we've ever dreamed last night. It was simply incomparable."

In July 2015, Scott Bernstein at YEMblog asked his readership to name the four best jams, the Mount Rushmore of Phish jams. The people answered and the Tahoe "Tweezer" won, taking first place above all other jams.

In 2013, *Relix* magazine published a list of top 40 "Tweezer" jams, and the Tahoe "Tweezer" took first place. Second- and third-place finishers were December 28, 2012, at MSG and September 3, 2011, at Dick's, respectively.

Really though, throughout the band's career, they've done more with "Tweezer" than any other song. Some "Tweezer" jams reach unparalleled musical heights and even still some showcase what could only be described as groupthink among the band and (in the case of Tahoe "Tweezer") the audience, too. "Oh, that's just the drugs," doubters may say. Well, if by drugs you mean incredible, spiritual moments of improvisational music, then yes, sir, you are correct.

While most versions of "Tweezer" offer something worth revisiting, there are a few particular performances that we insist you, dear reader, find a calm quiet place to hear and experience.

There's the 45-minute Bozeman "Tweezer" (November 28, 1994), featured in part on *A Live One* as the track "Montana." In fact, 1994 was a great year for "Tweezer," and includes the original Tweezerfest at the Bomb Factory (May 7, 1992) that features the band jamming in and out of "Tweezer" and other songs, including "Sparks," "Sweet Emotion," "Walk Away," and even "Cannonball" by The Breeders.

20 years later we would get a second Tweezerfest at Merriweather Post Pavilion (July 27, 2014), where Phish would weave "Tweezer" throughout the second set, in and out of a half dozen other songs.

The famous Memphis "Tweezer," the Mud Island "Tweezer," is the band's longest performance of the song and clocks in at more than 50 minutes.

Other notable performances of "Tweezer" include the Finger Lakes "Fleezer" (June 22, 1995) as part of a truly epic second set and 1997's TweezaBella (December 6, 1997), a dark, fuzzy jam that segues into Hendrix's "Izabella." See also 10 nights prior in Hampton (November 2, 1997) for an awesome "Tweezer" in what is an absolutely incredible second set.

Let's see, there are so many! Also check out September 9, 1999; June 24, 2000; and Madison Square Garden's December 28, 2012, and January 2, 2016.

Oh, and dial in Atlantic City's "Zeppeleezer" (October 30, 2010) featuring teases of four legendary Led Zeppelin songs.

And while no one could forget it, there's also the recent Magnaball "Tweezpian" aka "Tweezerpants" (August 22, 2015) where Phish does what they do best: jams the hell out of "Tweezer" and then surprises everyone with a well-jammed "Tweezer"-infused "Prince Caspian."

Look, we love "Tweezer," and there are a lot of exceptional performances out there. This book could have easily been "100 Tweezer Tweezers" Check out this pair from Alpharetta: 8/1/21 is one of the longest jams since the band returned to the stage in 2009 and was the first "Tweezer" since 2/22/20 during the forced 17-month pandemic hiatus; and 7/15/23 is a frothy beast of nearly 30 minutes. Oh, and the Greek "Tweezer" (4/17/23) hits the 45-minute mark. And don't sleep on the "Tweezer" from MSG (8/6/23), a full-band Type II jam with "Guy Forget," played for the first time in 425 shows (9/4/11).

For more on Phish's "Tweezer" jams, visit Phish.net's review archive, which features timed-out descriptions and details for every "Tweezer" performed between 1990 and today. Bundle up for the journey, because it's going to be cold, cold, cold, cold, cold. Can you answer the question: What's your favorite "Tweezer"?

94 3.0 Festivals: Festival 8, SuperBall, and Magnaball

Hopefully, you're reading this while relaxing at your campsite at Mondegreen. What will be Phish's 11th festival was only recently announced at the time of updating this book for the 2024 edition. Needless to say, we are very excited! Hope to see you there!

If you're looking for Curveball, the festival that didn't happen, check out chapter 47.

Their eighth festival, aptly titled Festival 8, took place over Halloween weekend in 2009. In June 2009, the band announced a fun save-the-date with the festival location to be announced, featuring an animated map on Phish.com where individual states were slowly removed to finally reveal California as the festival location, specifically the Empire Polo Fields in Indio, California, where the Coachella Festival also calls home.

Leading up to the festival, Phish.com had featured 100 albums that were systematically eliminated, "killed off" by animated axes and arrows, leaving just eight albums come festival weekend for which the eight campsites were named. The musical costume finalists included albums by The Rolling Stones, Radiohead, Genesis, Jimi Hendrix, Prince, David Bowie, and, somewhat surprisingly, MGMT's 2007 *Oracular Spectacular*.

Over three days, Phish played eight sets, including Saturday night's musical costume album, revealed on the day of the show to be The Rolling Stones' *Exile on Main Street* featuring Sharon Jones and horn players (see chapter 90).

That Saturday, after the *Exile* set, Phish returned for a third set, delighting the crowd with a jam-heavy five-song set that included "Fluffhead" as large metal structures installed on the festival grounds shot flames into the air in sync with the music. Another interesting, unique element to Festival 8 was the artwork—"BOREALIS," aka The Burble, a seemingly autonomous floating cluster of light-up orbs. Created by Hector Serrano in collaboration with Javier Esteban, this psychedelic creature floated above the crowds all weekend, reacting to the music with various light patterns.

Sunday afternoon featured Phish's "first full-length acoustic set," where coffee and figure-eight-shaped doughnuts were served to the attendees. After playing a 15-song set that included "Back on the Train," "The Curtain With," and "My Sweet One," Phish took a short break and returned to encore with "Driver," "Talk," and "Secret Smile," all performed acoustically, as well.

A festival in the desert, about a two-hour drive from Los Angeles, featuring an early-Sunday acoustic set the day after covering a Rolling Stones album with special guests? This is Phish, California style. An estimated 40,000 fans attended.

After taking a year off from festivals, Phish returned with SuperBall IX at Watkins Glen International for July 4 weekend in 2011.

The sold-out SuperBall IX welcomed more than 40,000 attendees and featured new and unusual amenities, including upscale camping, a craft beer tent, high-end cooked meals, sporting events, and dozens of art installations.

Phish performed seven sets of music that weekend featuring some tremendous jams, including a first-night, second-set opening "Jam" and Saturday's late-night, fourth-set, ambient "Storage Jam."

Over the weekend, Phish performed covers of "Golden Age," "No Quarter," and "The Star-Spangled Banner," and debuted covers of "Big Balls" by AC/DC and "Monkey Man" by The Rolling Stones.

Looking at the weekend as a whole, Phish pulled no punches and showcased the scope and breadth of their musicianship and showmanship. On Friday night, Phish busted out David Bowie's "Life on Mars?" and encored with "The Show of Life."

On Saturday night, Phish incorporated a Secret Language cue (a Simpsons signal after "Birds of a Feather") for the first time in almost 11 years to the day (July 3, 2000). And Sunday's show included a "Colonel Forbin's Ascent" > "Fly Famous Mockingbird" > "Destiny Unbound," with Gamehendge narration that spoke to the previous night's fourth set "Storage Jam." To put it bluntly, this weekend festival had it all!

And the success of the festival, paired with the support and assistance of the local communities, led Phish to return to Watkins Glen in August 2015 to host their 10th festival, Magnaball.

Phish played eight sets across three nights at Magnaball.

Magnaball's Friday-night show featured a number of highlights, including heavy bust-outs of "The Man Who Stepped into Yesterday" > "Avenu Malkenu" and in the first set, not to mention a "Happy Birthday to You" for Trey Anastasio's daughter Eliza to celebrate her 20th birthday, concluding with an epic "Bathtub Gin." The second set featured a few deep, dank, notable jams, including "Chalk Dust Torture" and "No Men in No Man's Land." Encoring with a strange pairing of "Farmhouse" and "First Tube," Phish recorded Magnaball night one in the books.

Saturday's show featured a number of highlights, including "Run Like an Antelope" and "Blaze On" and "Cities," but it is perhaps the "Tweezer" > "Prince Caspian" that will forever be remembered as the zenith of Magnaball. This heavily jammed pair of songs, a 35-minute block of music, feels more "Tweezer" than "Caspian," but the jam itself, with all four musicians at the helm, is an exceptional moment of Phish 3.0. This "Tweezpian," aka "Tweezpants," showcases the sheer talent of these collaborative musicians, true masters of their instruments.

After a third set and an encore of "Boogie on Reggae Woman" > "Tweezer Reprise" (perhaps a nod to 2014's TweezerFest show at Merriweather Post Pavilion on July 27, 2014, where they also

The now-infamous Drive-In theatre at Magnaball in Watkins Glen, 2015.
(Stephen Olker)

encored with "BORW" > "TR"), Phish would play a late-night ambient set.

For this late-night set, the band performed behind a large drive-in movie screen installed on-site, on which abstracted video of the live band was projected and various lighting techniques contributed to contrasting moments of screen opacity when the band could be seen through the screen. This is truly free and unique Phish, so please find an hour of free time, search "Drive-In Jam," and buckle up.

Sunday's show featured an awesome "Twist" > "Weekapaug Groove" -> "Martian Monster," the latter of which plays more as a hyped reprise from the set opener than a true version. Actually, that whole second set is fantastic. And after three days and nights of music, Phish chose to encore Sunday night and close out the festival with a 20-minute "You Enjoy Myself" and a fireworks show.

As I've said before, Phish continues to regularly force the question, "What band?" What band would host these mega festivals, perform surprise late-night artistically staged ambient sets, bust-out old songs, debut new ones, and conclude with fireworks? What band, I ask you?

95 *Fuego* (2014) and *Big Boat* (2016)

Released just two years, four months, and 28 days apart, these two albums were both produced by Bob Ezrin (Alice Cooper, Lou Reed, Pink Floyd).

June 2014: *Fuego* is Phish's 12th studio album and their first since 2009's *Joy*. Produced by Bob Ezrin, the 10-track album received critical acclaim and peaked on the Billboard chart at No. 7, tying Phish's chart record set by 1998's *Billy Breathes*.

In a 2014 Dean Budnick cover story for *Relix* magazine, Trey Anastasio speaks about the album's title: "Fire has always, throughout human history, been at the center of communities. People gather around the fire and talk or sing or connect." Of course, within the song "Fuego," the band references the French automobile: "Inside your Fuego, we keep it rolling."

At nine minutes, the title track has lead to numerous standout jams in live performances, perhaps most notably, or at least most recently, at the Baker's Dozen residency (July 25, 2017).

As further detailed by all band members in Budnick's article, the impetus behind what would become *Fuego* was to get together again and do what they love: jam. Not as full-on as the all-day-and-night sessions for *The Story of the Ghost*, but certainly a return to their roots. After many years out of the studio, the band had returned refreshed, not just as musicians in their own rights but also as friends.

Of course, fans were initially introduced to the album as *Wingsuit*, the working title when Phish performed the album as their musical costume "from the future" at their 2013 Halloween show in Atlantic City, New Jersey. For that, Phish performed 12 songs, including three songs that would not make it to the album. Some fans considered this a cheap cop-out for what has traditionally been a night when Phish covers a classic album by another band, while some fans considered themselves privileged to hear the debut of a new Phish album (see chapter 90).

Eight months later, we would meet *Fuego*.

In Will Hermes' *Rolling Stone* 3.5 out of 5 star review, he writes, "Lyrics remain an Achilles' heel, but sometimes Phish hit profundity sideways. 'The Line' is a soaring, Steely Dan–ish ballad inspired by Darius Washington Jr.'s famously flubbed free throws during a crucial 2005 college-hoop game. Yet the title metaphor also handily conjures an addict staring down his next dose. 'A hero's what I'm not,' Anastasio sings ruefully, before spinning out another set of guitar lines that prove him exactly wrong."

Phish would also perform "The Line" for their sixth appearance on *Late Night with David Letterman* on the evening of *Fuego*'s release (June 24, 2014). After the performance, Letterman thanked the band and said, "As you know, I was a founding member of the band, and then when I was lucky enough to get this show I had to stop touring. So it's good to have them back!"

Another point worth mentioning is the quality of song contributions from both Mike Gordon and Page McConnell with "555" and "Halfway to the Moon," respectively, the latter of which the band later confessed (November 1, 2013) was their favorite on the album. And sadly, some songs didn't make the final cut. As decided by Bob Ezrin, "Mercury" ended up on the studio floor.

Leading up to the album's release, NPR's *All Songs Considered* posted a "Waiting All Night" video of the painting *Edan* by Paco Pomet animated by George Loucas and Baked FX.

The delicate yet soaring "Wingsuit," which kicked off the Atlantic City set, closes out the album and has since been played live more than 40 times, featuring five or six significant jams.

And who doesn't love "Wombat," the supporting song of the gag from the Halloween performance? It's kinda like the theme from the "Fish" TV show. You know, with Abe Vigoda (October 31, 2013; see chapter 90).

October 2016: *Big Boat*, the second Phish album produced by Bob Ezrin, dropped just days before the band's Las Vegas Halloween run, though many of the songs had already been performed live during 2015's summer tour.

The album begins with a rolling drum lick and fuzzy guitar chords that kick off drummer Jon Fishman's "Friends." Its lyrics describe a big boat "Ascending from the depths of our imagination" and ultimately "heading across the great ocean from our shores to outer space."

Is this the big "boat" on the album's cover art? The trippy, ethereal image was created by Beijing-based artist Fang Er as part of her 2008 series *Don't Touch Me!*

Without a title track on the album, "Friends" may very well be that song. It's been performed live only twice.

However, of the 13 tracks on the album, a couple of them have become live-show staples. Most notably, "No Men in No Man's Land" has proved itself a heavy contender within Phish's jam conduits. Phish.net lists nearly half of all "NMINML" performances in its jam chart, where their writers highlight noteworthy jams, including the song's debut in Bend, Oregon (July 21, 2015), a year before the release of *Big Boat*.

"Blaze On," the album's fourth track, may read more like fan fiction than a Phish original with lyrics like, "You got your nice shades on, and the worst days are gone / So now the band plays on, you got one life, blaze on." Also please note the track's precise runtime of four minutes and twenty seconds. Heh.

The underlying theme to the album seems to be one of reflection, remorse, moving past the dark times, and embracing the good times ahead. Songs like "Home" and "Tide Turns" seem to be speaking specifically to Trey Anastasio's successful recovery from drug abuse.

And "Miss You" is about Anastasio's sister, Kristy Anastasio Manning, who passed away in April 2009 after a courageous battle with cancer. Anastasio spoke to Alan Paul at *The Wall Street Journal* in October 2006 about his song: "I was literally looking at my sister's picture, and those words just came tumbling out. Some of the lines were an attempt to speak for my parents and their experience. But as direct as it was, I hope that people think about their own lives when they hear the song. I believe that the more specifically a songwriter writes, the more universal the sentiment becomes, and I hope that happens here."

In his review at NPR, Mike Katzif writes, "What has changed this time out is the directness of Phish's lyrics. In the past, the band (along with longtime co-lyricist Tom Marshall) often relied on zany, imaginative wordplay—or fashioned fantastical mythologies—that treated words and syllables as rhythms that ping off the tongue, yet favor cryptic absurdity. But for *Big Boat*, Ezrin reportedly challenged the band members to share more of themselves in their songs, resulting in expressions of sadness, anger, and earnest positivity as well as themes of aging and mortality, internal angst, and desire for social change."

At the other end of the album's spectrum is the Page McConnell song "I Always Wanted It This Way," seemingly a tribute to early '80s synth and prog.

Though the penultimate song, "More," certainly has Ezrin's lyrical influence and has come to fill the first-set closer position at Phish's live shows quite nicely.

Now, let's discuss the elephant in the room: Anastasio's latest opus, the 13-minute "Petrichor." The word, as defined by the *Oxford English Dictionary*, means "a pleasant, distinctive smell frequently accompanying the first rain after a long period of warm, dry weather in certain regions."

Sam Sodomsky writes of "Petrichor" on Pitchfork: "It might not be a track to convince the naysayers (or even, with its 13-minute runtime, to necessarily warrant a second play). But it's the only moment on the album when Phish shows—and not just tells—that transcendence is possible, and that they're willing to go there with us."

The song itself may not stand up well against previous compositions like "YEM" or "Divided Sky," but it has its own unique emotive peaks and valleys all the same. Is this Phish's next big one? Perhaps not as much as Anastasio would hope. Is it just maybe a little too playful?

Perhaps more poetic and pedantic than other albums—I'm looking at you, Bob—*Big Boat* is not all sad, sappy ballads. Just mostly. Tracks like "No Men," "Breath and Burning," "I Always Wanted It This Way," and "Petrichor" keep it worthwhile and relevant.

Big Boat peaked at No. 19 on the Billboard charts.

96 NYE 2013–2017

Nostalgic, slapstick, psychedelic, and theatrical...

In 2013, Phish returned to New York City for four shows and what would be their eighth New Year's Eve at Madison Square Garden. It was, after all, the band's 30th anniversary.

Phish opened with "AC/DC Bag" and concluded the first set with "Fluffhead," after which Trey Anastasio and Page McConnell carried a cake shaped like a keyboard to the front of the stage with a theatrical flat of a mountain behind them, recreating the iconic photo from their 1988 tour in Colorado. After they cut and served the cake to the fans riding the rail, a video played showing Jon Fishman revitalizing a box truck, with a "JEMP" logo (an acronym using the first letters of each band member's name) referencing the band's own record company, founded in 2005. In the video, Fishman fixes the dilapidated truck and drives to NYC, shearing the top off when driving under an overpass.

And then, on the floor of Madison Square Garden, a pair of headlights shone. It was the JEMP truck, driving onto the floor at Madison Square Garden! Slowly, it positioned itself in the center of the floor and all of the band members made their way to the top of the box truck, where they performed a second set with a pared-down backline, including hockey sticks as microphone stands, referencing Phish's very first gig at UVM when they had indeed used a hockey stick in lieu of a mic stand.

The now-famous JEMP Truck Set featured nine songs, all from Phish's very early years, mostly from 1988, and a few classic Gamehendge songs, including an extended "Icculus."

After the JEMP set, Phish returned to the main stage and opened the third set with "Character Zero" > "Auld Lang Syne" >

"Fuego," the last of which Phish had only played once prior at their 2013 Halloween show, continuing the band's affinity for playing new material at the close of the year. The band then concluded the set with "You Enjoy Myself," and during the break before the encore, another video played, showcasing photographs and film clips from Phish's 30 years as a band. Back onstage, Phish encored with "Grind" and "Show of Life," and as the attendees left the arena the video screen showed a photograph of the band members, digitally aged to appear in their 80s, with a save-the-date message for Phish's 60th anniversary show on December 31, 2043.

In 2014, the Phish from Vermont opted instead of spending New Year's Eve in cold, snowy New York City to head to Miami Beach! Also, Skrillex and Diplo booked Madison Square Garden that year. Whether that was before or after Phish chose Miami, I don't know. Having played the American Airlines Arena on New Year's Eve in 2003 and 2009, this wasn't exactly new territory, but many fans were surprised not to have NYE at MSG. Still others welcomed the change and the chance to spend late January on South Beach.

The show progressed rather normally, with a solid first set. The second set is full of heavy-hitting jams. The whole set is fire start to finish: "Birds of a Feather," "Ghost" > "Theme From the Bottom" -> "Cities" > "Chalk Dust Torture," "Martian Monster."

After a break, Phish returned to the stage and debuted "Dem Bones," a cappella. Toward the end of the song, Fishman began to play the vacuum and confusion ensued. Anastasio informed the crowd, "We're sorry, this has never happened before; it seems the vacuum is stuck to his face." The band attempted unsuccessfully to remove the vacuum from Fishman's face before calling out their instrument technicians to give it a try. Unsuccessful, they then took Fishman backstage to work it out while Mike Gordon suggested, "You could try changing it from suck to blow," perhaps a reference to the 1987 Mel Brooks film *Spaceballs*. "Suck to blow" then repeated over and over through the PA system until a loud explosion sounded and the lights went out.

Then suddenly, a large inflated Fishman doll appeared from behind the stage and rose above the crowd while red Fishman doughnuts dropped and Phish counted down to Happy New Year. "Auld Lang Syne" was followed by "The Dogs" > "Tweezer" and more, concluding with "Julius" and then encoring with "Golgi Apparatus" > "Tweezer Reprise."

In 2015, Phish once again played four nights at Madison Square Garden, which would be the second time their New Year's Eve run would not end on New Year's Eve. In 2010, NYE was the second night of four, and again in 2015, NYE would be the second night of the run.

Phish opened December 31, 2015, with "The Moma Dance" > "Possum." Highlights from the first two sets include an audience sing-along during "I Didn't Know" and heavy jamming on "Kill Devil Falls" > "Piper" > "Twist" to conclude the second set.

For the third set, the band returned not to the main stage but rather a smaller stage on the floor on the opposite end of the arena. The band all faced inward, toward each other, and above them hung a large cone, point down, with a solid beam of light aimed directly down. They opened the set with "No Men in No Man's Land," and after about five minutes, as the composed section gave way to improvisation, the cone shed a layer of fabric down towards the band, engulfing the stage. The cone above them was now an hourglass from inside which they played while lights and projected images, some suggesting falling sand, some suggesting animals, adorned it. As trippy and psychedelic as the visuals were, the music was even more so.

Phish jammed into territories unknown, keeping a funky rhythm with layers of science fiction accompaniment. The guys go deep on this one.

The hourglass enveloping the band on a small platform opposite the stage at MSG, 2015. (Andy P. Smith)

Then, at some point toward the end of the ensuing 20-minute jam, the band set up an audio loop and unbeknownst to (most) of the crowd, snuck out of the hourglass and returned to the main stage for the countdown, after which they played "Auld Lang Syne" > "Blaze On" > "Carini" > "David Bowie," and more. Phish then encored with "Tube" and "Cavern."

For New Year's Eve 2016, Phish was back at The Garden. Opening each of the previous nights of the run with an a cappella song (including December 29, 2017, their first show since the 2016 presidential election, with "The Star-Spangled Banner"), Phish continued with an a cappella "Don't Bogart That Joint" to kick things off. While the first two sets certainly had their moments, including "2001" > "Carini" > "Twist," it was all about what would come for the third set.

And for most setlist-gambling fans, the odds-on favorite was Anastasio's new opus, "Petrichor," and that bet came in. Phish opened the third set with "Petrichor," *Big Boat*'s closing track. For this delicate-cum-joyful 18-minute performance, Phish welcomed a horn section, including longtime collaborator Jennifer Hartswick; James Casey; Natalie Cressman; Jeff Tanski on keyboards; and award-winning percussionist Andres Forero.

Furthermore, a crew of suit-clad dancers performed a choreographed number based on the rain theme of "Petrichor." The theatrics were reminiscent of paintings by René Magritte and Cirque du Soleil performances. Suspended, LED-lit umbrellas changed colors and moved in sync before the stage and then it "rained" tiny gels at the front of the stage and stress-relief-type raindrops on the crowd. Phish then played "Auld Lang Syne" > "Suzy Greenberg," during which the dancers ripped off their suits to reveal bright yellow costumes and continued to dance during the balloon drop, which included hundreds of inflatable dogs and cats. Yes…it rained cats and dogs after "Petrichor."

The horn section played with Phish through the rest of the set, including a wonderful rendition of "Ocelot" before concluding with the high-energy, bass-driven "First Tube." To end the night, all encored with "Loving Cup."

Phish once again returned to Madison Square Garden for a four-night run of shows across New Year's Eve weekend in 2017. These shows, paired with the Baker's Dozen residency, would make for 17 shows at MSG in 2017, i.e. #17in17.

And it seems that Phish was thinking about their 17 in '17 from the very beginning of the NYE 2017 run, opening Thursday's show (December 28, 2017) with "AC/DC Bag." Now, that selection is not exactly a rare opening number, but considering that the "Bag" performance at the Baker's Dozen is perhaps the only song undoubtedly flubbed and abandoned during the residency (July 23, 2017), I'm inclined to think Phish hit the stage determined to right their wrongs. As further evidence, Phish followed "Bag" with "Wolfman's Brother" on both nights.

But let's pause for a moment here. We need to discuss Chris Kuroda, because he most certainly leveled up on this run.

Having premiered his brand new intergalactic lighting rig earlier this year, Kuroda, I imagine, was thinking, *What else can we light up for New Year's Eve?* And so we get a little something extra: a 360-degree addition of lights in the ceiling spokes of The Garden. And Kuroda rocked these new, dynamic lights, illuminating the ceiling, the pit, creating expanding and contracting circles, ahem, doughnuts, on the crowd, even playing a bit of cat-and-mouse with the band by moving a spot of sorts round and round in circles around the venue. Kudos to Kuroda!

Highlights from December 28, 2017, include "Tube," "Back On The Train," and a 30-minute "No Men in No Man's Land," which segued into a "Twist" that's worth revisiting, though it seems as if Trey Anastasio pulled up just when things were heading for true greatness.

For night two, with a nod to our famous, cavernous venue, Phish bookended the first set with "Cavern" and "Walls of The Cave." Highlights from that show include a well-jammed "Blaze On," a very dark "555," and a stellar "Chalk Dust Torture."

Heading into night three, I think it was safe to assume that most people felt like Phish was performing well, but had yet to achieve a level of excellence on par with most of the Baker's Dozen shows. The first two nights were solid, absolutely—but then we have night three.

On December 30, 2017, Phish opened with "Mike's Song" and got the crowd going immediately. For me this seals the deal for Gordon as MVP of the run. The "Mike's" > "Hydrogen" > "Weekapaug" that comes is some damn fine Phish music: loose, fun, dare I say, ambitious? In some years it seems that maybe the band leans on this stalwart tryptic a little bit, but recently it seems to invigorate them, inspire them, and push them to new heights. The result? A first-set "Tweezer" to follow. And a damn fine "Tweezer" it is, not too crunchy, not too spacey, not too hot, and not too cold. Just right, really!

"Tweezer" concluded and Fishman delivered perhaps his best performance of "Ass-Handed," gently bringing everyone back to Earth to catch their breath after that 40-minute romp.

What followed was an incredible evening of music, with highlight jams in almost every form and context, including first-set "Kill Devil Falls" and "Bathtub Gin." The bust-out of "Brother," while not performed as well as we'd hoped, was still a welcomed surprise. Opening the second set with "Down with Disease" (Gordo for MVP!), the band took us on a journey into uncharted territory, with another 30-minute jam, besting the first night's "No Men," and continuing into powerful performances of "Steam" and "Light." Then "Farmhouse" came in the cool-down slot, followed by "Run Like an Antelope." Encoring with "Sleeping Monkey" > "Tweezer Reprise," Phish put December 30, 2017, in the books, which, as of writing this, has settled quietly into the No. 13 position on Phish.net's Top Rated Shows Chart.

Night Four, New Year's Eve: with all its inherent anticipation and expectations, the evening came with even more suspense after ticketholders were emailed a cryptic message that morning, detailing "cosmic wristbands" available at each seat that would be activated close to midnight.

Opening the first set of three, Phish played "Carini," perhaps the darkest, power-chord rocker in their arsenal. And the crowd went wild! "Suzy Greenberg" came second, a welcomed homage to the previous year's New Year's Eve performance. "My Friend, My Friend" was next, a quick and dirty performance, leading to the double-shot of "Fluffhead" and "Reba," stellar choices for a NYE first set. With a quick jaunt through "Poor Heart," Phish spent another 30 minutes running through "46 Days" > "Maze" > "Character Zero," all well-performed but perhaps a bit short of extraordinary.

Opening the second set with "Possum," Phish woke everyone up real good and performed a 70-minute, six-song second set with highlights including "Gotta Jibboo" and an extra eerie take on "What's the Use?" The 20-minute "YEM" felt like home, and everyone seemed to be having a good time. This was Phish playing Phish: classic compositions with just a dash of panache.

And now for our third and final act of the evening. After Phish had already played for two and a half hours, the band took the stage and played…a Trey Anastasio Band song?

Yes; after eight sets over three nights of Phish playing tried and true Phish and practically zero cover songs, they concluded 2017 with a "cover" of a brand-new Trey Anastasio Band song, "Soul Planet," premiered in Las Vegas only two months prior (October 27, 2017).

But wait! Suddenly stage techs were surrounding a 40-foot mast onstage and unfolding a giant ship sail. The spectacle added some validation of the song's lyrics: "We're screaming through space on

And the rain came down during "Petrichor" at MSG NYE 2016.
(Jason Gershuny)

a Soul Planet / the wind is the music / and everyone's together in this one big ocean, and the ocean is love."

The stage had transformed into a pirate ship, with a rotating mast and sail, including a Phish-infused Jolly Roger pirate flag. They even wheeled cannons on stage to shoot "cannonballs" into the crowd, complete with Acme-esque "cannon firing" sound effects and cannon ball "splashes" in the audience ocean.

And the "cosmic bracelets" worked! I was impressed. Illuminating 20,000 wrists is no easy task. And coordinating synchronized patterns and colors among the 20,000, between various levels of Madison Square Garden? Was it some kind of pyrotechnic hyper-color cornucopia? Not quite. But it was cool! And it went one more step toward bringing everyone together that night, under one roof, as one "ocean."

After the NYE countdown, projected on the billowing sail, "Happy New Year!" The balloons dropped and the band segued into "Auld Lang Syne."

"Free" was the first song of 2018, and Phish performed it well, "splashing in the sea."

Next up was "A Song I Heard the Ocean Sing," which offered one of the best jams of the run. Trey and Page exchanged melodies, building, building, then belaying each other upward to a gentle boil of a peak.

The band continued the third set with "The Moma Dance" > "Prince Caspian" > "Wading in the Velvet Sea," none of which offered any significant jamming, including that darling of Magnaball, but all do well to fit with the ocean/big boat/pirate theme of the set. Though that "Moma" is worth a relisten and includes a nice "Auld Lang Syne" tease at the end.

Then, to close out the set, the evening, the NYE run, and the 17 in '17, we got "First Tube," the big energy, bass-driven (Gordo MVP!) instrumental rocker, and a personal favorite of mine. And this one delivered, for sure.

Though, wait a minute—didn't they end the third set NYE 2016 with "First Tube"? They did. And then they encored with… yep. "Loving Cup," same as NYE 2017. Strange that they would repeat that pairing conclusion. Maybe they forgot about NYE 2016? I mean, they played 17 shows in MSG since then—ha!

Phish on New Year's Eve has always proved to be a unique experience: three sets, a gag, balloons…. Like most people, Phish often takes the evening as an opportunity to reminisce but also to bask in the glory of the moment, looking forward to the year to come. Sometimes funny, sometimes silly, surely a spectacle, Phish's New Year's Eve shows always deliver.

97 NYE 2018–2023

This batch of New Year's Eve runs features silver-suited space men, smoking rainbow aerialists, armies of monochromatic clones, platform malfunctions, a livestream from The Ninth Cube, a flying whale, kelp, a medley spanning 40 years, dozens of naked guys, and, of course, Gamehendge at its utmost level of production.

For New Year's Eve 2018, the band took the stage for the third set wearing silver spacesuits and played "Mercury" for the 16th time since its premiere in Bend, Oregon (7/22/15). As the band played, acrobats and aerialists danced and twirled with colored ribbons and smoke creating a rainbow across the stage. After the stroke of midnight and "Auld Lang Syne," the band played "Say It To Me S.A.N.T.O.S." as Mike and Trey were hoisted up and down in the air singing the chorus: "This is what space smells like (Dangling in thin air) / You will always remember where you were." And while it was only the second performance of that song, the entire arena sang along to ring in the new year.

New Years 2019 was the year of the Rescue Squad! Beginning the third set with an a cappella rendition of Stephen Sondheim's "Send in the Clowns" (made famous by Frank Sinatra and later Judy Collins) changing the lyrics to "Send in the *Clones*." Each band member, in monochromatic attire then took to individual platforms that rose in the air as they played "First Tube" and then "Auld Lang Syne." Meanwhile, groups of matching monochromatic "clones" sang and danced around the stage below the band as colorful balloons fell from the ceiling. Later, Trey's platform would get stuck high above the stage as the other band members' platforms descended. Trey's jokes barely masked his concerns as the band then played an encore of "Tweezer Reprise" before stagehands took

Fishman's platform up to Trey to help get him down. Descending on Fishman's platform, a joyful and relieved Trey played the drums singing an improvised song now known as "Rescue Squad."

Navigating the COVID-19 pandemic as a live touring band was certainly not easy. And Phish did the best they could. Unfortunately, just days before their 2021 New Years Run at MSG, the band issued a statement: "With the Omicron variant of Covid-19 surging in New York City, we have made the very difficult decision to reschedule next week's run of shows at Madison Square Garden. The health and safety of Phish fans, our crew, and venue staff is paramount in our minds. While Phish has played shows this year as the pandemic has continued, this variant's ability for rapid transmission is unprecedented." The band rescheduled the four-night run for April 2022, with tickets valid for those dates while also offering full refunds.

The April 2022 run at MSG is certainly one for the annals of Phish history, with stellar jams from each night of the run. But it's the flying, drone-operated whale and dolphins that made for a magical, underwater experience during the third set of the third night (4/22/22, see chapter 14). Only the band Phish would reschedule (not cancel) their four-night New Year's Eve run and still perform a three-set show with an unprecedented, awe-inspiring "gag." What's more is that the band *also* performed a New Years Eve show as a free live stream.

Webcast as part of the *Dinner and a Movie* series (see chapter 55), the band played live from "The Ninth Cube," with a recipe for fans of lemony dishes including a "giant bowl of lemonade," to poke fun at the webcast in lieu of a live audience performance. And what or where is The Ninth Cube? Well, quite literally the band played in a 52,000 sq. ft., 100 ft. tall box of matte black sheet metal called The Studio in a town called Lititz, Pennsylvania. The Studio is unarguably the greatest rehearsal space in the world, as part of a

Send in the clones! Phish playing on individual risers as an army of clones of the band members dance and perform below on 12/31/2019 at MSG, NYC (Jason Gershuny)

96-acre campus called Rock Lititz that includes a hotel and event production business facilities.

Of course, with Phish, nothing can be taken at surface value, and The Ninth Cube alludes to previous performances and lore first established as part of the Kasvot Växt Halloween performance (10/31/18, see chapter 83). For more on The Ninth Cube, turn to chapter 55).

Back at Madison Square Garden for New Year's Eve 2022, Phish performed a nostalgic hodgepodge of tunes from previous New Year's gags across their 40-year career. Beginning with a motif of a broken time machine, the performance featured dancers and performers from past New Years (Father Time from 12/31/99, the Famous Mockingbird from 12/31/92), as the band played a medley of previous New Year's songs, including: "Bohemian

Boundless confetti rains down on the crowd at the stroke of midnight as the band plays "Auld Lang Syne" on 12/31/22 at MSG, NYC. (Trevor Anderson)

Rhapsody" from 12/31/96, "Jungle Boogie" from 12/31/03, and the Theme from *New York, New York* from 12/31/97. And then, springing from a giant birthday cake came dozens of dancers in skin tone leotards with beards and boots to reference the lone streaker "Frenchie" from Dick's rain delay show (9/2/22)

I'm not sure what happened on New Year's Eve 2023. Were you there? (See chapter 5). Did you experience the culmination of nearly 40 years of Phish and bask in the emotional release of 20,000 fans? Are you okay? Is Poster Nutbag okay?

98 Sigma Oasis (2020)

Spring 2020 was a very strange time. The global pandemic nearly shut down the entire world, prompting lockdowns, cancellations, and ultimately millions of deaths. New York City, where I'm writing this from right now, issued a city-wide lockdown on March 23, 2020. It's an understatement to say that at the time we had no idea what our lives would soon become. It was a time of uncertainty, fear, and confusion.

Phish, of course, responded as best as they could by launching an archival webcast series called *Dinner and a Movie* (For more on *DaaM*, see chapter 55). Then, as if a free weekly webcast series wasn't enough, fans who tuned in to the second episode on 3/31/20 were treated to a very special chat. During the setbreak of the *DaaM* show (7/27/2014), the four members of Phish appeared onscreen in a group video chat during which Page McConnell announced that the band had recorded a new album titled *Sigma Oasis* in November 2019, and that they would host a live online listening party the following day, 4/1/2020 at 9:00 PM ET.

And sure enough, despite the April Fool's Day coincidence and Phish's propensity for pranks, the band did indeed drop a brand new studio album on April 1, 2020.

Sigma Oasis (2020) is Phish's 15th studio album and clocks in at 66 minutes across just nine tracks, including the title track. All nine songs had already been performed live by Phish. And "Mercury" and "Shade" were both previously recorded for the band's 2016 album *Big Boat* (chapter 95), but did not make it on the final album.

Sigma Oasis was available on streaming and digital purchase on April 2, 2020, the vinyl and CD release wouldn't come until

November 2020. The album's cover is a black and white photograph of the band members standing on the porch of The Barn studio in Vermont taken by photographer Rene Huemer.

Sam Sodomsky wrote of the album in his 6.5/10 review at Pitchfork: "Sigma Oasis cruises in the relaxed, muted groove this band has settled into over the past few years. None of these songs are new territory for them—the crunchy escapism of the title track, the rock opera Hallmark card of "A Life Beyond the Dream"—but they top anything they've recorded in the past decade-and-a-half by capturing their comfortable dynamic with a positivity that radiates from every note. Along the way, they nod to the stylistic diversions that pop up in their live shows: intricate prog ("Mercury"), Zappa freakouts ("Thread"), singing-in-the-shower balladry ("Leaves"), sci-fi atmospherics (the final moments of "Everything's Right"). You can listen from beginning to end and get a sense of the buoyant, utopian universe they create when they're playing at their best."

99 International Phish

In total, Phish has performed in 15 different countries around the world: the United States, Canada, Mexico, Japan, Germany, Italy, Denmark, France, Belgium, England, Ireland, Austria, Czech Republic, The Netherlands, and Spain.

In 2016, Phish started a new, annual tradition: playing a run of shows in Rivera Maya in Mexico. Each run (including 2016, 2017, 2019, 2020, 2022, 2023, and 2024) featured an all-inclusive ticketing packages with three or four nights of Phish performing on a stage mere feet away from the Caribbean Sea. Organized as a partnership between Phish and CID, a VIP entertainment package company, Phish's Riviera Maya events started at $2,200 per person for a shared, double-occupancy room for 4-nights.

Naturally, playing on the beach in Mexico, these Phish shows include a variety of ocean-themed songs for the relatively intimate audience on the beach, some of whom spend the shows dancing knee-deep in the Caribbean, eg "Wading in the Velvet Sea."

Other North American dates include our neighbor to the north, with Phish first performing in Canada on July 1, 1989, in Montreal, Quebec. Three years later, in 1992, Phish returned to Canada for a pair of shows in December to conclude their 21-show fall tour.

Following those shows, Phish has since performed in Canada a number of times: five shows in 1993, five shows in 1994, once in 1995, once in 1996, twice in 1999, once in 2000, and once in 2013 on July 22 after their previously scheduled July 9 show was cancelled due to severe thunderstorms and flash flooding. More recently, they played Toronto's Budweiser Stage in 2019 and 2022. Also worth noting is the November 23, 1996, show that featured their one and only performance of the bluegrass tune "Midnight on the Highway," which the band reportedly learned while detained at the border. During that show's second set, Phish played "Makisupa Policeman" and Anastasio improvised the lyrics, singing: "Woke up in the morning, border guard in my bunk, he took his fucking dog on the bus, and he found my dank."

Needless to say, there are real and present challenges to touring internationally, even in Canada.

And now, across the pond we go!

Phish initially toured Europe in 1992, performing in small theaters and clubs. Phish's 1992 Summer European Tour featured just eight shows across two weeks, which may have felt more like a fun vacation for our young musicians than the robust American tours they would come to headline in the years that followed. For this first foray into Europe, Phish was opening for The Violent Femmes, and then they performed at Denmark's annual Roskilde Festival alongside groups including Pearl Jam, Blur, and David Byrne.

Phish returned to Europe four years later, in July, 1996, for 18 shows through six countries in support of Santana, with whom Phish toured for nearly two dozen US dates in the late summer of 1992. Adding a few headlining shows of their own while in Europe, Phish was pleased to see so many dedicated American fans touring along by train.

And so Phish hit Europe again in 1997 with a 14-show winter tour and a 19-show summer tour, featuring some stellar performances to say the least. Nine songs from Phish's March 1, 1997, show in Hamburg, Germany, would be released as *Slip Stitch and Pass*, their second official live album, and their three shows at Amsterdam's Paradiso (February 17, July 1, July 2) would later be complied and officially released as a box set in 2015. Phish's February 16, 1997, show at Wartesaal in Cologne, Germany, was filmed and televised on German public television and is now readily available on YouTube.

Upon returning to the USA, Phish performed another 17 shows leading up to their second festival in Limestone, Maine, The Great Went, which hosted 70,000 fans.

To say 1997 was a prolific year for the band is an understatement, and not just for live recordings or touring dates (including Roskilde again and The Glastonbury Festival), but also in regard to live debuts. In 1997, Phish premiered nearly two dozen songs, including "Carini," "Twist," "Limb by Limb," "Piper," "Vultures," and "Ghost," to name a few.

This is a band hitting their stride, performing shows still heralded as some of their best.

In 1998, less than three months after the Island Tour (see chapter 21), Phish hit Europe again for a blitzkrieg of nine shows across just four venues, during which Phish debuted "Moma

Dance" (June 30, 1998) and notably taught the audience how to dance the moma dance. Phish's July 6, 1998, show in Prague would later be offered as an archival release on LivePhish.com.

And rounding out our international adventures, we have Phish's 1999 performances in Japan at the Fuji Rock Festival (July 30 through August 1, 1999), which included a Friday afternoon set and headlining shows on Saturday and Sunday nights. Saturday's performance (featuring Tibetan musician Nawang Khechog accompanying the band for the encore's "Jam" and "Brian and Robert") was later released in 2011 through LivePhish after the tragic earthquake and tsunami in Japan with proceeds benefiting Peace Winds America and its sister organization Peace Winds Japan to support disaster relief operations.

In 2000, Phish returned to Japan for a seven-show summer tour, hitting Tokyo, Nagoya, Fukuoka, and Osaka. Each show features its own noteworthy jams and the June 9, 2000, show in Tokyo, later rebroadcast on Japanese television, features the first performance of "Meatstick" to include Japanese lyrics. The June 14, 2000, show at Drum Logos in Chuo-Ku, Osaka, Japan, was later released as *Live Phish Vol. 4*.

Excluding the all-inclusive runs in Mexico and a handful of Canadian shows, Phish has not played internationally since Japan in 2000. Perhaps those days are forever behind us, though rumors abound every summer. We'll just have to wait and see. Keep your passports handy!

100 Phish.net, Mockingbird Foundation, WaterWheel, and Divided Sky Foundation

Phish.net is the premier website for all things Phish—other than Phish.com, of course. Featuring precise setlists, show recaps, song histories, jam ratings, and personal show tracking through user profiles, Phish.net offers everything and anything you may want to know about Phish. To say this is one of the *100 Things Phish Fans Should Know & Do Before They Die* seems superfluous. But we'd be remiss not to include it!

While Phish.net is the sum of collective efforts by a large group of generous volunteers, the executive team at Phish.net includes Marco Walsh, Adam Scheinberg, Charlie Dirksen, Ellis Godard, and Jack Lebowitz. Charlie Dirksen and Scott Marks helm the setlist team, which is perhaps the core of Phish.net. Every show, every set Phish has ever played, is meticulously detailed, catalogued, and (user) rated on Phish.net.

Phish.net also features a number of charts, databases detailing chronological rankings of guests who've performed with Phish, as wells as 20-plus-minute jams, song teases, and song debuts.

Phish.net has taken on many roles, duties, and digital iterations over the years. And it's all done for free, voluntarily.

In fact, Phish has a policy that stipulates any website dedicated to the band cannot be monetized. According to the Phish Fan Web Site Policy: "Fansites may not be commercial (as determined by Phish in its sole discretion). Therefore, they cannot accept advertising, offer links for compensation, exploit databases compiled from their traffic, sell humorous but heartwarming page-a-day calendars, or otherwise derive any commercial proceeds in any form, regardless of whether a net profit is realized. In exchange for this permitted use, the maintainers of such sites must agree to remove

Divided Sky Residential Recovery Program

The Divided Sky Foundation, a 46-bed nonprofit recovery center spearheaded by Phish frontman Trey Anastasio, is an abstinence-based, non-medical residence, one of the first of its kind in Vermont. Focusing on quality care and compassionate programming in recovery, the Foundation's beautiful campus in the Okemo Valley provides accommodations for guests who are ready to embrace recovery. Trey explains, "As a person in recovery, I understand how valuable it is to individuals in early sobriety to have access to an inclusive, welcoming, and supportive community where they can begin to build a solid foundation for their new sober lives."

any protected materials from their sites immediately upon the request of Phish."

Furthermore, Phish.net is a project of the nonprofit Mockingbird Foundation. As described at its website, mbird.org, The Mockingbird Foundation Inc. was founded in 1996 by Phish fans to raise funds for music education. With no salaries, staff, office, or endowment, the 14 directors live in 8 states, have supported grantees in 47 states, and work with volunteers worldwide. It exists almost exclusively online, using the Internet for publicity, fundraising, and all internal communications; and even to develop, produce, and distribute intellectual property.

The website Phish.net is now in its fifth iteration and *The Phish Companion*'s 3rd edition was published in June 2016 and quickly sold out. Over the years, The Mockingbird Foundation has distributed more than $1.1 million via more than 330 grants in all 50 states.

Relatedly, if you've been to a Phish show, you may have seen the WaterWheel tables with their green banners and white logos. The people behind WaterWheel, including the army of volunteers, are the kind folks who give purpose to our party.

According to Phish.com, WaterWheel is "the Phish community coming together to share in positive ways with the local communities we all visit on tour stops. The net proceeds raised at each show—fan donations plus the sale of WaterWheel logo merchandise and items autographed by the band—are donated to the organization tabling at the show, after deducting overhead costs."

In 1997, Phish created The WaterWheel Foundation to manage and oversee the band's various charitable activities, including the Lake Champlain Initiative, the Touring Division, and the Giving Program.

All of this was announced, including the launch of Ben and Jerry's Phish Food ice cream, at a special show on April 22, 1997, at the Flynn Theatre in Burlington, Vermont, where Ben Cohen and Jerry Greenfield shared that all royalties from the ice cream would fund The WaterWheel Foundation and support the Lake Champlain Initiative.

Continuing now more than 25 years later, proceeds from the sale of Phish Food continue to support the Lake Champlain Initiative and help with the environmental well-being of the lake and surrounding areas.

The WaterWheel Touring Division, from its debut in 1997 through the "final" Phish shows in 2004, was unique with its national reach and local focus. For each Phish show, the Touring Division selects a local nonprofit in each community and donates the proceeds from that show's WaterWheel sales and donations directly to the local organization. To date, Waterwheel has donated more than $1,000,000 to more than 425 organizations around the country.

For example, in 2011, after Vermont was hit with massive flooding and devastation from Hurricane Irene, Phish and WaterWheel hosted a benefit concert on September 14, 2011, that raised $1.2 million for the recovery effort. And beginning in 2012, WaterWheel has hosted preshow parties with early access to the venue before Phish's shows, raising as much as $55,000 per event.

For more than 25 years, The WaterWheel Foundation has rallied the Phish community to help those in need, and acted as a funnel between the fans and the nonprofit organizations dedicated to helping protect our environment as well as social services benefiting women and children.

You can learn more and make a donation at Phish.com/WaterWheel. Of course, if you're unable to donate financially, you can always donate your time and volunteer to help at shows or otherwise. See you at the WaterWheel table!

Acknowledgments

Heartfelt thanks to Triumph Books, particularly Josh Williams, our acquisitions editor, who really believed in this project. And to our editors, Michelle Bruton (2018) and Jesse Jordan (2024), who guided us through the manuscripts.

Furthermore, this book would not have happened without Scott Bernstein, editorial director at JamBase.com, who introduced us and launched this collaborative endeavor. Thanks, Scotty!

Additionally, we'd like to acknowledge a few people individually:

I want to take this opportunity to give Phish a literary standing ovation. You have been the soundtrack of my life, from my first show as a socially awkward high schooler trying to find myself, to one of my most recent shows, where I cried my eyes out with tears of joy when you played "Izabella" thinking of my beloved daughter of the same name. I have grown up with Phish, and I could never thank you all enough, but I can at least try. Thank you!

Much thanks to Ken Meyerson, Mark Feldman, and Noah Cole for hearing our ideas, reading our words, giving sage advice, and being honest with me throughout. Shout out to Sun Lee, for helping get the word out on KBOO radio, and a huge shoutout to Alex and Shawn at Imperial Bottle Shop for hosting an unbelievable book-release party.

Thanks also go out to HeadCount's executive director, Andy Bernstein, for taking the time for a phone interview, and 20 years ago giving me an opportunity to combine my political passion with my love of music .

I'd also like to give a shout-out to all my friends, near and far, who have continuously played a major role in my musical adventure. Much love goes out to my New City and New York City crew, who taught me as a young lad how to groove at the Wetlands, and somehow 30 years later still rock out together coast to coast.

Shout-out as well to my Buffalo crew, who teamed up with me to take my first cross-country Phish adventure, and who taught me the value of all-night syncopated taping sessions on six dual decks that became the stuff of legends.

Thanks go out to my Southern Arizona Crew (SAC), who still share adventures with me all around the country and who taught me to always search for the sound in the middle of a jam. And, finally, a big thank you goes out to my beloved Portland Crew, who for 20 -plus years have helped make Oregon and this incredible scene a true home. All of you PDXers have helped make this onetime visitor a permanent Visitor, and I am forever grateful.

I just want to say I love you all! This has been one hell of a ride. If anyone asks, I can truly say I have lived while I was young!

—Jason Gershuny

I've been going to see this band since 1998. It's one of the most stalwart aspects of my life. Hell, I haven't lived in the same city for as long as I've been seeing this band. And from that perspective, you could say Phish is home.

In some respects, I want to thank and acknowledge everyone I've been to a Phish show with, though I know that sounds silly. But that's how I feel! Thank you for sharing in the groove with me at a show. It truly is my happy place, and I cherish the moments shared with each and every one of you, whether it was one show or many, whether we became friends or just grooved for a set. Thank you!

That said, there are a few people in particular I want to shout-out.

First, my man Big Tim, who drove us thousands of miles, hitting countless shows. Those were the days! I wouldn't be writing this book had we not hit the road as often as we did. We had so many incredible adventures! I'll never forget Burgettstown. Thank you!

Also thanks to Bezer, Eric, Evan, Jake, and Zack, who have all been to Phish shows with me but were brave enough to come together for one more night of my bachelordom at the Baker's Dozen. Thank you! And thanks for the balloons!

Thanks to Josh High-Fives for a $1, Andy Sinboy, Anna, Matt and Steph, and my parents. Thanks to Leah, Luke, Lara, Christine, Sam, Mike, Scott, Mozy, Jimmy, Jeff, and Juice. I also want to thank Noah and my New Jersey crew for holding it down and taking care of each other the way we should. And Jason, my copilot on this project. Of course, Jenna, too!

And really, there's so many more. Some of whom I've probably forgotten your name, but I hope you reach out!

The Phish community is special, y'all. There's a kindness and a freedom that I hope remains and grows. This book is for all of you, everyone who helps keep Phish a fun, safe place.

Additionally, I want to give praise to Brando Rich at CashorTrade.com, who is fighting the good fight to provide a trusted platform for face-value ticket exchanges for Phish and a variety of other musical acts.

Thanks to the readers at PhanSite.com who shared and submitted so many wonderful photos of the band and life on tour. Also thanks to Julie S. and Ben Ray Ginwright for sharing their personal anecdotes and experiences of vending on Shakedown Street. Thanks also to Wally Holland for his eloquent, inspirational book, *A Live One*.

And many big thanks to our collaborative artists, including Stephen Olker for his incredible photographs and Mike Force and Andy Sinboy for their original illustrations. Also, Scott Harris for his spectacular cover photograph. I truly love every image in this book. You talented bastards, thank you!

Last, I want to acknowledge the band, these four musicians, who have tirelessly challenged themselves to stay creative and happy and aspirational. I take great inspiration from that—not just their music, but their unbridled pursuit of art and joy. Bravo, gentlemen. And thank you!

—Andy P. Smith

About the Authors

Andy P. Smith is a writer and copywriter who has been attending Phish shows since 1998. In addition to his writing on music, culture, and technology, he has produced creative work for Wieden+Kennedy, Budweiser, Airbnb, and Betaworks. Published in Quartz, Futurism, and The Village Voice, he is also the author of *The Last American Gypsy, Welcome to the Land of Cannibalistic Horses*, and *Can You Survive 2020.*

Jason and Andy (left to right) at MSG during Phish's Baker's Dozen residency.

Since 2006, Andy has lived in a converted warehouse loft in Greenpoint, Brooklyn. You can find him on social media @apsmithnyc or visit www.apsmith.net.

Jason Gershuny has photographed and written about concerts and festivals since 1999 for a variety of music news media outlets, including but not limited to *Jambase Magazine*, *Glide Magazine*, and *Billboard Mobile Beat*. During that time, he has covered a variety of festivals including High Sierra Music Festival, The Northwest String Summit, and The Portland Blues Festival. He has also reviewed and shot photographs for individual concerts such as Phish, moe., and String Cheese Incident. He has reviewed albums and interviewed various musicians such as George Porter Jr., Steve Kimock, and Karl Denson for publication.

Outside of the musical journalism realm, he was the Oregon team Leader for the national voter registration organization HeadCount for more than a decade. He attended the University of Buffalo and then graduated from the University of Arizona with an undergraduate degree in Sociology, and he received his Master's degree in teaching from Lewis and Clark College.

Since first seeing Phish in 1993 in a dusty fairgrounds in upstate New York, he has seen them more than 250 times. He lives in Portland, Oregon, with his loving wife, Mindy, his precious daughter, Izabella, and his cat, Leia. He has been a social studies teacher in a variety of grade levels for more than 20 years.

Authors' Favorites

To best give you some insight into where we come from as Phish fans, we've compiled a list of our 13 favorite Phish shows, as well as our 13 favorite Phish original compositions (some composed with a little help from their friends). This might just give you a better perspective as to where we are coming from, or so we hope!

In any case, here are our picks!

Jason's Top 13 Personal Favorite Phish Shows

Here is a baker's dozen list of my favorite seen shows in chronological order. This was a lot harder to compile than anticipated.

1. November 4, 1994, Onodaga War Memorial, New York
2. December 7, 1995, Niagara Falls, New York
3. October 31, 1995, Chicago, Illinois
4. December 31, 1995, Madison Square Garden, New York
5. October 31, 1996, Omni, Atlanta, Georgia
6. December 30, 1997, Madison Square Garden, New York
7. July 17, 1998, The Gorge, George, Washington
8. October 31, 1998, Thomas and Mack Arena, Las Vegas, Nevada
9. July 18, 1999, Oswego Airport, New York
10. December 31, 1999, Big Cypress, Florida
11. July 11, 2000, Deer Creek, Indiana
12. December 31, 2013, Madison Square Garden, New York
13. October 31, 2014, MGM Grand Garden Arena, Las Vegas, Nevada

(Honorable mentions: the Baker's Dozen and 10/28/21)

Jason's Top 13 Favorite PhishOriginals

1. "Tweezer"
2. "Mike's Song"
3. "Antelope"
4. "Weekapaug Groove"
5. "David Bowie"
6. "Sand"
7. "Ghost"
8. "Slave to the Traffic Light"
9. "Split Open and Melt"
10. "Maze"
11. "Harpua"
12. "Colonel Forbin's"
13. "Fluffhead"

Andy's Top 13 Personal Favorite Phish Shows

Here's a list of my top 13 personal favorite Phish shows, ranked.

1. December 31, 2023, Madison Square Garden, New York
2. September 6, 2015, Dick's Sporting Goods Park, Commerce City, Colorado
3. July 25, 2017, Madison Square Garden, New York
4. July 26, 2017, Madison Square Garden, New York
5. October 31, 2014, MGM Grand Garden Arena, Las Vegas, Nevada
6. July 29, 2003, Post-Gazette Pavilion, Star Lake, Burgettstown, Pennsylvania
7. July 28, 2023, Madison Square Garden, New York
8. February 28, 2003, Nassau Coliseum, Uniondale, New York
9. August 12, 2015, The Mann Center, Philadelphia, Pennsylvania
10. March 1, 2003, Greensboro Coliseum, in Greensboro, North Carolina

11. December 30, 2003, American Airlines Arena, Miami, Florida
12. June 25, 2016, Wrigley Field, Chicago, Illinois
13. July 16, 1998, The Gorge, George, Washington

Andy's Top 13 Favorite Phish Originals
1. "The Squirming Coil"
2. "Tweezer"
3. "Ghost"
4. "Sand"
5. "First Tube"
6. "Bathtub Gin"
7. "Moma Dance"
8. "2001"
9. "Mike's > Groove" (That's two songs, sorry, not sorry)
10. "Stash"
11. "Simple"
12. "What's the Use?"
13. "Tweezer Reprise"

Sources

Websites

AllMusic.com

BenJerry.com

Billboard.com

BurlingtonFreePress.com

BusinessInsider.com

CashOrTrade.com

CharlieRose.com

CleveScene.com

ConcertBoom

CPR.org

DenverPost.com

EW.com

Facebook.com

FastCompany.com

Fodors.com

HeadCount.org

HuffingtonPost.com

IMDB.com

JamBands.com

JamBase.com

LiveAtNectars.com

LiveForLiveMusic.com

LiveNation.com

mBird.org

Mike-Gordon.com

MimiFishman.org

MusicRadar.com

NPR.org

NYTimes.com

PageMcConnell.com

PhanSite.com

PhantasyTour.com

Phish.com

Phish.net

PhishThoughts.com

PollockPrints.com

PollStarPro.com

PostStar.com

Reddit.com

Relix.com

Reuters.com

RoarLionsRoar.com

RollingStone.com

SeattleTimes.com

Setlist.fm

SevenDaysVT.com

SoundCloud.com

Spin.com

StarTribune.com

Trey.com

TreysGuitarRig.com

Twitter.com

UnderTheScales.com

Wikipedia.org

YouTube.com

Magazines and Periodicals

Doniac Schvice

Sno magazine

Surrender to the Flow magazine

Books

Cassels, Kevin, and Richard Northrop. The Pharmer's Almanac: The Unofficial Guide to Phish, Vol. 6 (Atlanta: Pharmer's Almanac, 2000).

Gehr, Richard, and Phish. The Phish Book (New York: Villard, 1999).

Levine, Ed. Pizza: A Slice of Heaven: The Ultimate Pizza Guide and Companion (New York: Rizzoli Universe Promotional Books, 2010).

Mockingbird Foundation, The. The Phish Companion: A Guide to the Band and their Music (San Francisco: Miller Freeman Books, 2000).

Podcasts
Analyze Phish
Inside Out with Turner and Seth
The Light Side
The Helping Friendly Podcast

Photographers
Scott Harris
Trevor Anderson
Steph Polk
Stephen Olker